THE PLATFORM SUTRA
OF THE SIXTH PATRIARCH

Prepared for the Columbia College Program of
Translations from the Oriental Classics
Wm. Theodore de Bary, Editor

NUMBER LXXVI OF THE
Records of Civilization: Sources and Studies
EDITED UNDER THE AUSPICES OF THE
DEPARTMENT OF HISTORY, COLUMBIA UNIVERSITY

THE PLATFORM SUTRA
OF THE SIXTH PATRIARCH

THE TEXT OF THE TUN-HUANG MANUSCRIPT
with TRANSLATION, INTRODUCTION, AND NOTES
by PHILIP B. YAMPOLSKY

NEW YORK

COLUMBIA UNIVERSITY PRESS

*Philip B. Yampolsky is a Lecturer in Japanese
at Columbia University*

ISBN 0-231-08361-0

This study, prepared under the Graduate Faculties of Columbia University, was selected by a committee of those Faculties to receive one of the Clarke F. Ansley awards given annually by Columbia University Press.

To

YOSHITAKA IRIYA

Foreword

THE *Platform Sutra of the Sixth Patriarch* is one of the Translations from the Oriental Classics by which the Committee on Oriental Studies has sought to transmit to Western readers representative works of the major Asian traditions in thought and literature. These are works which in our judgment any educated man should have read. Frequently, however, this reading has been denied him by the lack of suitable translations. All too often he has had to choose between excerpts in popular anthologies on the one hand, and heavily annotated translations intended primarily for the specialist on the other. Here we offer translations of whole works, based on scholarly studies, but written for the general reader rather than the specialist.

At first glance the *Platform Sutra* may seem a poor example of this policy. It has already been translated several times, and most of the earlier versions have done with far less scholarly apparatus than Dr. Yampolsky has felt it necessary to include here. If we have risked some misunderstanding on these accounts, there are, we hope, good reasons for it. The first is that this work is a basic one in its own tradition, the Ch'an or Zen tradition, and so basic a text deserves frequent retranslation because it needs constant reexamination. Second, among the many religious "scriptures" it is one of the most cryptic and elusive, since it springs from a tradition which was loath to commit itself to writing. And third, as a consequence of this, its understanding has depended very much on the reader's familiarity with the context. Dr. Yampolsky's handling of it goes much further, we believe, in providing the reader with the relevant context, and should help to clear up many misconceptions and confusions that have surrounded the book.

We do not feel it out of place, therefore, to include a lengthy and detailed historical introduction which contains information hitherto unavailable even to scholars, and also a critical edition of the text. Some readers may choose to make less use of these than others, but their inclusion hardly renders the translation itself less readable, any more than similar scholarly apparatus has detracted from the widely used Edgerton translation of the *Gita*. At the same time it must be acknowledged that what Dr. Yampolsky has striven to provide is the historical context of the *Platform Sutra* insofar as it can be reconstructed from documentary sources, not the "living" context so important to the Zen believer. The latter derives from a teaching tradition that stresses practical training and the direct personal guidance of a master—not the kind of thing one would look for in a book.

WM. THEODORE DE BARY

Preface

DURING the course of the eighth century in T'ang China, Ch'an grew from a relatively unknown school of Buddhism into a sect of considerable prominence. Hui-neng, the Sixth Patriarch, is one of the most revered figures among Chinese Ch'an and Japanese Zen Buddhists. In many ways he is the most important personage in the Sect, regarded, together with Bodhidharma, as its founder, as the man who set Ch'an on the course it was to follow from the eighth century until today. The *Platform Sutra,* the book that purports to convey his teachings, has seen many editions and many changes since the Tun-huang manuscript version, the earliest text that is still extant.

In order to describe the rise of Ch'an and to make clear the position of Hui-neng in the early history of the Sect, I have discussed, in the introduction, the development of Ch'an in the eighth century, and have provided an annotated translation of the Tun-huang text of the *Platform Sutra,* as well as a corrected version of the text. In the introduction I have confined myself to the history and legends of Ch'an itself, attempting only very occasionally to relate Ch'an to other Buddhist groups that flourished at the same time. Nor have I touched, except in passing, upon the explosive development of Ch'an towards the end of the T'ang dynasty. In addition, the complicated political and social history of the times has been alluded to in only the most casual degree. Detailed consideration of these subjects would involve research quite beyond the intended scope of this book.

The history of the *Platform Sutra* spans the development of Ch'an Buddhism from the eighth century until modern times. Except for a discussion of some of the bibliographic problems involved, I have not concerned myself with the uses or the significance of the work from the Yüan dynasty to the present. This is an entirely unrelated and extremely complex problem, far removed from a discussion of the Tun-huang manuscript itself.

In the translation I have attempted to adhere as closely as possible to the original text. There are occasions, however, when the Tun-huang manuscript is unintelligible or clearly in error. Where possible the *Kōshōji* edition, derived from a Northern Sung text, has been relied on to supplement or adjust the Tun-huang version. For convenience, the translation and the text have been divided into sections, following the arrangement established by D. T. Suzuki in his edition of the *Platform Sutra*. Textual errors have in many cases been indicated in the notes to the translation, but no attempt has been made to include reference to all such errors. They have, however, been noted in the corrections to the text itself.

The study of the early history of Ch'an must rely heavily on the documents discovered at Tun-huang. The authorities of the British Museum have had the foresight to make all the documents of the Stein Collection available on microfilm, with the result that specialists, particularly in Japan, have been given the opportunity of making a fairly thorough study of this material, and thus contributing greatly to the advancement of sinological research. Other collections of Tun-huang materials are not so readily available for consultation, with the result that many vital documents may well remain undiscovered among these hoarded archives.

Mention of all the people, both in Japan and the United States, who helped towards the completion of this work, would be impossible. My first and principal acknowledgment must go to Professor Yoshitaka Iriya, head of the Chinese Literature Department of Nagoya University, and a member of the Research Institute for Humanistic Studies, Kyoto University. Professor Iriya has given me much of his time and has assisted me in all phases of my work. I have taken advantage of his great knowledge, and count myself privileged to have been able to work under his guidance. Various members of the Research Institute for Humanistic Studies have assisted me greatly: I am particularly indebted to Messrs. Tairyō Makita and Jikai Fujiyoshi for having provided me with a comfortable place for study in the Religion Research Room of the Institute and for their kind help in numerous ways. Professor Seizan Yanagida of Hanazono University has allowed me to benefit from his wide knowledge of the texts and history of Ch'an, by freely answering the numerous questions with which I plagued him. Professors Wm. Theodore de Bary, Yoshito Hakeda, Chih-tsing Hsia, and Burton Watson of Columbia University have read the manuscript with care, and their corrections and suggestions have proved to be of significant help. Lastly, I should like to express my thanks to my wife, Yuiko, who assisted in the copying of texts and in numerous other understanding ways.

PHILIP B. YAMPOLSKY

Contents

Abbreviations

INTRODUCTION: *Ch'an in the Eighth Century*

I. The Formation of the Legend

BY THE TIME that the T'ang dynasty had gained control of a unified China in 618, Buddhism was already firmly entrenched on Chinese soil. From its modest beginnings as a religion introduced by traveling merchants and both Indian and Central Asian missionaries in the first and second centuries, it had spread throughout all levels of Chinese society. Vast temple complexes, awe-inspiring in their magnificence, stood in the cities and towns; great monastic communities graced the top of many a lofty mountain. Imposing works of sculpture and painting and an elaborate and ornate ritual stirred the hearts and minds of the populace. The enormous body of Buddhist literature was, over the centuries, translated into Chinese. Native priests of great genius emerged, to explain, to systematize, and to adapt Buddhist teaching to Chinese ways of thinking. Great centers of learning arose, specializing in specific branches of Buddhist thought.

Buddhism had spread in China, despite the attacks of its Confucian and Taoist opponents. It had weathered several persecutions and had emerged stronger each time. Gradually Buddhism had adapted itself to the Chinese milieu, and had acclimated itself to the extent that new, sinified forms were beginning to appear. Throughout Buddhism's history, emperors of various dynasties had accepted its teachings and had, in many ways, used Buddhism to further their own causes. The T'ang was no exception. Although the founder of the T'ang was nominally a Taoist, he not only did not interfere with the continued rise of Buddhism; in fact he contributed much to it. Succeeding emperors, and especially the Empress Wu, were devout Buddhists. Buddhist ceremonies were adopted as an integral part of court ritual. China, by the eighth century, was virtually a Buddhist nation.

Some opposition did indeed exist: Confucianists continued to complain and memorialize against this religion that was so contrary to the traditional political and moral concepts they upheld; Taoists, shorn of their importance, resented the loss of power and respect for their beliefs. At times these voices of protest managed to gain a hearing. Occasionally during the T'ang dynasty, a particular emperor might favor the cause of the antagonists of Buddhism, but in most instances his successor soon restored whatever prerogatives the previous reign had seen fit to take away. But the imperial acceptance of Buddhism, while often blindly enthusiastic, was tempered by the realization that some restraints were necessary. There was, to a certain degree, a control maintained over the proliferation of temples; there were regulations concerning the number of monks and nuns who might join the monastic communities, as well as certain qualifications for entering the calling that had to be met; and the size of tax-free temple estates was regulated. However, as time and the T'ang dynasty wore on, these regulations came more and more to be ignored. Eventually, during the declining years of the T'ang dynasty, the disastrous persecutions of the Hui-ch'ang era (842–845) took place. Buddhism survived, but it was never to regain the dominant position it had once enjoyed.

In the early years of the T'ang the Chinese attitude toward the Buddhist religion was highly eclectic. A variety of schools, each centering on certain teachings or particular canonical works, flourished. Cults, addressing their faith to specific Buddhas and Bodhisattvas, gained wide popularity. The imperial court played no particular favorites— learned priests and teachers, advocating a variety of doctrines, were accorded equally the highest of honors. The high officials who patronized them, the literary figures who wrote their praises, did not necessarily confine themselves to one school or branch of Buddhism, but felt free to sample the great variety of teachings that Buddhism had to offer.

The Buddhist schools themselves, however, were not so unworldly as to neglect to champion the advantages of their own teachings. By the middle of the eighth century we find that internecine quarrels among various Buddhist groups had greatly intensified. Works attacking rival doctrines began to appear, contributing much to the development of sectarian Buddhism. The great T'ien-t'ai school of early T'ang lost its vitality; the Chen-yen teaching of the esoteric doctrines failed to fulfill the promise of its great T'ang masters. Ch'an, and to a lesser extent the Pure Land teachings, came to hold a dominant position. The persecution of the Hui-ch'ang era served as a death blow to many of the T'ang schools. Partly out of historical circumstance and partly because of the nature of its teachings, Ch'an emerged as the primary school of Chinese Buddhism.

In the following pages I concern myself with the history of Ch'an

Buddhism. Although they do not enter into the discussion, other schools and teachings, particularly in early T'ang, were of considerable importance. Long before Ch'an made its mark on Japanese soil, other T'ang schools had been imported into that island nation. There some of these teachings developed into major sects, far outdistancing the importance that they had held in T'ang China.

THE LAṄKĀVATĀRA SCHOOL

When Buddhism was first introduced to China, many Indian works on meditation techniques were translated and gained fairly wide circulation. Meditation had always been an essential part of Indian Buddhism and it was no less important in China. As the new religion spread and gained adherents, meditation techniques were adopted and put to use by the various schools of Buddhism; but the emphasis which was accorded them differed with each school. Eventually there came to be practitioners who devoted themselves almost exclusively to meditation. Contemporary records of them are scant[1] and little is known of what they taught. Probably originally wandering ascetics, some of them began to gain a following, and eventually communities of monks were established, where the practitioners meditated and worked together. Toward the end of the seventh century one such community, that of the priest Hung-jen,[2] of the East Mountain,[3] had gained considerable prominence. Hung-jen, or the Fifth Patriarch, as he later came to be known, had a great number of disciples who left their Master at the

[1] Almost the only sources of information are the sections devoted to meditation practitioners in the *Hsü kao-seng chuan*, т50, pp. 550–606. For a discussion of the historical background of the school which later developed into the first Ch'an sect, see Hu Shih, "Leng-chia tsung k'ao," *Hu Shih wen-ts'un*, IV, 194–235.

[2] For details of his biography, see below, pp. 13–14.

[3] In the *Li-tai fa-pao chi*, т51, p. 182a, we read: "He [Hung-jen] resided at Mount Feng-mu, east of Mount Shuang-feng; both were not far apart. People of the time referred to [Hung-jen's teaching] as the teaching of the East Mountain (Tung-shan famen), in other words, that of Mount Feng-mu." Mount Shuang-feng was the home of Tao-hsin, Hung-jen's teacher, and in his biography in the *Li-tai fa-pao chi*, т51, p. 181b, we find: "He resided at Mount P'o-t'ou, which later was named Mount Shuang-feng." The *Leng-chia shih-tzu chi*, т85, p. 1289b, refers to Hung-jen's teaching as the "teaching of the East Mountain," and in the *Tsu-t'ang chi*, I, 90, there is a reference merely to East Mount Feng-mu. Hung-jen's temple is frequently referred to as Huang-mei, after the district in which it was located. It is in present-day Ch'i-ch'un in Hupeh. (Page references to the *Tsu-t'ang chi* are to the mimeographed edition published in Kyoto, n.d.)

completion of their training, moved to various areas of the nation, and established schools of their own. It is with these men that the story of Ch'an as a sect begins.

Once Ch'an began to be organized into an independent sect, it required a history and a tradition which would provide it with the respectability already possessed by the longer-established Buddhist schools. In the manufacture of this history, accuracy was not a consideration; a tradition traceable to the Indian Patriarchs was the objective. At the same time that Ch'an was providing itself with a past which accommodated itself to Buddhism as a whole, various competing Ch'an Masters, each with his own disciples and methods of teaching, strove to establish themselves. Throughout the eighth century a twofold movement took place: the attempt to establish Ch'an as a sect within the Buddhist teaching in general, and the attempt to gain acceptance for a particular school of Ch'an within the Chinese society in which it existed. Obviously, the first step to be taken was for each group within Ch'an to establish a history for itself. To this end, they not only perpetuated some of the old legends, but also devised new ones, which were repeated continuously until they were accepted as fact. Indeed, in the eyes of later viewers the two are virtually indistinguishable. These legends were, in most instances, not the invention of any one person, but rather the general property of the society as a whole. Various priests used various legends; some were abandoned, some adopted, but for the most part they were refined and adjusted until a relatively palatable whole emerged. To achieve the aura of legitimacy so urgently needed, histories were compiled, tracing the Ch'an sect back to the historical Buddha, and at the same time stories of the Patriarchs in China were composed, their teachings outlined, their histories written, and their legends collected. Treatises were manufactured to which the names of the Patriarchs, the heroes of Ch'an, were attached, so as to lend such works the dignity and the authority of the Patriarch's name.

Owing to the fragmentary condition of the literary remains of the period, to serious doubts about the authenticity of much of what is left, and to the absence of supporting historical evidence, it is virtually impossible to determine the actual process whereby Ch'an developed. Thus the story is a negative one; one can come to no definite conclusions. The legend, as it has come down to us in the Ch'an histories, is a pretty one; it makes a nice tale, but it is almost certainly untrue. The few facts that are known can, perhaps, also be molded into a nice story, but it is one surrounded by doubts, lacunae, and inconsistencies. Alleged occurrences may be denied because there is no evidence to support them, but at the same time there is little to prove that these events did not happen. This is so of the history of Ch'an in the eighth century; it is so of the story of Hui-neng, the Sixth Patriarch; and it is true as well of the book that purports to give his history and his teachings: the *Platform Sutra of the Sixth Patriarch*.

Yet, by examining the growth of the legends in the light of the histories of the time, by considering them in relation to the facts that are known, we may be able to learn something of the history of Ch'an in the eighth century. At least we should be able to learn what parts of it can and what parts of it cannot be accepted with any degree of assurance.

It goes without saying that no history of Ch'an in this period can be undertaken without reference to the documents discovered at Tunhuang. It is this material, discovered at the turn of this century in a sealed cave in Central Asia, which first provided evidence to controvert the entrenched legendary history of Ch'an.

The first of these documents to concern us is a Ch'an history, the *Ch'uan fa-pao chi*.[4] Although undated, it can, through internal evidence, be placed in the first decade of the eighth century,[5] and represents the history of Ch'an as it was conceived of in one particular school. It does not necessarily begin the legend, but it represents an early version of it, drawing from the existing tradition those elements which fit its purposes best. Tu Fei,[6] of whom virtually nothing is

---

[4] A complete copy of this work was discovered in Paris by Kanda Kiichirō and is reproduced in facsimile form in Kanda Kiichirō, "Dembō hōki no kanchitsu ni tsuite," *Sekisui sensei kakōju ki'nen ronsan*, pp. 145–52, 7 plates. This was later reproduced in printed form in Shiraishi Hōru (Kogetsu), *Zoku Zenshū hennen shi*, pp. 972–77. Its number in the Pelliot collection (hereinafter abbreviated P) is P3559. A fragment of the same work, consisting primarily of the preface, is found in T85, p. 1291 (P2634). For a discussion of the work, see Yanagida Seizan, "Dembō hōki to sono sakusha," *Zengaku kenkyū*, no. 53 (July, 1963), pp. 45–71.

[5] Although undated, the last Ch'an Patriarch discussed is Shen-hsiu, who died in 706. It may be assumed that the work was completed shortly after his death, as his successor is not mentioned.

[6] The *Ch'uan fa-pao chi* mentions Tu Fei as its compiler, and notes that his personal name was Fang-ming. No biographical information is available concerning him. He is, however, mentioned as the "Dharma-master Fei" in an inscription by Yen T'ing-chih, *Ta-chih ch'an-shih pei-ming ping-hsü*, CTW, ch. 280 (VI, 3596). (Citations to volume

known, is given as the compiler. A brief work, it contains a short preface and then presents brief biographies of the Patriarchs in China. References to and quotations from the Laṅkāvatāra Sutra demonstrate that the school which the *Ch'uan fa-pao chi* represents concentrated its teachings on this sutra. In the preface one finds the first evidence of an attempt to connect the Chinese Ch'an masters with the Patriarchs in India. The authority drawn upon is the *Ta-mo-to-lo ch'an ching*,[7] a work of uncertain origin, whose preface and text mention several Indian Patriarchs. This sutra is frequently cited in later Ch'an histories to prove the legitimacy of the Ch'an tradition. At this time the T'ien-t'ai school had an established lineage, going back to the historical Buddha and maintaining that the Faith had been handed down from Patriarch to Patriarch until it reached Siṁha bhikṣu, the twenty-fourth, who was killed during a persecution of Buddhism, after which time the transmission was cut off.[8] T'ien-t'ai traces itself by a separate lineage to Nāgārjuna, the Fourteenth Partriarch. Thus Ch'an efforts were turned towards proving that the teaching had, in fact, not been cut off, but that Siṁha bhikṣu, before his death, had passed his teaching on to a disciple. In this way Ch'an was attempting to establish that the Faith had indeed been handed down directly from Patriarch to Patriarch until it reached China. The setting-up of a patriarchal tradition both within Buddhism and within Ch'an itself, was the concern of most Ch'an histories of the eighth century. The compiler of the *Ch'uan fa-pao chi* did not attempt to establish a direct link with the historical Buddha; he did, however, suggest one. There is no way of determining

and page number of the *Ch'üan T'ang wen* are to the reduced size edition in 20 vols., Taipei, 1961.) Kanda, "Dembō hōki . . . ," p. 152, suggests that he may have been a monk who later returned to lay life, adopting the patronym Tu.

[7] T15, pp. 301–25. For the identification of Dharmatrāta, to whom this sutra is attributed, see Lin Li-kuong, *L'aide mémoire de la vraie loi*, appendix, pp. 341–46. The preface of this sutra lists several Patriarchs after the Buddha; the first section of the text repeats their names. The last five (although not mentioned in the *Ch'uan fa-pao chi*) figure importantly in the later Ch'an transmission tradition. They are given as: Kāśyapa, Ānanda, Mādhyāntika, Śaṇavāsa, Upagupta, Vasumitra, Saṅgharakṣa, Dharmatrāta (T15, p. 301c). The preface erroneously omits Kāśyapa. See Table 1.

[8] T'ien-t'ai follows the tradition as given in the *Mo-ho chih-kuan*, T46, p. 1, which in turn is based on the *Fu fa-tsang yin-yüan chuan*, T50, pp. 297–322, a work which purports to be a translation of a Sanskrit text, but which was most likely made in China (see Mochizuki Shinkō, *Bukkyō daijiten*, V, 4493–94). The *Fu fa-tsang yin-yüan chuan* lists only twenty-three Patriarchs. The *Mo-ho chih-kuan* adds as the third Patriarch Madhyāntika, who is listed in the former work as belonging to a collateral branch. Thus the figure twenty-four was arrived at.

whether this work reflects an entirely new departure or an attempt to associate Ch'an with the Indian Patriarchs, or whether it serves merely as our earliest record of certain contemporary beliefs and legends. That a variety of legends relating to the early Chinese Patriarchs did exist at this time is indicated by the compiler. In his preface he states that his account pays strict attention to authenticity, and that he rejects the mysterious legends associated with these Patriarchs.

After the preface which mentions the Indian Patriarchs, the *Ch'uan fa-pao chi* now turns to the transmission as seen in China. Presented are brief biographies of seven Patriarchs: Bodhidharma, Hui-k'o, Seng-ts'an, Tao-hsin, Hung-jen, Fa-ju, and Shen-hsiu. The text, unlike later works, does not assign numerical designations to these men, nor does it refer to them specifically as Patriarchs, although a successive transmission of the teaching is indicated. The first five men listed are the traditional Patriarchs of Ch'an; at no time did the sect ever question the legitimacy of their position. By the beginning of the eighth century, then, the legend of the succession of these Patriarchs was firmly entrenched. Their biographies, the stories about them, the legends which are found in later histories were, however, by no means fixed. These were first recorded, expanded, and systematized during the eighth century; they form a part of the evolution of the Ch'an legend. While the *Ch'uan fa-pao chi* represents this legend as known in only one particular school in the early years of the eighth century, it reveals to a certain extent the degree to which the legend had evolved by this time.

The biographies are, generally, uncomplicated; their subjects are still shadowy figures, unadorned, for the most part, with the fanciful stories and pseudofactual detail added later to bring both emotional appeal and authenticity to their characters. The account of Bodhidharma[9] is a simple one: he was a Brahman from southern India who came by sea to China to propagate Buddhism. At Sung-shan[10] he acquired two

[9] For a historical study of Bodhidharma, see Hu Shih, "P'u-t'i-ta-mo k'ao," *Hu Shih wen-ts'un*, III, 293–304. His studies are summarized in English in Hu Shih, "The Development of Zen Buddhism in China," *The Chinese Social and Political Science Review*, XV (no. 4, January, 1932), 476–87. He concludes that Bodhidharma arrived in Canton around 470 and traveled north, where he remained for some fifty years.

[10] Located near Loyang, this mountain has long been associated with Ch'an Masters. The Shao-lin ssu, where Bodhidharma is said to have lived, was located here. Sung-shan was the home of various Masters of Northern Ch'an, and achieved great prominence because of royal patronage. The names of many of the famous priests who lived here are found in P'ei Ts'ui, *Shao-lin ssu pei*, CTW, ch. 279 (VI, 3584–87).

TABLE 1. THE TWENTY-EIGHT

Fu Fa-tsang chuan		*Ta-mo-to-lo ch'an ching*	*Ch'uan fa-pao chi*	*Leng-chia shih-tzu chi*
Mahākāśyapa	[1]	Mahākāśyapa	Mahākāśyapa	
Ānanda	[2]	Ānanda	Ānanda	
[Madhyāntika]		Madhyāntika	Madhyāntika	
Śaṇavāsa	[3]	Śaṇavāsa	Śaṇavāsa	
Upagupta	[4]	Upagupta		
Dhṛtaka	[5]			
Miccaka	[6]			
		Vasumitra		
Buddhanandi	[7]			
Buddhamitra	[8]			
Pārśva	[9]			
Puṇyayaśas	[10]			
Aśvaghoṣa	[11]			
Kapimala	[12]			
Nāgārjuna	[13]			
Kāṇadeva	[14]			
Rāhulata	[15]			
Saṅghānandi	[16]			
Gayaśāta	[17]			
Kumārata	[18]			
Jayata	[19]			
Vasubandhu	[20]			
Manorhita	[21]			
Haklenayaśas	[22]			
Siṁha bhikṣu	[23]			
		Saṅgharakṣa		Guṇabhadra
		Dharmatrāta	Bodhidharma	Bodhidharma

disciples, Tao-yü and Hui-k'o. The latter stayed with him for four or
five years and received from him the teachings of the Laṅkāvatāra
Sutra. The text then makes brief mention of the tale in which Hui-k'o
cuts off his arm to attest to the earnestness with which he sought the
teachings, and adds a note denying the allegation that Hui-k'o's arm

INDIAN PATRIARCHS *

Shen-hui		Li-tai fa-pao chi		T'an-ching		Pao-lin ch'uan	
				Seven Buddhas of the Past			
Kāśyapa	[1]	Mahākāśyapa	[1]	Mahākāśyapa	8	Mahākāśyapa	1
Ānanda	[2]	Ānanda	[2]	Ānanda	9	Ānanda	2
Madhyāntika	[3]	Madhyāntika	[3]	Madhyāntika	10		
Śaṇavāsa	[4]	Śaṇavāsa	[4]	Śaṇavāsa	11	Śaṇavāsa	3
Upagupta	[5]	Upagupta	[5]	Upagupta	12	Upagupta	4
		Dhṛtaka	[6]	Dhṛtaka	13	Dhṛtaka	5
		Miccaka	[7]			Miccaka	6
						Vasumitra	7
		Buddhanandi	[8]	Buddhanandi	14	Buddhanandi	8
		Buddhamitra	[9]	Buddhamitra	15	Buddhamitra	9
		Pārśva	[10]	Pārśva	16	Pārśva	10
		Puṇyayaśas	[11]	Puṇyayaśas	17	Puṇyayśas	11
		Aśvaghoṣa	[12]	Aśvaghoṣa	18	Aśvakhoṣa	12
		Kapimala	[13]	Kapimala	19	Kapimala	13
		Nāgārjuna	[14]	Nāgārjuna	20	Nāgārjuna	14
		Kāṇadeva	[15]	Kāṇadeva	21	Kāṇadeva	15
		Rāhulata	[16]	Rāhulata	22	Rāhulata	16
		Saṅghānandi	[17]	Saṅghānandi	23	Saṅghānandi	17
		Gayaśāta	[18]	Gayaśāta	24	Gayaśāta	18
		Kumārata	[19]	Kumārata	25	Kumārata	19
		Jayata	[20]	Jayata	26	Jayata	20
		Vasubandhu	[21]	Vasubandhu	27	Vasubandhu	21
		Manorhita	[22]	Manorhita	28	Manorhita	22
		Haklenayaśas	[23]	Haklenayaśas	29	Haklenayaśas	23
		Siṁha bhikṣu	[24]	Siṁha bhikṣu	30	Siṁha bhikṣu	24
		Śaṇavāsa	[25]	Śaṇavāsa	31	Basiasita	25
		Upagupta	[26]	Upagupta	32	Puṇyamitra	26
Śubhamitra	[6]	Śubhamitra	[27]	Saṅgharakṣa	33	Prajñātāra	27
Saṅgharakṣa	[7]	Saṅgharakṣa	[28]	Śubhamitra	34		
Bodhidharma	[8]	Bodhidharmatrāta	[29]	Bodhidharma	35	Bodhidharma	28

* When the numerical designations for the Patriarchs do not appear in the original text, they are enclosed in brackets.

had been cut off by bandits.[11] In a note to his own text, Tu Fei mentions Bodhidharma's teachings of wall-gazing and the four categories of conduct,[12] and comments to the effect that these are only temporary

[11] In reference to a story in the *Hsü kao-seng chuan*, T50, p. 552b.
[12] Reference is to Bodhidharma's concept of the "Two Entrances and Four Categories

and provisional teachings and are by no means to be considered first-rate treatises. The biographical notice goes on to state that several attempts were made to poison Bodhidharma, but they were all unsuccessful, for he was immune to harm. We are told then, however, that in the end Bodhidharma did eat poison and die, and that at the time he himself claimed to be a hundred and fifty years of age. Now Tu Fei, despite the claims for the rejection of legendary material that he makes in his preface, tells us the following story:

On the day that Bodhidharma died, Sung Yün[13] of the Northern Wei, while on his way back to China, met Bodhidharma, who was returning to India, in the Pamirs. Upon being asked what was to happen to his school in the future, Bodhidharma replied that after forty years a native Chinese would appear to spread his teaching.[14] When Sung Yün returned to China, he told Bodhidharma's disciples of his interview. When they opened the grave they found that the body was no longer there.[15]

The above account is a version of the Bodhidharma legend as it appeared around the year 710 in one school of Ch'an. Whether what is described here reflects the beliefs of all schools at the time cannot be ascertained, for there is no evidence remaining from which such information can be derived. There were numerous disciples of the Fifth Patriarch, each proclaiming his own brand of Ch'an, and it would seem likely that there were various legends in common circulation, which were used by the different Ch'an teachers of the time as best fitted their needs. The *Ch'uan fa-pao chi* drew largely upon the *Hsü kao-seng chuan* for its information, in most instances abbreviating the notice considerably. There are, however, several new elements, such as the tale of Hui-k'o's self-mutilation, the account of the attempts that were made to poison Bodhidharma, and the description of his encounter with Sung Yün. The chief departure, however, is the implication of a

of Conduct (*erh-ju ssu-hsing*)" found in the *Hsü kao-seng chuan*, т50, p. 551c. It is discussed in Heinrich Dumoulin, *A History of Zen Buddhism*, pp. 70–71. This is probably the only teaching ascribed to Bodhidharma which can be regarded as authentic. See below, p. 21, n. 57.

[13] A lay official, sent by the empress dowager in search of Buddhist works. His travel record has been translated by Samuel Beal, *Travels of Fa-hian and Sung-yun: Buddhist pilgrims from China to India*, London, 1869.

[14] It is unclear to whom this prediction refers.

[15] This story appears in a more elaborate form in *Tsu-t'ang chi*, I, 76, and *Ching-te ch'uan-teng lu*, т51, p. 220b.

patriarchal succession. Tao-hsüan, in his *Hsü ḳao-seng chuan,* gives
notices of Bodhidharma, Hui-k'o, and the Fourth Patriarch, Tao-hsin,
along with a large number of other Ch'an teachers, but he makes no
mention of the transmission of the Ch'an teaching from Patriarch to
Patriarch. Since Tao-hsüan, who died in 667, kept adding to his work,
which had been completed in 645, it may be assumed either that the
concept did not exist in his time, or that he was unaware of it. Therefore, unless Tao-hsüan deliberately ignored it, it is probable that the
concept of a patriarchal succession developed in the late seventh century, and had become generally accepted in Ch'an circles by the first
decade of the eighth century, when the *Ch'uan fa-pao chi* was compiled.

In its account of Hui-k'o, the Second Patriarch, the *Ch'uan fa-pao
chi* again relies, to a certain extent, on the *Hsü ḳao-seng chuan.* We
are told that his name was Seng-k'o, although he was sometimes called
Hui-k'o, and that he was of the Chi family, and a native of Wu-lao.[16]
Originally a scholar of Confucianism and an authority on various secu-
lar works, he later turned to Buddhism and became a monk. Meeting
Bodhidharma at the age of forty, he practiced the Way for six years,
and to show the earnestness with which he sought the Indian's teachings, he cut off his left arm, betraying no sign of emotion or pain.
Hui-k'o received his Master's sanction, and, after Bodhidharma had
returned to the West, stayed at the Shao-lin Temple at Sung-shan,
where he carried on his teachings. During the T'ien-p'ing period (534–
537) of the Northern Wei dynasty, he went to the capital at Yeh, where
he continued his preaching with success, gained many converts, and
led many persons to enlightenment. Here, as with Bodhidharma, many
attempts were made to poison him, but they were all unsuccessful. He
appointed Seng-ts'an as his successor, we are told, and transmitted to
him the Laṅkāvatāra Sutra, predicting that after four generations the
Sutra would change and become no more than an empty name.[17]

Although quite similar to the *Hsü ḳao-seng chuan* biography, and
obviously derived in part from it, there are significant points of departure: the story of the cutting-off of his arm is again included; the ac-

[16] The *Hsü ḳao-seng chuan* gives Hu-lao, in Ssu-shui hsien, Honan.
[17] Here again we have a prediction whose import is unclear. It may possibly indicate
some internal dissension within the school that advocated the Laṅkāvatāra teaching. As
will be noted later (see p. 14), the *Ch'uan fa-pao chi* lists a priest in the fourth generation, whose name is not found in what came to be the accepted lineage of this school.

count of Hui-k'o's enemy, Tao-heng, who attempted to destroy him
(so vividly described in the *Hsü kao-seng chuan*)[18] is only briefly alluded to; and most significantly, where Tao-hsüan's work records that
Hui-k'o left no heirs, the *Ch'uan fa-pao chi* states specifically that he
transmitted his teaching to Seng-ts'an, the Third Patriarch. This again
indicates that, if there was a patriarchal tradition in Ch'an at this time,
Tao-hsüan had no knowledge of it. Indeed, we have no evidence to
show that such a tradition existed before the *Ch'uan fa-pao chi.*

The biography of Seng-ts'an[19] is brief, and it is the first account we
have of this extremely ambiguous figure in the ranks of the Ch'an
patriarchate. The *Hsü kao-seng chuan* contains no separate biography;
under the account of Fa-ch'ung,[20] however, Seng-ts'an is listed as one
of Hui-k'o's disciples. The *Ch'uan fa-pao chi,* therefore, was unable to
rely on the *Hsü kao-seng chuan* for its information, but there is no way
of determining what source it used. Thus it may be presumed to be
a distillation of the legends current at the time. We learn that the place
of Seng-ts'an's origin was unknown, and that as a youth he showed
great promise, eventually becoming Hui-k'o's disciple. During the Buddhist persecution of Emperor Wu of the Chou dynasty (574), he concealed himself at Huan-kung Mountain[21] for ten years. We are told
that before Seng-ts'an came here the mountain was filled with wild
beasts, but that with his arrival they all vanished. Three priests who
studied under him are mentioned by name. Then we hear that Seng-
ts'an told his disciple Tao-hsin that he wished to return to the south,
whereupon he handed down to him Bodhidharma's teaching. After he
left no one knew what had happened to him or where he had gone.

This simple story of a virtually unknown man is all the *Ch'uan fa-
pao chi* has to tell us. Throughout the eighth century much material
was added to his legend, his biography became more complex, and details were added to the story of his life, but Seng-ts'an always remains
a relatively obscure figure in the history of Ch'an.

With the Fourth Patriarch, Tao-hsin, the account again becomes
more concrete, largely because the *Hsü kao-seng chuan* provides fairly

---

[18] T50, p. 552a.
[19] For a discussion of the biography and thought of Seng-ts'an, see Masunaga Reihō,
"Sanso Sōzan to sono shisō," *Nikka Bukkyō kenkyūkai nempō*, no. 2 (1937), pp. 36–63.
[20] T50, p. 666b.
[21] Located in the northwest part of T'ai-hu hsien, Anhui.

detailed information.[22] In several passages the wording is identical with that in Tao-hsüan's compilation and, although there is a degree of variation and considerable abbreviation, the *Ch'uan fa-pao chi* version is clearly derived from the former work.

We are told that Tao-hsin was a native of Ho-nei[23] and that his patronym was Ssu-ma. Leaving home at the age of seven, he studied with an unidentified priest for six years. Sometime in the K'ai-huang era (581–601) he went to study under the Third Patriarch, remaining with him for eight or nine years. When the Third Patriarch left to go to Lo-fu[24] Tao-hsin wanted to accompany him, but was told to remain behind, to spread the teaching, and only later to travel. During the disorders of the Ta-yeh era (605–617), just before the fall of the Sui dynasty, he went to Chi-chou,[25] which for seventy days had been surrounded by a band of robbers and where the springs had all run dry. But when the Fourth Patriarch arrived, the waters again flowed, and his recitation of the Prajñāpāramitā Sutras caused the bandits to disperse. In 624 he went to Mount Shuang-feng where he stayed for thirty years. He is said to have advocated intensive sitting in meditation, and to have opposed the recitation of sutras as well as talking with other people. In the eighth month of 652 he ordered his disciples to make a mausoleum on the side of the mountain, and with this they knew that he was soon to die. He then transmitted his teachings to Hung-jen. When informed that his mausoleum had been completed, he passed away, to the accompaniment of strange natural phenomena: the ground trembled and the earth was enveloped in mists. At the time of his death he was seventy-two years old. The story goes on to state that three years after he died the doors to his stone mausoleum opened of themselves, and his body was revealed, retaining still the natural dignity it had possessed while he was alive. Thereupon his disciples wrapped the body in lacquered cloth and did not dare to shut the doors again.

The account of the career of the Fifth Patriarch, Hung-jen, is exceedingly brief. We are told that he was a native of Huang-mei, of

[22] T50, p. 606b. The biography is contained at the very end of the section on Ch'an practitioners, and was presumably added by Tao-hsüan sometime between 645, when his work was completed, and 667, the year of his death.
[23] Ch'in-yang hsien, Honan.
[24] Unidentified. Ui Hakuju, *Zenshū shi kenkyū*, I, 137, identifies it as being "near to Canton." There is a mountain of the same name in Kiangsu.
[25] Chi-an hsien, Kiangsi.

the Chou family, and that he left home at the age of thirteen. Tao-hsin soon recognized his capacities: Hung-jen spent the whole night sitting in meditation and, without reading the sutras, attained enlightenment. He died in 675[26] at the age of seventy-four, after having transmitted his teachings to Fa-ju.

The above summarizes what the *Ch'uan fa-pao chi* has to say about the first five Patriarchs of Ch'an. Its information is drawn largely from the *Hsü kao-seng chuan,* with a few legendary details from unknown sources added. For the Third and Fifth Patriarchs, of whom no account is given in Tao-hsüan's work, it has little to say. This then is the status of the knowledge of the Patriarchs held by one school of Ch'an in the first decade of the eighth century. It is obvious that at this time the legends concerning them had yet to be highly elaborated; the *Hsü kao-seng chuan* was the basic source for the compiler of the *Ch'uan fa-pao chi.* Other schools undoubtedly knew further details and possessed other legends, but we have no contemporary records of them. Later works give more precise accounts, but we have no way of telling to what degree they represent newly invented material, the first recording of older legends, or the transmission of historical fact. As we watch the history and legend of Ch'an grow in its elaborateness with the passage of time, it would seem logical to assume that the absence of historical detail and biographical fact in the early works indicates that much of the later material is either the product of the imagination of later writers or the recapitulation and embroidering of earlier unrecorded legends.

The successor to Hung-jen was Fa-ju,[27] the *Ch'uan fa-pao chi* informs us. Although his name soon disappears from the records of Ch'an history, and he is mentioned only as one of the disciples of the Fifth Patriarch in eighth-century works, he was evidently a personage of no little prominence towards the end of the seventh century. His name is found in the biographical notices of two of the famous Ch'an priests[28]

---

[26] Various sources differ as to the date of his death. For a discussion, see Osabe Kazuo, "Tōdai Zenshū kōsō no shisho kyōka ni tsuite," *Haneda hakushi shōju ḳi'nen Tōyōshi ronsō,* pp. 297–98. The most probable date seems to be 674.

[27] His biographical monument is to be found, under anonymous authorship, as *T'ang Chung-yüeh sha-men Shih Fa-ju cha'n-shih hsing-chuang pei, Chin-shih hsü-pien,* ch. 6, pp. 5b–7a. Its contents are similar to the account given in the *Ch'uan fa-pao chi.*

[28] His name appears in the inscription commemorating I-fu by Yen T'ing-chih, *Ta-chih ch'an-shih pei-ming ping-hsü,* CTW, ch. 280 (VI, 3596), and the pagoda inscription in honor of P'u-chi by Li Yung, *Ta-chao ch'an-shih t'a-ming,* CTW, ch. 262 (VI, 3360). Both mention only his name.

in the capital cities, and the inscription relating the history of the Shao-lin Temple refers to him.[29] Fa-ju, we are told, was a native of Shang-tang[30] and was surnamed Wang. He left home at nineteen, studied the canonical works in detail, and then traveled widely in search of the Way. Hearing of the genius of Hung-jen, he went to Mount Shuang-feng. Here his talents were recognized and the teaching was transmitted to him. Later he went to the Shao-lin Temple where he resided for several years. In the seventh month of 689 he called his disciples together and instructed them quickly to ask questions of him, so that they might be able to resolve their doubts. Then he seated himself in meditation beneath a tree and passed away. He was fifty-two years of age at death, and his heir was Shen-hsiu of the Yü-ch'üan Temple.[31]

Shen-hsiu (606?–706), whom the *Ch'uan fa-pao chi* lists as the heir of Fa-ju, was one of the great leaders of Ch'an in the early years of the century. Later we will see his name slandered and his teachings damned, but at the turn of the century he was a priest of great fame, honored by court and populace alike. In all other works he is known as the heir of the Fifth Patriarch; the *Ch'uan fa-pao chi* alone makes him a disciple of Fa-ju. There is no adequate explanation for this attribution; it must be left as one of the many puzzles and unsolved problems which so clutter the history of Ch'an of this period. One might hazard a guess that he was a priest of considerable prestige at the Shao-lin Temple near to the capital, who perhaps had a school of his own but died before he had produced any disciples of note.

Shen-hsiu,[32] the *Ch'uan fa-pao chi* tells us, was a native of Ta-liang[33] and a member of the Li family. Extremely bright as a child, he disliked the normal games of youth, and at thirteen, after witnessing the disasters and famine brought about by the disturbances of the time, he chanced to meet a good teacher, and decided to become a monk. He wandered about to various Buddhist establishments, and at twenty re-

---

[29] *Shao-lin ssu pei,* p. 3586.

[30] Chang-chih hsien, Shansi.

[31] Located at the southeast foot of Mt. Yü-ch'üan in Hupeh.

[32] His biography is found in *Leng-chia shih-tzu chi,* ⊤85, p. 1290a-c; ⊤s 191, pp. 13b–14b; *Sung kao-seng chuan,* ⊤50, pp. 755c–756b. His biographical monument is by Chang Yüeh, *T'ang Yü-ch'üan ssu Ta-tung ch'an-shih pei ming ping hsü,* cᴛw, ch. 231 (V, 2953–54). There is also a notice celebrating his arrival at the capital by Sung Chih-wen, *Wei Lo-hsia chu-seng ch'ing fa-shih ying Hsiu ch'an-shih piao,* cᴛw, ch. 240 (V, 3076). For a detailed study of his biography, see Lo Hsiang-lin, *T'ang-tai wen-hua shih,* pp. 105–58. It is also discussed in Ui, *Zenshū shi kenkyū,* I, 269–75.

[33] All other sources make him a native of Wei-shih hsien in Honan.

ceived the precepts. When he was forty-six he went to Hung-jen at the East Mountain, and the Master, at a glance, discerned his talents. Here he gained enlightenment after several years of study. He went then to Ching-chou,[34] where he stayed for some ten years, yet all the time he was there the general populace was unaware of his accomplishments. In the I-feng era (676–678) he came to the Yü-ch'üan Temple, where again for ten years he did not transmit the doctrine. After Fa-ju's death (689) students flocked to him from great distances and he was instrumental in leading many people to salvation. In the year 701 or 702 [35] he was invited to court by the Empress Wu, and was greeted with great splendor and ceremony, receiving the adulation of both monks and laymen. He died in Loyang at the T'ien-kung Temple on the twenty-eighth day of the second month of Shen-lung 2 (= April 15, 706); at the time he was over a hundred years of age. His body was interred in a pagoda at the Yü-ch'üan Temple, and he was given the posthumous title "Ta-t'ung ch'an-shih."

The account of Shen-hsiu's career, summarized above, is substantially the same as in other contemporary records, and with it the *Chu'an fa-pao chi* concludes its story of the Chinese Patriarchs. The last two biographies it provides are extremely factual and devoid of legendary elements, and probably represent a fairly accurate account of the careers of these two men.

This is what one school of Ch'an, which flourished in the first decade of the eighth century, knew about its ancestors. The next Ch'an historical work which has been preserved stems from the same or a closely related line, and similarly was recovered from among the documents discovered at Tun-huang. Known as the *Leng-chia shih-tzu chi*,[36] it details the lineage of the school of Shen-hsiu and his disciples. Before discussing this new work, let us turn to a passage in a book that it quotes, the *Leng-chia jen-fa chih*. This work, now lost, was compiled by Hsüan-tse, a disciple of Hung-jen, the Fifth Patriarch, probably shortly after Shen-hsiu's death in 706. As quoted by the *Leng-chia shih-tzu chi*,[37] it gives the names of ten principal disciples of the Fifth Patriarch: Shen-hsiu, Chih-hsien, the assistant magistrate Liu, Hui-

---

[34] Chiang-ling hsien, Hupeh.

[35] The date cannot be set exactly. See Osabe, "Tōdai Zenshū kōsō . . . ," p. 296.

[36] т85, pp. 1283–90. The most recent collated text is by Shinohara Hisao, "Ryōga shiji ki kōchū," *Uchino Tairei sensei tsuitō rombunshū*, pp. 132–64.

[37] т85, p. 1289c.

tsang, Hsüan-yüeh, Lao-an, Fa-ju, Hui-neng, Chih-te, and I-fang. Hsüan-tse, as compiler, does not add his name to the list of the ten chief disciples, but he may legitimately be included as the eleventh. These eleven men, it may be presumed,[38] were the most active exponents of the Ch'an of Hung-jen. Some were of considerable eminence; others are known by name alone. Some founded schools and left disciples; others survive only in casual reference in other works. They do, however, indicate the great ferment and activity within Ch'an at this time.

Shen-hsiu, the great leader of the Laṅkāvatāra school, which came later to be known as Northern Ch'an, has an unquestionable place as one of the most eminent priests of his time. He is the only one of the eleven priests to whom a biographical notice in the *Leng-chia shih-tzu chi* is devoted; however, other sources reveal something of several of the other men included in the list.

Chih-hsien, of whom we shall have occasion to speak later,[39] was the founder of a school in Szechuan, which attained a fair degree of renown. On the assistant magistrate Liu and on Hui-tsang we have no information whatsoever. Hsüan-yüeh is also virtually unknown, although one source states that he was summoned to court by the Empress Wu.[40]

Lao-an was a priest of unusual renown, partly because of the extraordinary age he is said to have attained. Most works give his name as Hui-an,[41] which was his real Buddhist name. Of the Wei family, he was born in 582 in Chih-chiang in Ching-chou.[42] Wandering from temple to temple, he gave his efforts to helping the starving. Sometime in the Chen-kuan era (627–649) he went to Mount Shuang-feng, where he studied under Hung-jen. After completing his training, he resided in a number of temples; in 664 he was at Mount Chung-nan in Shensi and, although summoned by Emperor Kao-tsung, declined to come to

[38] Hu Shih, "Ch'an (Zen) Buddhism in China, Its History and Method," *Philosophy East and West*, III (no. 1, April, 1953), 10, regards the list given here as reasonably authentic.

[39] See below, p. 42ff.

[40] *Li-tai fa-pao chi*, т51, p. 184b.

[41] For his biography, see *Sung kao-seng chuan*, т50, p. 823b–c, and *Ching-te ch'uan-teng lu*, т51, p. 231c. His biographical inscription is by Sung Tan, *Sung-shan Hui-shan ssu ku ta-te Tao-an ch'an-shih pei-ming*, cTw, ch. 396 (IX, 5104–5). The text contains lacunae. Although referred to as Tao-an here, there seems to be no doubt that the subject of the inscription is Hui-an. See Ui, *Zenshū shi kenkyū*, I, 150–52.

[42] Chih-chiang hsien, Hupeh.

court. At different times he was at the Hui-shan Temple in Loyang, the Yü-ch'üan Temple, and the Shao-lin Temple. He was called to court by the Empress Wu, and is said to have been honored on a par with Shen-hsiu. He died in 709. His heir, Yüan-kuei (644–716), and the latter's disciple Ling-yün (d. 729) were both priests of sufficient consequence to have biographical monuments inscribed in their honor.[43]

Fa-ju, seventh on the list of disciples, we have seen before in the *Ch'uan fa-pao chi.* Hui-neng, the Sixth Patriarch, destined to become, with Bodhidharma, the most famous of the Ch'an Masters, is mentioned here for the first time in this or any other text.[44] To him is ascribed the *Platform Sutra,* and his history and teachings appear constantly in the literature of the latter part of the eighth century. He is a younger contemporary of Shen-hsiu, a fellow disciple under Hung-jen, but it is only later that he comes to be known. The biography of Hui-neng typifies the problems of Ch'an historiography: the later the work, the more detailed is the information provided. The works which concern him cannot be dated with any certainty, nor can we be sure that they do not represent information which has been revised by later hands. We need not doubt the accuracy of the information about men who had temporary renown, and whose fame receded into historical obscurity, men such as Shen-hsiu and most of the other disciples of Hung-jen. They did not become absorbed into the legend, although in some ways they helped to promote a part of it, as they strove to strengthen the position of their own Ch'an schools. But, as we shall see later, there is no way of distinguishing fact from legend in the case of Hui-neng. All one can do is to point out what might have happened and what probably did not happen, and suspend judgment until more evidence becomes available—if ever it does.

Chih-te and I-fang, ninth and tenth on the list, are unknown. Of Hsüan-tse, the compiler of the lost *Leng-chia jen-fa chih,* we also know virtually nothing. He is said to have been called to the imperial court;[45] thus he was most likely a man of no little importance. His disciple,

[43] For Yüan-kuei, see Hsü Ch'ou, *Sung-yüeh Kuei ch'an-shih ying-t'ang chi,* CTW, ch. 790 (XVII, 10435–36) and Jen-su, *Ta-T'ang Sung-yüeh Hsien-chü ssu ku ta-te Kuei ch'an-shih t'a-chi,* CTW, ch. 914 (XIX, 12022); for Ling-yün, see Ts'ui Ch'i, *T'ang Shao-lin ssu Ling-yün ch'an-shih t'a-pei,* CTW, ch. 303 (VII, 3893–94).
[44] The sources of Hui-neng's biography are discussed in chapter 2. Some works give precise dates for events in Hui-neng's life for a much earlier period, but these are either of dubious authenticity or of late origin.
[45] *Leng-chia shih-tzu chi,* T85, p. 1290a; *Li-tai fa-pao chi,* T51, p. 184b.

Ching-chüeh, of whom also little is known, was the compiler of the *Leng-chia shih-tzu chi,* and was evidently a man of some consequence, since no less a person than Wang Wei wrote his pagoda inscription.[46] He was born, most likely, in 683 and died some time in the period between 742 and 753.[47]

Of the eleven heirs of Hung-jen, then, we have three men of prime importance, men who founded major schools of Ch'an, or to whom the foundation is attributed: Shen-hsiu, Chih-hsien, and Hui-neng. We have four men, Hsüan-yüeh, Lao-an, Fa-ju, and Hsüan-tse, of whom we have slight, and at times negligible information, but who may well have been fairly important Ch'an Masters in the early eighth century. And we have four men of whom nothing whatsoever is known.

The *Leng-chia shih-tzu chi,* which contains this information concerning Hung-jen's disciples, is, chronologically, the second text still extant that deals with the history of Ch'an. An exact dating of the work cannot be made, but it may be placed somewhere in the K'ai-yüan era (712–741)[48] and, as we have seen, it contains material which can be dated to the first decade of the eighth century. At least five different copies or fragments have been found among the Tun-huang documents, which would indicate that the work had a fairly wide circulation.

The *Leng-chia shih-tzu chi* makes several contributions to the advancement of the Ch'an legend, and also adds new material, which later Ch'an writers were to reject as untrue. It is the first work to give numerical designations to the Patriarchs, listing eight: (1) Gunabhadra, (2) Bodhidharma, (3) Hui-k'o, (4) Seng-ts'an, (5) Tao-hsin, (6)

[46] See Wang Wei, *Ta-T'ang Ta-an-kuo ssu ku ta-te Ching-chüeh shih t'a-ming,* CTW, ch. 327 (VII, 4193–94).

[47] See Chikusa Masaaki, "Jōkaku katchū 'Hannya haramita shingyō' ni tsuite," *Bukkyō shigaku,* VII (no. 3, October, 1958), 66.

[48] Hu Shih, "Leng-chia shih-tzu chi hsü," *Hu Shih wen-ts'un,* IV, 237, estimates that it was completed sometime in the K'ai-yüan era. In a later work, however, "Hsin-hsiaoting te Tun-huang hsieh-pen Shen-hui ho-shang i-chu liang-chung," CYLYYC, XXIX (no. 2, February, 1958), 869, he places the date as "before 716." Shinohara Hisao, "Ryōga shiji ki ni tsuite," *Komazawa Daigaku kenkyū kiyō,* no. 13 (March, 1955), p. 94, agrees with the attribution to the K'ai-yüan era. Sekiguchi Shindai, "Hiniku kotsuzui," *IBK,* no. 22 (March, 1963), p. 15, dates the work at 708, and Nakagawa Taka, "Daruma zenji ron (Tonkō shutsudo) kō," *Shūkan Tōyōgaku,* no. 2 (1959), p. 96, dates it at 710. Since the work lists Shen-hsiu's disciple, P'u-chi, as the Eighth Patriarch, and gives no death date for him, it may be assumed that the work was completed before his death in 739.

Hung-jen, (7) Shen-hsiu, and (8) P'u-chi.[49] No mention is made of the early Indian Patriarchs. By placing Gunabhadra (394–468) as the First Patriarch, the *Leng-chia shih-tzu chi* seems to be attempting to establish a new legend, although it may possibly be perpetuating an older one of unknown origin. The selection of Gunabhadra as the First Patriarch of the sect is based on an obvious reason: he was the translator of the four-*chüan* version of the Laṅkāvatāra Sutra, the scripture on which this school founded its teachings. Furthermore, the *Hsü kao-seng chuan* mentions that Bodhidharma transmitted this sutra in four *chüan* to Hui-k'o.[50] The introduction here of this novel theory of the descent of the Chinese Patriarchs is indicative of the newness of the patriarchal tradition within Ch'an. The legend which was eventually to gain acceptance had yet to be devised, the connection with India had yet to be established, and there was still room for invention. Later, in a work dating around 780, we find the *Leng-chia shih-tzu chi* severely taken to task for its assertion that Gunabhadra was Bodhidharma's teacher.[51]

The notice in the *Leng-chia shih-tzu chi* tells us very little of Gunabhadra.[52] He was a priest from central India, a follower of the Mahāyāna teaching, who arrived in Canton by ship during the Yüan-chia[53] era (425–453) of the Sung dynasty. Welcomed by the emperor, he soon undertook the translation of the Laṅkāvatāra Sutra. The remainder of this rather lengthy notice is devoted to quotations attributed to Gunabhadra, as well as others drawn from various canonical works. Gunabhadra is associated with the Pao-lin Temple, where Hui-neng made his home, and later texts attribute to him a prediction in which he foretells the arrival of the Sixth Patriarch.[54] Gunabhadra translated a great number of works, but there is nothing to indicate that he gave particular emphasis to the Laṅkāvatāra Sutra. Futhermore, there is no evidence to show that he ever met Bodhidharma.[55] The whole

---

[49] An identical list, unnumbered, is given in the preface to Ching-chüeh's commentary on the Heart Sutra. See Chikusa, "Jōkaku katchū . . . ," p. 65.

[50] T50, p. 552b.

[51] *Li-tai fa-pao chi*, T51, p. 180b.

[52] For his biography, see *Kao-seng chuan*, T50, pp. 344a–46b.

[53] The *Kao-seng chuan* gives the year as 435 (T50, p. 344a).

[54] See below, p. 61.

[55] Lo Hsiang-lin, *T'ang-tai Kuang-chou Kuang-hsiao ssu yü Chung-Yin chiao-t'ung chih kuan-hsi*, English summary, pp. 14–15, believes that Bodhidharma studied under Gunabhadra at the Kuang-hsiao Temple, basing his conclusions on the statement in the *Leng-chia shih-tzu chi*. If credence can be given to Hu Shih's studies, however, Gunabhadra must have been dead by the time Bodhidharma arrived in China. See Hu Shih, "P'u-t'i-ta-mo . . . ."

story is obviously fictional, either devised by the compiler of this work or borrowed by him from elsewhere. That it was not perpetuated is evidence of its absurdity for, throughout the creation of the legend of the patriarchal transmission, Ch'an has tended to reject any attributions that were completely untenable, and that might leave it open to attack by other schools of Buddhism. This will be seen later in the rejection of an equally indefensible theory of thirteen Patriarchs from Buddha through Hui-neng, and the elimination of certain obvious errors in the lineage as it developed through the course of the eighth century.

Bodhidharma is listed as the Second Patriarch, and the text specifically states that he received the teaching from Gunabhadra. Included is the text of Bodhidharma's doctrine of the "Two Entrances and the Four Categories of Conduct," which is described as having been compiled by Bodhidharma's disciple, T'an-lin.[56] We are also informed that Bodhidharma made a commentary on the Lankāvatāra Sutra, the *Leng-chia yao-i,* otherwise known as *Ta-mo lun.*[57] There is no significant enlargement of the legend of Bodhidharma here, and this is true also of the biographies of the other Patriarchs; they consist primarily of brief notices of the career and a series of quotations, drawn largely from a variety of sutras, which are attributed to each Patriarch.

The *Leng-chia shih-tzu chi* makes no further mention of Fa-ju, whose cause had been championed by the *Ch'uan fa-pao chi,* and it carries the line of transmission one generation further, by adding P'u-chi as eighth in the line of succession. Along with P'u-chi are listed three other heirs of Shen-hsiu: Ching-hsien, I-fu, and Hui-fu. Almost no information is provided here for any of these men; they were, however, significant figures in the Ch'an of the capital cities. P'u-chi and his disciple I-fu both had access to the imperial court, were accorded

---

[56] Biography unknown.

[57] This may well be the same work as the Tun-huang text, known as *Ta-mo ch'an-shih lun,* published by Sekiguchi Shindai, *Daruma Daishi kenkyū,* pp. 445–50. Sekiguchi believes that this work represents, along with the "Two Entrances and Four Categories of Conduct," the true thought of Bodhidharma. It may, however, be of a much later period. See Nakagawa, "Daruma zenji ron . . . ," pp. 85–96. Many works are attributed to Bodhidharma; almost all of them are products of a later age. The fabrication during the seventh and eighth centuries of works to which Bodhidharma's name was attached is another facet of the Ch'an legend. A large number of these attributions have been found among the Tun-huang documents. In addition, there is a work known as the *Shōshitsu rokumon* (T48, pp. 365–76), which contains six works attributed to Bodhidharma. This collection, however, was made in Japan during the Tokugawa period, and does not exist as such in China. The entire subject is discussed by Sekiguchi in the work cited above.

exceptional patronage, and were honored as national teachers. Their biographies are known from contemporary records.

P'u-chi,[58] a native of Ho-tung,[59] left home at an early age, and went to study under Shen-hsiu at the Yü-ch'üan Temple. He did not officially become a monk until his Master was called to court by the Empress Wu. In 735 he was summoned by the emperor and gained immense popularity, not only in court circles, but among the general populace as well. When he died in 739 a grand funeral service was held, attended by numerous high officials, and by so many of the general public that the villages were said to have been emptied of people.

I-fu,[60] from T'ung-ti,[61] studied Taoism and the *Book of Changes* as a youth and then, turning to Buddhism, concentrated on the Saddharmapuṇḍarīka, Vimalakīrti, and other Mahāyāna sutras. He went to the Shao-lin Temple, intending to study under Fa-ju, but when he arrived he found that this priest had already passed away. Thus he became a disciple of Shen-hsiu and studied under him until the latter was called to court. After Shen-hsiu's death he served at various temples in Ch'ang-an, and was active in propagating the teachings among both the high officials and the common people. When he died in 736, the emperor sent a messenger to convey his condolences.

Of the two other heirs of Shen-hsiu mentioned in the *Leng-chia shih-tzu chi,* Hui-fu is completely unknown, but Ching-hsien,[62] although forgotten in later biographies, seems to have been a man of considerable importance. A native of Fen-yin,[63] he came to Shen-hsiu shortly before the latter's death in 706. He was called to court by

---

[58] His biography is found in CTS, 141, p. 14b. His pagoda inscription is by Li Yung, *Ta-chao ch'an-shih t'a-ming,* pp. 3360–63. The *Sung k͟ao-seng chuan* account (T50, p. 760c–761b) is largely based on this inscription. Later works ignore him. His name is mentioned in the *Ching-te ch'uan-teng lu,* T51, p. 224b, but no biographical material, anecdotes, or sayings are given.

[59] Yung-chi hsien, Shansi.

[60] His biography is found in CTS 191, pp. 14b–15a. His biographical monument is by Yen T'ing-chih, *Ta-chih ch'an-shih pei-ming,* pp. 3596–98; his pagoda inscription is by Tu Yü, *Ta-chih ch'an-shih t'a-ming, Chin-shih hsü-pien,* VII, 17b–19a. The *Sung k͟ao-seng chuan,* T50, p. 760b–c, also carries his biography, but, as with P'u-chi, only his name is listed in the *Ching-te ch'uan-teng lu,* T51, p. 224b.

[61] Ch'in hsien, Shansi.

[62] His name does not appear in any of the Ch'an histories, nor in the *Sung k͟ao-seng chuan.* His pagoda inscription is by Yang Yü, *Sung-shan Hui-shan-shan ssu k͟u Ching-hsien t'a-shih shen-t'a shih-chi,* CTW ch. 362 (VIII, 4649–50). In this inscription his name is written Ching (Matthews' number 1129)-hsien; the *Leng-chia shih-tzu chi* writes Ching (Matthews' number 1138)-hsien.

[63] Jung-ho hsien, Shansi.

the Emperor Chung-tsung, who had heard of his great popular appeal, but soon left the palace precincts, finding the monastic environment more to his liking. He died in 723 at the age of sixty-four.

We have examined in considerable detail the careers of the men prominent in the Ch'an movement in the first three decades of the eighth century. These men were all associated with the Ch'an of Shen-hsiu or related schools. They are described in the histories of their own sect, and many of those of whom brief mention alone is made were important enough personages to have had inscriptions in their honor composed on their deaths. There may well have been other schools of Ch'an extant at the time, but of them we have no record. The Ch'an of Shen-hsiu and his disciples had gained a great following, both within the imperial court and among the people at large, especially in the capital cities. With this popularity went prestige, much power, and resplendent temples. With it also went recognition as the orthodox Ch'an teaching of the time, and also recognition of the lineage of the sect.

Yet neither the tradition adopted by the *Ch'uan fa-pao chi* nor that of the *Leng-chia shih-tzu chi* was accepted as the final version of Shen-hsiu's school. In Chang Yüeh's inscription for Shen-hsiu the lineage is given as: (1) Bodhidharma, (2) Hui-k'o, (3) Seng-ts'an, (4) Tao-hsin, (5) Hung-jen, and (6) Shen-hsiu.[64] Three other contemporary inscriptions attest to the same lineage, and they extend the line by one generation, by including P'u-chi as the Seventh Patriarch.[65] This, then, became the orthodox line of transmission in the school of Ch'an founded by Shen-hsiu.

SHEN-HUI

While the Ch'an of Loyang and Ch'ang-an was enjoying this immense popularity and power, a then unknown priest in Nan-yang,[66] Shen-hui by name, was intent upon building a new school of his own. To this end he launched an attack upon the Ch'an of Shen-hsiu's

[64] *T'ang Yü-ch'üan ssu Ta-t'ung ch'an-shih pei-ming ping hsü*, p. 2953.
[65] Li Yung, *Sung-yüeh ssu pei*, cтw, ch. 263 (VI, 3380); *Ta-chao ch'an-shih t'a-ming*, p. 3362; *Ta-chih ch'an-shih pei-ming*, p. 3597. This last item speaks of both P'u-chi and I-fu as being "in the seventh generation."
[66] Nan-yang hsien, Honan.

descendants and, after many years of struggle, eventually carried the day. The story of this new kind of Ch'an was unearthed by the late Dr. Hu Shih, who found among the Tun-huang documents housed at the Bibliothèque Nationale several manuscripts containing the sayings and writings of Shen-hui and his followers. These he collated and published, and through his studies rewrote the history of Ch'an during the T'ang dynasty. The career of Shen-hui fascinated this multifaceted scholar, who, toward the close of his diversified life, returned to the study of this champion of what came to be known as "Southern Ch'an." Since Hu Shih's studies caught the imagination of both Western and Oriental scholars, a considerable body of material concerning Shen-hui has been produced.[67]

[67] Hu Shih first published his findings in *Shen-hui ho-shang i-chi*. The work contains a biographical study of Shen-hui and four fragmentary texts: 1) P3047 (1), entitled by Hu Shih *Shen-hui yü-lu*, fragment 1; 2) P3047 (2), called by Hu Shih *Shen-hui yü-lu*, fragment 2; it is entitled *P'u-t'i-ta-mo Nan-tsung ting shih-fei lun*, and was compiled with a preface by Tu-ku P'ei; includes only the first part of the text of this treatise; 3) P3488, entitled by Hu Shih *Shen-hui yü-lu*, fragment 3; the text is a portion of the same work represented by fragment 2; and 4) an item from the Stein collection at the British Museum (hereinafter abbreviated S), S468, which Hu Shih referred to as *Shen-hui yü-lu*, fragment 4; it bears the title, *Tun-wu wu-shang pan-jo sung*, and is otherwise known as *Hsien-tsung chi*; in its complete form it can be found in *chüan* 30 of the *Ching-te ch'uan-teng lu*, T51, pp. 458c–459b; it is also found in the *Tsung-ching lu*, *chüan* 99 (T48, p. 949a–b) under the title *Hsien-tsung lun*.

Hu Shih's collection of Shen-hui's works was translated by Jacques Gernet, *Entretiens du Maître de Dhyāna Chen-houei du Ho-tsö* (Publications de l'école française d'extrême-Orient XXXI).

In 1932 a facsimile reproduction of a Tun-huang manuscript in the possession of Ishii Mitsuo was published under the title *Tonkō shutsudo Jinne roku*. The text is similar to P3047 (1), published by Hu Shih, and was later collated and edited by D. T. Suzuki and Kuda Rentarō, *Tonkō shutsudo Kataku Jinne zenji goroku* (it was issued together with an edition of 1) the Tun-huang text of the *Platform Sutra*, 2) the Kōshōji edition of the *Platform Sutra*, and 3) a volume of explanatory material, 4 vols. in 1 case). This edition lacks the beginning few pages (pp. 97–103) of the Hu Shih text, but contains additional text at the end: pp. 49–67 in the Suzuki edition (hereinafter referred to as *Shen-hui yü-lu* [Suzuki text]).

A translation of those portions of the Suzuki edition of the Ishii text which are not represented in the Hu Shih edition has been made by Jacques Gernet, "Complément aux entretiens du Maître de Dhyāna Chen-houei," *BEFEO*, XLIV (no. 2, 1954), 453–66. Included is a summary of the contents of a then newly discovered text, P2045, the first part of which contains the *P'u-t'i-ta-mo Nan-tsung ting shih-fei lun*. The second part (not summarized by Gernet) contains the complete text of a work entitled *Nan-yang ho-shang tun-chiao chieh-t'o ch'an-men chih-liao-hsing t'an-yü*. This latter work has been translated by Walter Liebenthal, "The Sermon of Shen-hui," *Asia Major*, new series, III (no. 2, 1952), 132–55. Two unpublished fragments, S2492 and S6977, have been identified by Professor Iriya as representing portions of this work.

A copy of a text similar to P2045 (2) was found in Peking and published by D. T. Suzuki, *Kōkan Shōshitsu issho oyobi kaisetsu*, pp. 57–71, and was later repub-

To understand the revolution in Ch'an Buddhism brought about by Shen-hui, it is necessary to examine his career in some detail.[68] His

lished by Suzuki, "Jinne oshō to kangaubeki Tonkō shutsudo bon ni tsukite," *Ōtani gakuhō*, XVI (no. 4, December, 1935, 1–30; text, pp. 22–30).

Hu Shih resumed his study of Shen-hui with "Hsin-chiao-ting te Tun-huang hsieh-pen Shen-hui ho-shang i-chu liang-chung [Two newly edited texts of the Ch'an Master Shen-hui from the Pelliot collection of Tun-huang manuscripts at the Bibliothèque Nationale of Paris]," *CYLYYC*, XXIX (no. 2, 1958), 827–82. Included in this study are collated texts of P2045 (2): *Nan-yang ho-shang tun-chiao chieh-t'o ch'an-men chih-liao-hsing t'an-yü*, and of P2045 (1): *P'u-t'i-ta-mo Nan-tsung ting shih-fei lun* in 2 chüan, of which Hu Shih had originally published two fragments in his text of 1930.

A new text, S6557, was collated and discussed in detail by Paul Demiéville, "Deux documents de Touen-houang sur le dhyāna chinois," *Tsukamoto hakushi shōju ki'nen Bukkyō shigaku ronshū*, pp. 1–27. The text is entitled *Nan-yang Wen-ta tsa-cheng i*, and was compiled by Liu Ch'eng. This text, first identified by Professor Iriya, is in several places parallel to the first text published by Hu Shih (P3047 [1]) and the Ishii text published by Suzuki, so that Hu Shih in his "An Appeal for a Systematic Search in Japan for Long-hidden T'ang Dynasty Source Materials of the Early History of Zen Buddhism," *Bukkyō to bunka*, p. 16, has concluded that this is the correct title for the text that has been referred to as *Shen-hui yü-lu*.

A collated text of the above was published by Hu Shih, "Shen-hui ho-shang yü-lu te ti-san-ko Tun-huang hsieh-pen [A third Tun-huang text of the Discourses of the Monk Shen-hui with its original title "Nan-yang ho-shang Wen-ta tsa cheng i," collated by Liu Ch'eng]," *CYLYYC*, extra vol. 4 (no. 1, September, 1960) [Studies presented to Tung Tso Pin on his sixty-fifth birthday], 1–31.

On the basis of the above studies, we can identify four basic texts by Shen-hui:

1. *Nan-yang ho-shang wen-ta tsa-cheng i*
   a) P3047 (1) — Hu Shih, *Shen-hui ho-shang i-chi*, frag. 1.
   b) S6557 — Hu Shih, "Shen-hui ho-shang yü-lu te ti-san-ko Tun-huang hsieh-pen."
   c) Suzuki text — D. T. Suzuki, *Tonkō shutsudo Kataku Jinne zenji goroku*.
2. *Nan-yang ho-shang . . . t'an-yü*
   a) P2045 (2) — Hu Shih, "Hsin-chiao-ting te Tun-huang hsieh-pen Shen-hui ho-shang i-chu liang-chung."
   b) Peking text — D. T. Suzuki, *Kōkan Shōshitsu issho oyobi kaisetsu*.
   c) S2492 — Unpublished fragment.
   d) S6977 — Unpublished fragment.
3. *P'u-t'i-ta-mo Nan-tsung ting shih-fei lun*
   a) P2045 (1) — Hu Shih, "Hsin-chiao-ting. . . ."
   b) P3047 (2) — Hu Shih, *Shen-hui ho-shang i-chi*, frag. 2.
   c) P3488 (1) — Hu Shih, *Shen-hui ho-shang i-chi*, frag. 3.
4. *Tun-wu wu-shang pan-jo sung*
   a) S468 — Hu Shih, *Shen-hui ho-shang i-chi*, frag. 4.
   b) *Hsien-tsung chi* — *Ching-te ch'uan-teng lu*, ch. 30.
   c) *Hsien-tsung lun* — *Tsung-ching lu*, ch. 99.

[68] There are two excellent biographical studies of Shen-hui: 1) Hu Shih, *Shen-hui ho-shang i-chi*, pp. 1–90; 2) Jacques Gernet, "Biographie du Maître Chen-houei du Ho-tsö," *Journal Asiatique* (1951), pp. 29–60. The latter is a translation of the notice contained in the *Sung kao-seng chuan*, with extensive commentary. The biographical material given below is drawn largely from these studies.

surname was Kao, and he was a native of Hsiang-yang in Hupeh. As a child he took easily to study, and soon mastered the intricacies and the obscurities of the classics. He found much to his satisfaction in the *Lao Tzu* and the *Chuang Tzu,* but when he read the *History of the Later Han Dynasty* he became aware of Buddhist doctrines and, shunning an official career, turned to their study. After entering a temple near his home, he went, when he was about forty years of age,[69] to Ts'ao-ch'i,[70] where he studied under Hui-neng. Here he stayed for a few years, perhaps from around 708 until Hui-neng's death in 713.[71] After this he traveled about, and in 720 was ordered by imperial command to reside at the Lung-hsing Temple in Nan-yang. From this time until 732 our information is scanty. It may be presumed that he studied and preached, spreading his own teachings, and gained both in popularity and in the number of converts made. Then, on the fifteenth day of the first month of 732 (= February 15, 732)[72] he organized a great conference at the Ta-yün Temple in Hua-t'ai,[73] at which he mounted a grand attack on the Ch'an of P'u-chi, the successor to Shen-hsiu. Details of this and subsequent condemnations of his rivals are recorded in the *P'u-t'i-ta-mo Nan-tsung ting shih-fei lun,* compiled by Tu-ku P'ei.[74] At this time, as well as on later occasions, he pressed his assault on the established school of Ch'an.

He made many charges and many pronouncements. Among other things, he told the history of his sect. According to Shen-hui, Bodhidharma, the third son of an Indian king, arrived in Liang and held

[69] Sources differ as to Shen-hui's age when he visited Hui-neng. The *Sung kao-seng chuan,* T50, p. 765c, and Wang Wei's inscription for Hui-neng (Chao Tien-ch'eng, annotator, *Wang Yu-cheng chi-chien-chu,* p. 449) indicate that he arrived at Hui-neng's temple when he was in his middle age. The *Ching-te ch'uan-teng lu,* T51, p. 245a, and Tsung-mi in his *Yüan-chüeh ching ta-shu ch'ao,* zzl, 14, 3, 277a, give his age as fourteen. In the *Platform Sutra* (sec. 48) Hui-neng addresses Shen-hui as "young monk." As Hu Shih points out (*Shen-hui ho-shang i-chi,* p. 7), since Wang Wei's inscription was made while Shen-hui was still alive, it is more probably correct. The story of his visit to Hui-neng as a youth, and various details of his life, especially as found in the *Ching-te ch'uan-teng lu* and Tsung-mi's work, may best be regarded as legends of the type which tended to grow up around any priest of exceptional fame.

[70] The site of Hui-neng's temple in Kuangtung.

[71] See Gernet, "Biographie . . . ," p. 37.

[72] Hu Shih originally dated this meeting as having taken place in 734, but more recently, on the basis of new information, revised the date to 732. See Hu Shih, "Hsin-chiao-ting . . . ," pp. 872–73.

[73] Hua hsien, northeast of Loyang.

[74] The complete text is given in Hu Shih, "Hsin-chiao-ting . . . ," pp. 838–56. Nothing is known of the compiler.

discourse with the Emperor Wu.[75] To the emperor's question as to whether he, the emperor, had gained merit by building temples, helping people, making statues, and copying sutras, Bodhidharma replied: "No merit." The emperor did not understand and Bodhidharma left for Wei, where he met Hui-k'o. The latter sought desperately to become his disciple, and Bodhidharma finally relented when Hui-k'o, to show his earnestness, seized a sword and cut off his left arm. Bodhidharma later handed his robe to Hui-k'o as a symbol of the transmission of the Dharma. Hui-k'o then handed it to Seng-ts'an, Seng-ts'an to Tao-hsin, Tao-hsin to Hung-jen, and Hung-jen transmitted it to Hui-neng. For six generations, we are told, the robe was handed down from Patriarch to Patriarch.[76]

Shen-hui is making two points here: he is establishing Bodhidharma's robe as a symbol of the transmission of the Dharma, and he is refuting the accepted line of the transmission, by substituting Hui-neng for Shen-hsiu. Up to now we have heard nothing of Hui-neng, except for the brief mention of him as one of the heirs of the Fifth Patriarch in the *Leng-chia shih-tzu chi;* his name does not appear in sources other than those of dubious reliability.[77] Furthermore, Shen-hui, by introducing the stories of Bodhidharma and the Emperor Wu and of Hui-k'o's severed arm, is deliberately embroidering the legendary aspects of the early patriarchs. These stories are repeated *ad nauseum* in later Ch'an works and have proven to be the most popular and enduring of Ch'an legends. Hu Shih has suggested that they were made up by Shen-hui,[78] but it appears more likely that they were common stories, current at the time,[79] and that Shen-hui merely borrowed them for the effect they might have. Certainly, his use of them served to perpetuate them in the developing Ch'an legend.

Elsewhere, Shen-hui went on to say: "During his lifetime the Ch'an Master Shen-hsiu stated that the robe symbolic of the Dharma, as transferred in the sixth generation, was at Shao-chou;[80] he never called

[75] The story of Bodhidharma and the Emperor Wu appears also in the *Platform Sutra* (sec. 34).
[76] Hu Shih, "Hsin-chiao-ting . . . ," p. 869; Hu Shih, *Shen-hui ho-shang i-chi,* p. 160; Gernet, *Entretiens . . . ,* p. 83.
[77] See below, chapter II.
[78] Hu Shih, "Ch'an (Zen) Buddhism in China . . . ," p. 8.
[79] The story of Hui-k'o's cutting off his arm, for example, has appeared already in the *Ch'uan fa-pao chi.*
[80] Hui-neng's temple at Ts'ao-ch'i was located near this city.

himself the Sixth Patriarch. But now P'u-chi calls himself by the title
of the Seventh Patriarch and falsely states that his Master was the
Sixth. This must not be permitted." [81]

In the same vein, we read: "The Dharma-master Yüan asked: 'Why
should P'u-chi not be allowed to do this?' The priest [Shen-hui]
answered: 'Although the Ch'an Master P'u-chi speaks of the Southern
School, he is only plotting to destroy it.'" Shen-hui then goes on to
charge that in the third month of 714 P'u-chi sent a certain Chang
Hsing-ch'ang,[82] disguised as a priest, to take the head from Hui-neng's
mummified body, and that he inflicted three knife wounds upon it.
Furthermore, Shen-hui claims, P'u-chi sent his disciple Wu P'ing-i[83]
to efface the inscription on the Master's stele and to substitute another
one that said that Shen-hsiu was the Sixth Patriarch. P'u-chi, Shen-hui
continues, erected a stone inscription at Sung-shan,[84] constructed a
building known as the "Hall of the Seventh Patriarch," and compiled
the [*Ch'uan*] *fa-pao chi*,[85] in which he failed to make mention of Hui-
neng's name. Shen-hui continued his attack, stating that Fa-ju was a
fellow student with Shen-hsiu and was also not in the line of transmission, yet in the *Ch'uan fa-pao chi* he is called the Sixth Patriarch.
Shen-hui concludes sarcastically: "Now P'u-chi erects a stele for Shen-
hsiu in which he calls him the Sixth Patriarch, and then he compiles
the *Ch'uan fa-pao chi,* in which he makes Fa-ju the Sixth Patriarch. I
don't understand how these two worthies can both be the Sixth Patriarch. Which is right and which is wrong? Let's ask the Ch'an Master
P'u-chi to explain it himself in detail." [86]

In the passage summarized above, Shen-hui makes particular mention of P'u-chi's attempts to destroy the Southern School (Nan-tsung).

[81] *Shen-hui yü-lu* (Hu Shih text, frag. 3). Hu Shih, *Shen-hui ho-shang i-chi,* p. 176;
Gernet, *Entretiens* . . . , pp. 94–95.
[82] Unidentified.
[83] In the biography of Hui-neng in the *Sung kao-seng chuan,* T50, p. 755b, Wu
P'ing-i is described as having visited Hui-neng's grave, and as having written a verse
to be inscribed on a giant bell that one of the Master's disciples was casting. His
biography is in HTS 119, pp. 1a–2a. At one time he studied Buddhism at Sung-shan,
and was associated with Sung Chih-wen and Chang Yüeh in literary endeavors. He died
toward the end of the K'ai-yüan era (*ca.* 741). One account has Wu doing honor to
Hui-neng; the other has him desecrating his inscription. I know no way of reconciling
the contradiction.
[84] This may refer to the *Sung-yüeh ssu-pei,* pp. 3379–81.
[85] P'u-chi, of course, was not the compiler of the *Ch'uan fa-pao chi.*
[86] Hu Shih, "Hsin-chiao-ting . . . ," p. 847 (*P'u-t'i-ta-mo Nan-tsung ting shih-fei
lun*).

There seems to have been considerable confusion at this time concerning the use of this term.[87] In the preface to a commentary on the
Heart Sutra by Ching-chüeh,[88] mention is made of the Southern
School in reference to the teachings which Gunabhadra handed down
to Bodhidharma. Thus, what came to be known as the Northern
School of Ch'an, that of Shen-hsiu and P'u-chi, was at one time known
as the Southern School. That this caused Shen-hui considerable conster-
nation is evident from another passage in the *P'u-t'i-ta-mo Nan-tsung
ting shih-fei lun:* "When the priest [Shen]-hsiu was alive, all students referred to these two great Masters, saying, 'In the South, [Hui]-neng;
in the North, [Shen]-hsiu,' . . . therefore we have the two schools,
the Southern and the Northern. . . . [P'u-chi] now recklessly calls his
[teaching] the Southern Sect. This is not to be permitted." [89]

Furthermore, the story of the attempt to cut off the head from Hui-
neng's mummified body, which figures so prominently in some of the
later works,[90] appears here for the first time. Similarly, the story of
the effacement of Hui-neng's inscription and the substitution of an alternate version appears also in a subsequent biography.[91] There is no
way of determining whether these stories were inventions of Shen-hui
or were merely tales current at the time.

In another work Shen-hui discusses the lineage of Ch'an: "Bodhidharma received the teaching from Saṅgharakṣa, Saṅgharakṣa received
it from Śubhamitra, Śubhamitra received it from Upagupta, Upagupta
received it from Śaṇavāsa, Śaṇavāsa received it from Madhyāntika,
Madhyāntika from Ānanda, Ānanda from Kāśyapa, Kāśyapa from the
Tathāgata. When we come to China, Bodhidharma is considered the
Eighth Patriarch. In India Prajñāmitra[92] received the Law from Bodhi-

---

[87] In the biography of Fa-ch'ung in the *Hsü kao-seng chuan,* ᴛ50, p. 666b, there is
mention of the "One vehicle sect of India (Nan-t'ien-chu i-ch'eng tsung)," in reference
to Bodhidharma's teaching, and it is possible that the term derived from here. See Hu
Shih, "Hsin-chiao-ting . . . ," p. 869. The problem of the confusion in terms is discussed in Sekiguchi Shindai, "Nanshū to Nanshū Zen," *IBK,* no. 20 (March, 1962),
pp. 70–76.

[88] See Chikusa, "Jōkaku katchū . . . ," p. 65. The commentary does not have a
distinctive title, but contains the text of the sutra in large characters, with Ching-chüeh's
commentary in small characters attached.

[89] Hu Shih, "Hsin-chiao-ting . . . ," p. 847.

[90] It is found in the *Sung kao-seng chuan,* ᴛ50, p. 155b, in a variant form, as well
as in the *Ching-te ch'uan-teng lu,* ᴛ51, pp. 236c–237a, in a highly elaborated version.

[91] *Sōkei daishi betsuden,* ᴢᴢ2B, 19, 5, 486b. This work is discussed below, pp. 70ff.

[92] The *Ta-mo-to-lo ch'an-ching,* ᴛ15, p. 301c, adds in its list of the Indian Patriarchs
after Dharmatrāta's name: "up to Puṇyamitra," and it may be that Prajñāmitra
represents a miscopying of this name.

dharma. In China it was Hui-k'o ch'an-shih who came after Bodhidharma. Since the time of the Tathāgata there were, in all, in India
and China, some thirteen Patriarchs."[93]

This extraordinary version of the patriarchal lineage involves a host
of problems. It is drawn directly from the body of the *Ta-mo-to-lo
ch'an-ching,* not from the preface as Shen-hui himself states.[94] The
latter work does not pretend to give a definitive list of all the Patriarchs, but Shen-hui seems to have regarded it as such. The absurdity
of having only thirteen Patriarchs from the time of the Buddha to
the eighth century seems not to have occurred to Shen-hui; however,
we see no later adoption of this example of his inventiveness in other
works.[95] The theory has been advanced that Shen-hui accepted the
lineage of twenty-eight Patriarchs, which was afterwards to become
the official one, but this seems quite doubtful.[96]

In his list of thirteen Patriarchs, Shen-hui made one serious mistake.
He inverted the first two characters of the name of the sixth Indian
Patriarch, Vasumitra, as given in the *Ta-mo-to-lo ch'an-ching,* arriving
at the name Śubhamitra. This error was later perpetuated in the Tun-
huang edition of the *Platform Sutra* (sec. 51), as well as in the *Li-tai
fa-pao chi.*[97] In addition, Shen-hui arbitrarily changed the name of
Dharmatrāta to Bodhidharma; the *Ta-mo-to-lo ch'an-ching,* of course,
makes no mention of Bodhidharma.

Shen-hui made a considerable number of statements about Hui-neng.
We do not know the source of his information and there is no cor-

[93] *Shen-hui yü-lu* (Hu Shih text, Frag. 3); see Hu Shih, *Shen-hui ho-shang i-chi,*
p. 179; Gernet, *Entretiens* . . . , pp. 97–98. See also Table 1.
[94] Later in the same passage (Hu Shih, *Shen-hui ho-shang i-chi,* p. 179) Shen-hui
identifies the source of his information as the "preface to the *Ch'an-ching.*" The list
in the preface, however, omits Kāśyapa in error, whereas his name is listed in the body
of the text (T15, p. 301c).
[95] Fang Kuan (697–763), in his inscription for the Third Patriarch, Seng-ts'an (*Pao-
lin chuan,* III, 561), says that up to the time of the Third Patriarch there were in all
seven Patriarchs in India and three in China. This follows Shen-hui's theory. For Fang
Kuan, see below, p. 78.
[96] Hu Shih, *Shen-hui ho-shang i-chi,* pp. 30–31, feels that Shen-hui, later in his life,
turned to the twenty-eight-Patriarch theory, on the basis of a statement in the version
of the *Hsien-tsung chi* contained in chüan 30 of the *Ching-te ch'uan-teng lu,* T51,
p. 459a, to the effect that there were in all twenty-eight Indian Patriarchs. The Tun-
huang version of the *Hsien-tsung chi,* contained in Hu Shih's own text (*Shen-hui ho-
shang i-chi,* pp. 193–95), does not mention the twenty-eight Patriarchs, so that their
inclusion in the *Ching-te ch'uan-teng lu* may represent a later interpolation. See Matsumoto Bunzaburō, *Bukkyō shi zakkō,* p. 160; Yanagida (Yokoi) Seizan, "Tōshi no
keifu," *Nihon Bukkyōgaku nempō,* no. 19 (1954), p. 20.
[97] T51, p. 180b.

roborating evidence of sufficient reliability to enable us to determine whether he was inventing stories or merely passing along legendary material current at the time. Shen-hui, in his efforts to justify his claim that Hui-neng was legitimately the Sixth Patriarch, tells the story that when the Empress Wu invited Shen-hsiu to court, in the year 700 or 701, this learned priest is alleged to have said that in Shao-chou there was a great master [Hui-neng], who had in secret inherited the Dharma of the Fifth Patriarch.[98] This story appears in one or another form in almost every biography of Hui-neng, its most common form being an imperial proclamation requesting Hui-neng, on Shen-hsiu's recommendation, to appear at court. It is included in the *Ch'üan Tang wen*,[99] the monumental collection of T'ang documents. Writers who emphasize the importance of Hui-neng, and seek to establish the historicity of his biography, constantly refer to it, but it would seem to be highly suspect, and scarcely serviceable as early evidence of Hui-neng's activity. The *Ch'üan T'ang wen* was compiled in 1814, using indiscriminately all available sources, many of them of a very late date, so that an unbounded faith in the validity of all the material it contains seems hardly justified. The alleged recommendation made to the Empress Wu by Shen-hsiu is, depending upon the source, ascribed also to Emperor Chung-tsung,[100] and even to Emperor Kao-tsung.[101] This hardly contributes to a feeling of confidence in its reliability. It would appear rather incautious to afford it the historical respectability which many writers have accorded it.[102]

Shen-hui, in addition to accusing P'u-chi of sending representatives to cut off the head of Hui-neng's mummified body and to efface his inscription, gave a biographical sketch of Hui-neng, along with those of the five other Patriarchs.[103] The information given is substantially the same as the autobiographical sections and the description of Hui-

---

[98] Hu Shih, "Hsin-chiao-ting . . . ," p. 848 (*P'u-t'i-ta-mo Nan-tsung ting shih-fei lun*).

[99] CTW, ch. 17 (I, 241).

[100] The *Ch'üan T'ang wen* attributes the invitation to the Emperor Chung-tsung. This would require it to have been issued after the twenty-fifth day of the first month, when Chung-tsung reascended the throne.

[101] *Sōkei Daishi betsuden*, p. 485b. The date given for the invitation is 705, and it is said to have been issued by Kao-tsung. Kao-tsung died in 683.

[102] Ui, *Zenshū shi kenkyū*, II, 223, does not question its reliability when quoting the version found in the *Ch'üan T'ang wen*. Dumoulin, *A History of Zen Buddhism*, p. 83; Gernet, "Biographie . . . ," p. 30; and Wing-tsit Chan, *The Platform Scripture*, p. 14, all accept its validity. For a further discussion, see pp. 65–66.

[103] *Shen-hui yü-lu* (Suzuki text), pp. 60–64. See also pp. 67 ff.

neng's death found in the *Platform Sutra,* although in a much more
concise form.[104] The authenticity of the *Platform Sutra* will be discussed later,[105] but it must be pointed out here that, despite his
championing the cause of his teacher, Shen-hui never quotes from the
writings or sayings of Hui-neng. If such had existed, it would seem
logical that he would have used them as his authority. As will be seen,
there are a number of instances in which the texts of Shen-hui's works
and the *Platform Sutra* are identical, and there can be no question
that the Tun-huang version of the latter work is chronologically later
than the surviving works of Shen-hui. These and other factors have
prompted Hu Shih to assert that the *Platform Sutra* was "composed by
an eighth-century monk, most likely a follower of Shen-hui's school,
who had read the latter's *Discourses* and decided to produce a *Book
of the Sixth Patriarch,* by rewriting his life-story in the form of a
fictionalized autobiography and by taking a few basic ideas from Shen-
hui and padding them into [the] Sermon of Hui-neng." [106] The al-
ternative view is that there existed an early version of Hui-neng's sayings which has not survived, from which Shen-hui derived his ideas.
This view, adopted by many, cannot be altogether rejected for reasons
which will be discussed later, but it certainly seems probable that
Shen-hui either perpetuated, organized, or perhaps deliberately fabri-
cated much of the legend of Hui-neng.

Shen-hui did not attack P'u-chi and Northern Ch'an only on the
basis of the alleged usurpation of the position of the Sixth Patriarch.
He accused them of holding erroneous views as well. His comments
on the meditation practice of the Northern school are reflected in the
following passage:

The Master Yüan said: "P'u-chi ch'an-shih of Sung-yüeh and Hsiang-
mo[107] of Tung-shan, these two priests of great virtue, teach men to 'con-

[104] The reader is referred to the translation, secs. 2–11, the first paragraph of sec. 48,
and sec. 54. There are some slight variations in the details.

[105] See chapter III, below.

[106] Hu Shih, "Ch'an (Zen) Buddhism in China . . . ," p. 11, fn. 9.

[107] Evidently a fairly important priest of Northern Ch'an. His biography appears in
Sung kao-seng chuan, T50, p. 760a. Very little is known of him: he studied a variety
of Buddhist doctrines before coming to Shen-hsiu for instruction, and is said to have
lectured on the Southern Teaching (Nan-tsung), a further indication that this term
was at one time used to refer to the Northern School of Ch'an (see p. 29, n. 87).
He died at the age of ninety-one, but the year of his death is not given. His biography
also appears in the *Ching-te ch'uan-teng lu,* T51, p. 232b, but no additional information is provided.

centrate the mind to enter *dhyāna,* to settle the mind to see purity, to stimulate the mind to illuminate the external, to control the mind to demonstrate the internal.' On this they base their teaching. Why, when you talk about Ch'an, don't you teach men these things? What is sitting in meditation (*tso-ch'an*)?'

The priest [Shen-hui] said: "If I taught people to do these things, it would be a hindrance to attaining enlightenment. The sitting (*tso*) I'm talking about means not to give rise to thoughts. The meditation (*ch'an*) I'm talking about is to see the original nature." [108]

On the identity of *prajñā* and *dhyāna,* Shen-hui states, in a passage closely paralleling one in the *Platform Sutra* (sec. 13):

The Dharma-master Tieh asked: "What does the statement, 'meditation (*dhyāna*) and wisdom (*prajñā*) are alike' mean?"

[Shen-hui] answered: "Not to give rise to thoughts, emptiness without being, this is the true meditation. The ability to see the non-rising of thoughts, to see emptiness without being, this is the true wisdom (*prajñā*). At the moment there is meditation, this is the substance of wisdom; at the moment there is wisdom, this is the function of meditation. Thus, the moment there is meditation, it is no different from wisdom. The moment there is wisdom, it is no different from meditation. Why? Because by their nature, of themselves, meditation and wisdom are alike." [109]

Statements such as those above have prompted Hu Shih and others to conclude that Shen-hui swept aside all meditation, rejected sitting practices, and produced a "new Ch'an which renounces *ch'an* itself and is therefore no *ch'an* at all." [110] This view, however, seems somewhat extreme. Shen-hui was attacking a particular type of meditation practice, which he attributed to Northern Ch'an. It would seem that what Shen-hui is saying is that meditation need not be limited to a formalized method of sitting alone; it can be practiced at any time. This is certainly the concept held by the new schools of Ch'an which rose at the end of the eighth century.[111] Shen-hui states that once there is true meditation then there is wisdom; wisdom is not a thing to be aimed at by "settling the mind to see purity." It is the method, not the meditation, that he is attacking. If we assume that Shen-hui discarded meditation and rejected Ch'an completely, then we must con-

---

[108] Hu Shih, *Shen-hui ho-shang i-chi,* pp. 175–76; Gernet, *Entretiens* . . . , pp. 93–94.

[109] Hu Shih, *Shen-hui ho-shang i-chi,* p. 128; Gernet, *Entretiens* . . . , p. 50.

[110] Hu Shih, "Ch'an (Zen) Buddhism in China . . . ," p. 7.

[111] It should be noted, too, that Hui-neng in the *Platform Sutra* (sec. 53) tells his students to sit in meditation after he has gone.

clude that his ideas were totally ignored by later Ch'an teachers, for
certainly meditation was practiced by the later schools. No matter how
varied the practices, Ch'an has always been within the framework of
Buddhism as a whole.

That Shen-hui was not beyond fabrication is indicated by his assertion that all the Patriarchs, from Bodhidharma through Hui-neng,
advocated the efficacy of the Diamond Sutra, and that it was this work,
rather than the Laṅkāvatāra Sutra which was handed down in the
school.[112] The *Hsü kao-seng chuan,* the *Ch'uan fa-pao chi,* and the
Leng-chia shih-tzu chi all refute this claim. Frequent quotations from
the Diamond Sutra and lengthy discussions devoted to it[113] emphasize
its importance in Shen-hui's teachings, but to claim that it was taught
by Bodhidharma and all later Patriarchs is pure fabrication.

The most frequent charge made against the Northern School was
that it taught a gradual method of attaining enlightenment, as opposed
to the sudden method advocated by the Southern School. Shen-hui's
advocacy of the sudden method is advanced in his works,[114] but it is
most strongly emphasized throughout the *Platform Sutra.* This attack
was clever and effective; it may, however, have been quite unjustified,
for there is evidence to show that Shen-hsiu also advocated the sudden
method, while insisting on the initial mastery of meditation techniques
for those just "entering upon the Way." [115] We know few details of
the teachings of Northern Ch'an, for most of its works have not been
preserved.[116] Indications are, however, that the school did not merely
practice the gradual method of introspection that Shen-hui described,
nor did it confine itself solely to the Laṅkāvatāra Sutra. It seems to
have advocated a far more sophisticated teaching, reflecting Hua-yen
concepts and Prajñāpāramitā thought,[117] and may well have been

[112] *Shen-hui yü-lu* (Suzuki text), pp. 60–64.
[113] Hu Shih, "Hsin-chiao-ting . . . ," pp. 850–51; Hu Shih, *Shen-hui ho-shang i-chi,* pp. 127–28; Gernet, *Entretiens* . . . , pp. 49–50.
[114] Hu Shih, *Shen-hui ho-shang i-chi,* p. 130; Gernet, *Entretiens* . . . , p. 53.
[115] We know too little of Northern Ch'an to have any clear idea of what its teachings were. An excellent study of the subject has been made by Kuno Hōryū, "Hokushū Zen," *Taishō daigaku gakuhō,* no. 30–31 (March, 1940), pp. 131–76. Included is the full text and an analysis of Shen-hsiu's *Ta-ch'eng wu fang-pien Pei-tsung,* discovered at Tun-huang. The subject is also discussed by Ui, *Zenshū shi kenkyū,* I, 269–327.
[116] A partial listing of Northern Ch'an works which have been preserved is given in Kuno, "Hokushū Zen," p. 175, n. 1.
[117] See the commentary on the Heart Sutra by Ching-chüeh, Chikusa, "Jōkaku katchū . . . ," pp. 64–67.

much closer to the teaching of the Fifth Patriarch than was the Ch'an which Shen-hui advocated.

There is little evidence to account for Shen-hui's activities between the years 732 and 745. He seems to have continued preaching, making many converts, and to have associated frequently with officials of high rank, traveling rather widely in the course of his work. This was a particularly trying time in the political history of the T'ang dynasty.[118] Emperor Hsüan-tsung, who had begun his forty-four-year reign in 712, was at the outset an astute and competent ruler. His efforts were directed towards the expansion of empire as well as the concentration of power in the hands of the central government. Great military victories brought numerous outlying areas under Chinese control; internally a variety of fiscal, economic, and political reforms was initiated. Buddhism, which had enjoyed great patronage and indulgence during the reigns of the Empress Wu and her two successors (690–712), found the imperial munificence drastically curtailed. Restrictions were imposed on the size of temple estates and the building of temples, and more stringent requirements were established for those who would become monks and nuns. Although Hsüan-tsung gave certain priorities to Taoism, the Buddhists were not greatly deprived. In fact, it may well have been that these new economic restrictions helped to further the intellectual development of the religion, for some of the greatest figures in Chinese Buddhism flourished during this period. As Hsüan-tsung's reign continued, the inevitable intrigues between rival political factions striving for power arose, seriously eroding the programs advocated by the emperor. Hsüan-tsung himself, during the latter half of his reign, seems to have lost interest, and to have dissociated himself from the intrigues surrounding him. We do not have much information concerning Buddhism's involvement with the plots and counterplots that beset the empire, but we do know that many of the great ministers and military leaders were present at public sermons and attended Buddhist services and ceremonies. Certainly, the fact that certain priests gained fame while others remained in obscurity may well have depended on the astuteness with which they selected their political associations.

---

[118] An excellent discussion of the political aspects of this period of the T'ang dynasty may be found in Edwin Pulleyblank, *The Background of the Rebellion of An Lu-shan* (London, 1955).

In 745 Shen-hui was invited by the vice-president of the army ministry, Sung Ting,[119] to come to Loyang, and to take up residence at the Ho-tse Temple. Here he held forth on the doctrines of the Southern School of Hui-neng, continuing his attack on the followers of P'u-chi's school. P'u-chi himself had died in 739. Shen-hui, after eight years of brilliant success as a preacher, fell afoul of the censor Lu I,[120] who was prejudiced in favor of Northern Ch'an,[121] and who reported that Shen-hui was plotting moves inimical to the government. Shen-hui was called to Ch'ang-an, where he was interviewed by Emperor Hsüan-tsung, and eventually sent into exile. During his banishment the nation was shaken to its roots by the rebellion of An Lu-shan, a general of Sogdian and Turkish ancestry. The rebel armies swept down upon the capital cities, capturing both Loyang and Ch'ang-an, and drove the imperial court into exile in 756. The emperor fled, leaving the affairs of state in the hands of the heir-apparent, who rallied the government forces and eventually succeeded in suppressing the rebellion. The T'ang dynasty survived for over a century and a half after this revolt, but it was never to regain even a measure of the glory of the early years of Hsüan-tsung's reign.

While the government forces were striving to subdue the revolt, they found themselves in extreme financial difficulties. To raise money to support the armies, ordination platforms were set up in each prefecture for the investiture of monks and the selling of certificates. Shen-hui was called back from exile to assist in this money-raising campaign, and he directed the ordinations in Loyang with such spectacular success that he contributed substantially to the beleaguered government. Although Loyang was in ruins, the director of palace construction was ordered to erect a Ch'an sanctuary for him within the grounds of the Ho-tse Temple. He remained active until his death, the date of which is variously given: the *Yüan-chüeh ching ta-shu ch'ao* has 758,[122] the *Sung kao-seng chuan*, 760.[123] Hu Shih has recently established the correct date as 762.[124]

After a long and strenuous career Shen-hui succeeded in establishing

---

[119] Biography unknown. His name appears in CTS 197, 4a and HTS 222, 14b.
[120] Biography in CTS 187, 5a–b; HTS 191, 12b–13a.
[121] So the *Sung kao-seng chuan* tells us (T50, p. 756c).
[122] ZZ1, 14, 3, 277a.
[123] T50, p. 757a.
[124] Hu Shih, "Hsin-chiao-ting . . . ," p. 875.

his school of Ch'an as the dominant one in the capital cities. Our records are scanty for this period, but it should not be assumed that Northern Ch'an gave up without considerable struggle. Although ignored in the histories, there is evidence to show that P'u-chi's school continued for several generations after his death in 739.[125] Hung-cheng, of whom we know little, is described as being in the "eighth generation" of Ch'an.[126] Another priest, more prominent in Japan than China, was Tao-hsüan (702–760), a disciple of P'u-chi, who arrived in Japan in 736. He taught Vinaya and Hua-yen philosophy, and was the teacher of Gyōhyō (722–797), who in turn was the instructor of the famous Saichō (767–822), who later went to China himself and brought back the T'ien-t'ai teachings to his country. Another Northern Ch'an priest of note was T'ung-kuang (700–770), whose name does not appear in the biographical works, but of whom we know through his inscription.[127] He had a large number of followers, and was himself probably one of the "sixty-three of the myriad disciples of P'u-chi who entered the hall (became active Ch'an teachers)." [128] Though precise information is lacking, it would seem that the Northern Ch'an school probably continued into the ninth century, without developing any priests of prominence, and most likely died out with the persecutions of the Hui-ch'ang era (842–845).

Shen-hui's school may well have suffered a similar fate. Although we hear of several disciples,[129] none achieved particular renown with the exception of Tsung-mi (780–841),[130] his descendant in the fifth

[125] For a discussion of the disciples of Northern Ch'an under P'u-chi and I-fu, see Ui, *Zenshū shi kenkyū*, I, 269–375; Takao Giken, "Futatabi Zen no Namboku ryōshū ni tsuite," *Ryūkoku gakuhō*, no. 306 (July, 1933), pp. 115–120.

[126] See Li Hua, *Ku Tso-ch'i ta-shih pei*, CTW, ch. 320 (VII, 4101).

[127] Kuo Shih, *T'ang Shao-lin ssu T'ung-kuang ch'an-shih t'a-ming*, CTW, ch. 441 (IX, 5685–86).

[128] See Tu-ku Chi, *Shu-chou Shan-ku ssu Chüeh-chi t'a Sui ku Ching-chih ch'an-shih pei-ming*, CTW, ch. 390 (VIII, 5002). This inscription, erected in 771, is designed to point up the conflict between Northern and Southern Ch'an. It praises Hung-cheng and says of Hui-neng that "he withdrew and grew old in Ts'ao-ch'i, and of his disciples nothing has been heard."

[129] For a discussion of Shen-hui's descendants, see Ui, *Zenshū shi kenkyū*, I, 195–268.

[130] Tsung-mi was a prolific writer and Buddhist scholar, who is listed also as one of the Patriarchs of the Hua-yen sect. Among his works are three that contain information about the Ch'an of this period: 1) *Ch'an-yüan chu-ch'üan tu-hsü*, T48, pp. 397–413; 2) *Ch'an-wen shih-tzu ch'eng-hsi-t'u*, ZZ2, 15, 5, 433b–38b; and 3) *Yüan-chüeh ching ta-shu ch'ao*, ZZ1, 14, 3–5; 15, 1. The first two have been translated into Japanese with annotations by Ui Hakuju, *Zengen shozenshū tojo*. Tsung-mi's biography is discussed, pp. 236–41.

generation. Tsung-mi left no disciples of note, and as with Northern Ch'an, it may be presumed that the school died out with the persecutions of Hui-ch'ang.

While Shen-hui was raising Hui-neng to the recognized status of the Sixth Patriarch,[131] either perpetuating an old legend or creating a new one, other Ch'an schools were busy building "histories" of their own lineage, as well as of Ch'an as a whole. The legend of the Ch'an Patriarchs continued to develop, and new versions began to appear. In the inscription by Li Hua for the T'ien-t'ai priest Tso-ch'i Hsüan-lang (673–754),[132] probably written shortly after the latter's death, mention is made of several schools of meditation, including those associated with the T'ien-t'ai sect. Four of these may be classified as belonging to Ch'an:

1. The school which started with the Buddha, who transmitted the mind-dharma to Kāśyapa, from whom it was handed down through twenty-nine Patriarchs until it reached Bodhidharma, who transmitted the Laṅkāvatāra Sutra, which passed through eight generations, reaching the Ch'an Master Hung-cheng. This was the Northern School of Ch'an.

2. The school which reached the Ch'an Master Ta-t'ung [Shen-hsiu] in the sixth generation from Bodhidharma, and was transmitted from him to the Ch'an Master Ta-chih [I-fu], who in turn transmitted it to the Ch'an Master Jung[133] of the Shan-pei Temple in Ch'ang-an. This school is referred to as the "one fountain-head of Northern Ch'an."

3. The school referred to as Southern Ch'an, which descended from Bodhidharma to the Fifth Patriarch Seng-ts'an,[134] from whom it was transmitted to Hui-neng.

4. The school transmitted from Bodhidharma to Tao-hsin in the fourth generation, and from him to the Ch'an Master [Fa]-jung[135]

---

[131] According to the *Yüan-chüeh ching ta-shu ch'ao*, zz1, 14, 3, 277b, the Emperor Te-tsung issued a proclamation in 796, establishing Shen-hui as the official Seventh Patriarch. Thus Hui-neng would seem to have been recognized as the legitimate Sixth Patriarch.

[132] *Ku Tso-ch'i ta-shih pei*, p. 4101.

[133] Unknown.

[134] An error for Hung-jen.

[135] His biography (*Hsü kao-seng chuan*, T50, p. 603c–605b) makes no mention of Bodhidharma or his school. Hu Shih, "Chan (Zen) Buddhism in China . . . ," p. 12, suggests that because of the popularity of Hui-neng as the Sixth Patriarch in the eighth century, "monks of the Oxhead school were willing to acknowledge that their founder

(594–657) of Mount Niu-t'ou, from whom it passed to the Ch'an Master Ching-shan.[136]

From this inscription it would seem evident that Li Hua considered the Northern School of Ch'an as the dominant one, although he recognizes the presence of the Southern School, without mentioning Shen-hui's name. If the assumption that this inscription was made shortly after Hsüan-lang's death is correct, then it may have been composed during the time Shen-hui was in exile, which might account for the failure to acknowledge him. The statement that there were twenty-nine Patriarchs from the Buddha to Bodhidharma is a new departure, seen here for the first time. They are not specifically itemized, so that no details of the names of the Patriarchs are determinable, but the inscription shows that in Northern Ch'an a theory of twenty-nine Indian Patriarchs had gained currency.[137]

This theory is continued in another Tun-huang document, the *Li-tai fa-pao chi*,[138] chronologically the next of the Ch'an histories. Again,

was at one time a student of Tao-hsin, 'the Fourth Patriarch after Bodhidharma,' thus establishing a connection with the Sixth Patriarch." Ui, *Zenshū shi kenkyū,* I, 94–96, cites several inscriptions of the late eighth and early ninth centuries, which he feels prove that Fa-jung was definitely a pupil of the Fourth Patriarch.

[136] Reference is to Ho-lin Hsüan-su (668–752), in the third generation after Fa-jung. His inscription is by Li Hua, *Jun-chou Ho-lin ssu ku Ching-shan ta-shih pei-ming,* CTW, ch. 320 (VII, 4106–08). A biography appears in the *Sung kao-seng chuan,* T50, pp. 761c–62b. Conceivably the reference might be to Hsüan-su's disciple, Ching-shan Fa-ch'in (714–792). For his biography see Li Chi-fu, *Hang-chou Ching-shan ssu Ta-chüeh ch'an-shih pei-ming ping-hsü,* CTW, ch. 512 (XI, 6599–6601), and *Sung kao-seng chuan,* T50, pp. 764b–65a.

[137] There is evidence to show that a theory of twenty-eight Indian Patriarchs was also held by the teachers of Northern Ch'an. The variation from twenty-eight to twenty-nine is determined by the omission or inclusion of Madhyāntika, the third Patriarch, who in some instances is included in the lists and in others excluded as representing a collateral branch. The Japanese Tendai (T'ien-t'ai) priest Saichō, who studied under the heir of a Northern Ch'an priest who came to Japan, provides a list of twenty-eight Patriarchs in his *Naishō Buppō sōjō ketsumyaku fu* (*Dengyō Daishi zenshū,* II, 516–29). This list is cited from a lost work of the Northern Ch'an school, known as the *Hsi-kuo Fo-tsu tai-tai hsiang-ch'eng ch'uan-fa chi.* Saichō lists twenty-eight Patriarchs from Kāśyapa through Bodhidharma, omitting Madhyāntika. The list continues, giving the line of Northern Ch'an from Hui-k'o through Hung-jen, then proceeding to Shen-hsiu—P'u-chi —Tao-hsüan (who came to Japan in 736)—Gyōhyō (of the Daianji in Nara)—Saichō. Thus we have the curious case of a Tendai priest advocating a Ch'an line of transmission. T'ien-t'ai, of course, held that the transmission had been cut off with the death of Siṁha bhikṣu, the twenty-fourth Patriarch, and traced its own teaching to the fourteenth, Nāgārjuna. To do justice to Saichō, he includes in the same work the traditional lines of transmission of the Tendai and Shingon schools.

[138] T51, pp. 179–96. For a discussion of this work, see Yabuki Keiki, *Meisha yoin kaisetsu,* pp. 504–20. The information given is somewhat out-dated. Copies exist in both the Stein and Pelliot collections.

the exact dating is uncertain, but it seems safe to place it at around the year 780.[139] Representing an entirely different line of Ch'an than has been seen up to now, it shows the influence of both the Northern and the Southern schools in its account of the patriarchal succession. The name of each of the Patriarchs is given;[140] for the first twenty-four the *Yin-yüan fu fa-tsang chuan* is the authority, for the next five Shen-hui is followed. There are slight variations in the list: Madhyāntika is given as the third Indian Patriarch, whereas the *Yin-yüan fu fa-tsang chuan* omits him as being of a collateral branch; however, substantially the list is the same. The *Li-tai fa-pao chi,* for the twenty-fifth through twenty-ninth Patriarchs, depends on the fourth through eighth Patriarchs in Shen-hui's list of thirteen Patriarchs. Shen-hui had drawn these from the *Ta-mo-to-lo ch'an-ching,* but the present work, since it repeats his errors, was obviously based on Shen-hui. Here the fourth and fifth Patriarchs are repeated as the twenty-fifth and twenty-sixth,[141] and Shen-hui's carelessness in reversing the first two characters in Vasumitra's name, thus arriving at Śubhamitra,[142] is perpetuated. Furthermore, where Shen-hui arbitrarily changed the name of Dharmatrāta to Bodhidharma, the *Li-tai fa-pao chi* has seen fit to combine the two names, coming up with Bodhidharmatrāta.

This work, then, in so far as the Indian Patriarchs are concerned, seems to have borrowed the tradition of Northern Ch'an, for it follows the number described in Li Hua's inscription. Yet at the same time it was influenced by Shen-hui's list of Patriarchs. Southern Ch'an may at this time also have had a theory of twenty-nine Patriarchs, for the version in the *Platform Sutra* (sec. 51) is based largely on the *Li-tai fa-pao chi.*[143] There is obviously a close connection between parts of this work and the biographical sketches of the Chinese Patriarchs as given by Shen-hui. An alternate title for the *Li-tai fa-pao chi* is the *Shih-tzu hsieh-mo chuan.* A work of the same title is mentioned, in Tu-ku Pei's preface to the *P'u-t'i ta-mo Nan-tsung ting shih-fei lun,*[144]

---

[139] Ui, *Zenshū shi kenkyū,* I, 9, dates this work at around 774. The book closes with the biography of Wu-chu, who died in 775.

[140] See Table 1.

[141] The fourth is Śaṇavāsa (Shang-na-ho-hsiu) and the fifth Upagupta; the twenty-fifth is again Śaṇavāsa (but written with different characters: She-na-p'o-ssu), and the twenty-sixth again Upagupta.

[142] See above, p. 30.

[143] See below, p. 45. The numbering system in the *Platform Sutra* differs, and some variations appear, but these are owing to the corrupt state of the Tun-huang text.

[144] Hu Shih, *Shen-hui ho-shang i-chi,* p. 159; Gernet, *Entretiens . . . ,* p. 81. The original is lost.

as a book which gives the genealogy of Shen-hui's school. Furthermore, the biographies here and in Suzuki's text of the *Shen-hui yü-lu*[145] are quite similar, and one is obviously derived from the other. Unfortunately there is no way of determining what the exact relationship between these various works is.

The *Li-tai fa-pao chi* begins by listing the twenty-nine Indian Patriarchs by name. Included is a sharp condemnation of the *Leng-chia shih-tzu chi,* which makes Gunabhadra the First Patriarch. The text points out that Gunabhadra was but one of several translators of the Laṅkāvatāra Sutra, none of whom were Ch'an Masters. Furthermore, we are told, the Laṅkāvatāra represents the transmission of a written teaching, whereas Bodhidharma did not use one word in handing down the Dharma, for his was a "silent transmission of the seal of the mind." [146]

After listing the Indian Patriarchs, this work then proceeds to the individual biographies of Bodhidharma and the other Ch'an Masters. In general, it details events which have appeared in earlier works. Bodhidharma is identified, as usual, as a prince from India, and we are told that he taught the "sudden doctrine," but no mention is made of his transmission of either the Laṅkāvatāra or the Diamond Sutra. Several stories of Bodhidharma's conversations with other priests and laymen are recorded, including his encounter with the Emperor Wu. This legend has by now become entrenched in the Ch'an tradition. We are furnished with a new story, which tells of how Bodhidharma, in transmitting his teaching, gave to one disciple his bones, to another his flesh, and to a third, Hui-k'o, his marrow.[147] Again we hear that Bodhidharma gave his own age as one hundred and fifty. The biography concludes with the story that after his death Bodhidharma was seen returning to India, wearing only one shoe, and that the missing shoe was found later in his grave.[148] He is said to have left one disciple in India, Prajñāmitra, and three in China.

The biographies of the other Chinese Patriarchs contain slight variations from the earlier versions that have appeared. Most significantly,

---

[145] *Shen-hui yü-lu* (Suzuki text), pp. 53–64.

[146] T51, p. 180c.

[147] The *Ching-te ch'uan-teng lu* version of this story is translated in Dumoulin, *A History of Zen Buddhism,* p. 73. It is not included in the biography in the *Shen-hui yü-lu* (Suzuki text).

[148] The identical story is in the *Shen-hui yü-lu* (Suzuki text), p. 55. This is an elaboration of the story of Bodhidharma's encounter with Sung Yün, first seen in the *Ch'uan fa-pao chi.*

Hui-neng is accepted as the Sixth Patriarch. Thus, twenty years after the death of Shen-hui, his theories have been adopted by a school of Ch'an which made no attempt to connect its own teachers with Hui-neng himself. The *Li-tai fa-pao chi* gives a fairly detailed account of the Sixth Patriarch, quite similar, as we have seen, to that given in the Suzuki text of the *Shen-hui yü-lu*. It then moves on to a discussion of the priests who represent its own school; but before their biographies are given, it furnishes an introductory story.

We are told that on the twentieth day of the second month of Ch'ang-shou 1 (= March 14, 692) the Empress Wu dispatched the secretary Chang Ch'ang-chi as a messenger to Ts'ao-ch'i to summon Hui-neng to court; pleading illness, however, he declined. A second messenger was dispatched in 696 to request that Bodhidharma's robe be sent to court so that reverence might be done it and offerings made to it. To this Hui-neng assented, and the robe was brought to the palace, much to the empress' delight. In the seventh month of the next year, Chang Ch'ang-chi was again sent as a messenger, this time to Chih-hsien in Szechuan, with a request that he come to court. Chih-hsien complied. In the year 700, the story continues, Shen-hsiu, Hui-an, Hsüan-tse, and Hsüan-yüeh were all called to court. Chih-hsien was conspicuous for the conversions he made, and for his knowledge of the Dharma, but falling ill, he requested permission to return home. His wishes were granted, and when he left he was given Bodhidharma's robe to take back with him to Szechuan. Then we are told, in the eleventh month of 707 [149] the Empress Wu sent the chief palace attendant, Hsüeh Chien, to Hui-neng with a gift of a special robe and 500 bolts of silk.

This preposterous story, patently an invention designed to advocate the legitimacy of the school descended from Chih-hsien and to make the claim that the robe, symbolic of the transmission, was in Szechuan, appears nowhere but in this work. History continues to be invented by the various Ch'an schools, and the Empress Wu seems to have been the most popular subject for the attribution of proclamations and requests to eminent priests, inviting them to serve within the palace precincts.

[149] The text reads: "the eleventh month of Ching-lung 1 (707)." This is probably an error for Shen-lung 1 (705). In any event the Empress Wu had already been replaced on the throne by Emperor Chung-tsung.

With this new legend established, at least to its own satisfaction, the *Li-tai fa-pao chi* moves into the biographies of Chih-hsien and his school. As has been noted before, no attempt is made to link the school with that of Hui-neng. Chih-hsien,[150] we are told, was a native of Ju-nan in Honan. At thirteen he left home to enter a monastery, and first studied the canonical works under the famous Hsüan-tsang. Later, hearing of the Fifth Patriarch, he discarded his books and went to study under him. After leaving Hung-jen, he went to the Te-ch'un Temple in Szechuan, where he busied himself making converts, and wrote several commentaries, including one on the Heart Sutra. In 697 he was called to court by Empress Wu, where the events described above took place. In 702 he called his disciple Ch'u-chi to his side and handed to him Bodhidharma's robe, which the Empress Wu had entrusted to him. He passed away at the age of ninety-four on the sixth day of the seventh month of Chang-an 2 (= August 4, 702).

Ch'u-chi,[151] his disciple, was a native of Mien-chou[152] of the family T'ang and he is occasionally referred to as the "Priest T'ang" (T'ang ho-shang). Following his father's death, Ch'u-chi left home at the age of ten, going to Chih-hsien for instruction. For a while he stayed at other temples, but eventually returned to his Master in Szechuan, where he spent some twenty years in making conversions among the general populace. The date of his death is given as 732 and his age as sixty-eight.[153] Although not expressly stated, it is evident that his teachings contained various elements of the Amidist tradition. Among his disciples was Ch'eng-yüan,[154] who became a prominent teacher in the Pure Land school.

Ch'u-chi handed down Bodhidharma's robe to his disciple Wu-

---

[150] The events described here are the only source of information we have on Chih-hsien, with the exception of brief mention in the biographies of his disciples found in the *Sung kao-seng chuan* (т50, p. 836b [under Ch'u-chi]; т50, p. 832b [under Wu-hsiang]), and a brief notice of his school in the *Yüan-chüeh ching ta-shu ch'ao*, zz1, 14, 3, 278a–b.

[151] His biography in the *Sung kao-seng chuan* (т50, p. 836b), gives conflicting information for his family name, place of origin, and death date. The present work may be presumed to be more accurate.

[152] Mien-yang hsien, Szechuan.

[153] The version in the *Taishō Tripitaka* is based on the Pelliot manuscript. The Stein text gives his dates as 669–736 (т51, p. 184c, fn. 21); the *Sung kao-seng chuan* has 648–734 (т50, p. 836b).

[154] A study of Ch'eng-yüan has been made by Tsukamoto Zenryū, "Nangaku Shōen den to sono Jōdokyō," *Tōhō gakuhō*, Kyoto, no. 2 (November, 1931), pp. 186–249.

hsiang.[155] Of Korean origin, he is commonly referred to as the "Priest Chin" (Chin ho-shang). The biography given in the *Li-tai fa-pao chi* is a lengthy one, and contains various details of his teaching. He is said to have based his doctrine on three phrases: no recollection, no thought, and no forgetting, and to have advocated a form of invocation which required a gradual lowering of the voice as the intonation progressed. Here again, Pure Land elements are evident in the teaching of this school. After coming to China, Wu-hsiang spent two years with Ch'u-chi, left him for a while, but later returned, eventually receiving Bodhidharma's robe from his Master. He lived at the Ching-ch'üan Temple in Szechuan for over twenty years, and was eminently successful in gaining converts. His death date is given as the nineteenth day of the fifth month of Pao-ying 1 (= June 15, 762) at the age of seventy-nine.

Wu-chu,[156] his successor, is the last person to whom this work devotes a biography. This, too, is extensive, and details his teachings and many conversations in which he participated. A native of Feng-hsiang in Mei hsien, Shensi, he became a Buddhist believer at twenty and a follower of the layman Ch'en Ch'u-chang,[157] who was commonly believed to have been a reincarnation of Vimalakīrti, and under whom he studied the doctrine of sudden awakening. Leaving him after several years, he studied under various priests, including Shen-hui and Tzu-tsai,[158] a disciple of Hui-neng. It was under Tzu-tsai that he received the precepts and became a monk. He continued to travel from temple to temple, and in 759 came to Wu-hsiang, whose heir he became. Later he moved to the Pao-t'ang Temple, also in Szechuan, and established a teaching which varied somewhat from his Master's. He held that no-thought and no-mind were the very Buddha, and that no ceremonies whatsoever were to be carried out. He died in 775 at the age of sixty-one.

The *Li-tai fa-pao chi* was written for the purpose of detailing the

---

[155] His biography in *Sung kao-seng chuan* (T50, pp. 832b–33a) contains conflicting details. He is said to have studied under Chih-hsien, who died in 702; yet his arrival in China is dated as 726. His dates are given as 680–756. This information cannot be regarded as reliable.

[156] There are few other sources for his biography. The *Ching-te ch'uan-teng lu*, T51, pp. 234b–35a, contains a notice but supplies no further information about him.

[157] Biography unknown. He is identified with the school of Hui-an, a disciple of the Fifth Patriarch in the Northern Ch'an tradition.

[158] Biography unknown.

history and describing the teachings of Chih-hsien's school. By emphasizing the transmission of Bodhidharma's robe, it was, in effect, claiming that the true symbol of Ch'an was in its own possession. For an account of its Indian heritage, it followed the theories held by Northern Ch'an; for the Chinese Patriarchs, it relied on the teachings of Southern Ch'an, accepting Hui-neng as the Sixth Patriarch. The school it represented had, by the time this work was written, split into two probably closely related branches, one represented by the heirs of Wu-hsiang at the Ching-ch'üan Temple; the other by the heirs of Wu-chu at the Pao-t'ang Temple.[159] Both of these schools seem soon to have died out, for we hear of no further priests of significance who are descended from them.

The *Platform Sutra* poses almost insurmountable problems when we attempt to place it chronologically, but it seems obvious that certain portions of the work must stem from the period between 780 and 800. The conflict between North and South, initiated by Shen-hui, appears much more prominently in the *Platform Sutra* than it does in Shen-hui's works themselves. Thus, these sections must have been composed at a time when the struggle between the two schools was still in progress. By the end of the eighth century there would have been no point in introducing such material; by then the struggle was over. Consequently, certain parts of the autobiography (secs. 5–11), those sections which contain remarks decrying practices attributed to Northern Ch'an (secs. 14, 16–18, 24–25, 39), and those that contain stories showing the superiority of Hui-neng's teaching over that of Shen-hsiu (sec. 40–41) may well be placed in this category.

The transmission of the teachings through the Indian Patriarchs to China appears also in the *Platform Sutra* (sec. 51). The version given is substantially the same as that in the *Li-tai fa-pao chi*; however, certain variations exist. The *Platform Sutra* adds to the head of the list the Seven Buddhas of the Past, the seventh being the historical Buddha, thus arriving at a total of thirty-five Indian Patriarchs. One would expect the *Platform Sutra,* by adding seven Patriarchs, to list a total of thirty-six. The error is accounted for by the accidental omission of Miccaka, the Seventh Patriarch. The repetition of the names of Sanavāsa and Upagupta is perpetuated here, as well as the mistake, first made by Shen-hui, of changing the name Vasumitra to Śubhamitra.

[159] See below, p. 46.

One further error is the inversion of the names of the thirty-third and thirty-fourth Patriarchs. The *Platform Sutra,* however, gives largely the same list as does the *Li-tai fa-pao chi,* and thus may be said to have followed the theory of twenty-nine Patriarchs. We may assume, then, that the Southern School of Ch'an had by this time also adopted a similar theory, finding Shen-hui's original version of thirteen Patriarchs untenable. The addition of the names of the Seven Buddhas of the Past indicates that the list given here is an elaboration on the theory of twenty-nine Patriarchs, and thus is of a later date.

In Tsung-mi's *Yüan-chüeh ching ta-shu ch'ao*[160] we find a report of the various types of Ch'an that were current at the beginning of the ninth century. This work lists seven different schools of Ch'an and furnishes a brief history and summary of their teachings. The schools are:

1. The Northern school, derived from the Fifth Patriarch, and headed by Shen-hsiu and P'u-chi.

2. The school in Szechuan, derived from the Fifth Patriarch, and founded by Chih-hsien. His heirs were Ch'u-chi (T'ang ho-shang) and Wu-hsiang (Chin ho-shang).

3. The school of Lao-an (Hui-an), derived from the Fifth Patriarch. Lao-an's heirs were Chen Ch'u-chang and Wu-chu.[161]

4. The school of Nan-yüeh Huai-jang,[162] derived from the Sixth Patriarch. This becomes, in later centuries, one of the two important schools of Ch'an. Its leader was Ma-tsu Tao-i,[163] who, according to Tsung-mi, first studied under Wu-hsiang (Chin ho-shang). Of the seven schools listed here, this is the only one that survived the T'ang dynasty.

5. The Niu-t'ou, or Oxhead school, which traces its origins to Tao-hsin, the Fourth Patriarch. Tsung-mi lists the Patriarchs through the eighth generation. The last one mentioned is Fa-ch'in.

6. The school of Ch'an propagated by Hsüan-shih, which traces itself to the Fifth Patriarch. Located in Szechuan, it practiced a form of

---

[160] zz1, 14, 3, 277b–80a. Tsung-mi's comments are discussed in Hu Shih, "Ch'an (Zen) Buddhism in China . . . ," pp. 14–16.

[161] In the *Li-tai fa-pao chi,* т51, p. 186a, Chen Ch'u-chang is mentioned as one of the early teachers of Wu-chu, but Wu-chu himself is listed as an heir of Wu-hsiang. Tsung-mi here considers that Wu-hsiang and Wu-chu represented two distinct schools of Ch'an.

[162] See below, p. 53.

[163] See below, p. 53.

meditation based on the invocation of the Buddha's name. Nothing is known of the school or of its founder.

7. Shen-hui's school of Southern Ch'an, to which Tsung-mi belonged. Shen-hui is here given the title of the Seventh Patriarch.

These are the schools of Ch'an as Tsung-mi knew them. No mention is made of the other school of Ch'an which survived the T'ang dynasty, that of Ch'ing-yüan Hsing-ssu,[164] which traces itself to the Sixth Patriarch.

Both Northern and Southern Ch'an, which developed in the capital cities, received the patronage of the court and of high officials, but in the last decades of the eighth century they began to lose their vitality and strength, and failed to produce disciples of distinction who could preserve and develop their teachings. Meanwhile, in far-off Kiangsi and Hunan, a new school of Ch'an was rising, gaining in popularity and prestige. Its origins are obscure, but the legends it passed along and created were destined to persist to this day.

The work which established the Ch'an legend and wrote the "history" of the sect as it has come down to us, was a product of this new school. Known as the *Pao-lin chuan*,[165] it was lost in China for many centuries, and was not rediscovered until the 1930s. Chih-chü, an obscure monk of whom nothing is known, was its compiler, and it was completed in 801.[166]

The purpose of the *Pao-lin chuan* was to champion the cause of this new school of Ch'an, which traced its origins in China to Hui-neng, the Sixth Patriarch. To this end it devised an entirely new tradition of

[164] See below, p. 54.

[165] In 1932 Prof. Tokiwa Daijō discovered an old manuscript copy of *chüan* 6 of the *Pao-lin chuan* in the Shōrenji at Awataguchi, Kyoto. His study of the work, "Hōrinden no kenkyū," *Tōhō gakuhō, Tōkyō*, IV (November, 1933), 205–307, was followed by the publication of a facsimile of the manuscript, together with a reprint of the above essay (Tokiwa Daijō, *Hōrinden no kenkyū*). A revised and enlarged version of the essay was published in Tokiwa Daijō, *Shina Bukkyō no kenkyū*, II, 203–326.

In 1933 a set of the Chin tripitaka was found at the Kuang-sheng Temple in Shansi (for a discussion of this discovery, see Tsukamoto Zenryū, "Kinkoku Daizōkyō no hakken to sono kankō," *Nikka Bukkyō kenkyūkai nempō*, I [August, 1936], 167–95). Among the works included were *chüan* 1–5 and 8 of the *Pao-lin chuan* (full title: *Shuang-feng shan Ts'ao-hou-ch'i Pao-lin chuan*). These were published, together with *chüan* 6 found in Kyoto, in *Sung-tsang i-chen*, case 3, v. 10; case 4, v. 1–2. A mimeographed edition in 3 vols. has been published by Yanagida Seizan. *Chüan* 7, 9, and 10 of the *Pao-lin chuan* have yet to be found.

[166] The preface and the first few pages of *chüan* 1 of the *Pao-lin chuan* are missing. *Zenseki shi, Dai-Nihon Bukkyō zensho*, I, 286, provides the date and the name of the compiler. He is also known as Hui-chü.

the Seven Buddhas of the Past and of the twenty-eight Indian Patriarchs, one which was adopted by all later Ch'an histories, and came to
represent the tradition as accepted today. As we have seen, the patriarchal succession had continued as a particularly vexing problem for
Ch'an.[167] The eighth century had seen constant experimentation in an
attempt to devise a theory which would be acceptable within the sect,
and at the same time not be vulnerable to the criticism of other Buddhist groups. The *Pao-lin chuan* solved this problem by eliminating the
inconsistencies which had existed in earlier versions and devising a new
list of its own, which, with the gradual growth of Ch'an as a whole,
gained general recognition. To be sure, T'ien-t'ai and other sects which
held that the transmission from Patriarch to Patriarch had been cut
off at the twenty-fourth generation did not accept the Ch'an version,
but this, in later centuries, was scarcely of concern to Ch'an, which
gradually became the dominant sect of Buddhism in China.

The *Pao-lin chuan* begins by incorporating the Seven Buddhas of
the Past, including Śākyamuni, at the head of the list of Patriarchs, but
does not count them among the twenty-eight.[168] It then proceeds to give
the Patriarchs in order, much on the basis of the *Yin-yüan fu fa-tsang
chuan.* The Third Patriarch, Madhyāntika, is omitted; however, for the
seventh we have Vasumitra. His name appears first in the *Ta-mo-to-lo
ch'an-ching,* where he is the fourth Patriarch mentioned, but the latter
work was not concerned with an attempt to set up a tradition of the
succession of the Indian Patriarchs. Vasumitra, however, had been
adopted by Shen-hui, who changed his name in error to Śubhamitra,
and this mistake was later perpetuated in the *Li-tai fa-pao chi* and the
Platform Sutra. From the eighth Patriarch through the twenty-fourth,
the conventional order is maintained. Then, to eliminate the confusion
and the weak point of other theories, the repetition of the names of the
fourth and fifth Patriarchs, Śaṇavāsa and Upagupta, as the twenty-fifth
and twenty-sixth, the *Pao-lin chuan* hit upon a novel solution. It simply
threw them out and substituted new names of its own. The twenty-

---

[167] In addition to the works already discussed, several fragments of manuscripts dealing
with the subject have been found among the Tun-huang documents. For a discussion,
see Tanaka Ryōshō, "Tonkō shutsudo 'Soshi dengyō Seiten nijūhasso Tōrai rokuso' ni
tsuite," *IBK,* no. 21 (January, 1963), pp. 251–54, and Tanaka Ryōshō, "Fu hōzō den to
Zen no dentō," *IBK,* no. 19 (January, 1962), pp. 243–46.

[168] The first few pages of *chüan* 1 are missing; thus we do not have details of the
Seven Buddhas of the Past before Śākyamuni. The *Platform Sutra,* as we have seen, includes them, and adds them to the numerical order as well.

fifth Patriarch, we are told, was Basiasita; the twenty-sixth, Puṇyamitra; the twenty-seventh, Prajñātāra; and the twenty-eighth, Bodhidharma.[169]

But the *Pao-lin chuan* was not content merely to list the Patriarchs
by name. It provided involved information about them, numerous quotations, details about their lives, and for each Patriarch it supplied a
"transmission verse." [170] These verses symbolized the handing down of
the teaching from one Patriarch to his heir, and the practice of quoting
these verses was taken up by later Ch'an histories. The *Platform Sutra*
(secs. 49, 50) includes transmission verses for the Chinese Patriarchs,
from Bodhidharma through Hui-neng.[171] These verses were not necessarily invented by the *Pao-lin chuan* (most probably they were not)
but they are systematized here for the first time and incorporated into
the legend.

The source for the information contained in the *Pao-lin chuan* is
difficult to determine, but it seems probable that it represents a large
body of miscellaneous material, rather than the inventive genius of its
compiler. We have seen the Ch'an legend as it has grown throughout
the eighth century, how some stories have taken hold and how some
have eventually been rejected. The *Pao-lin chuan* represents the culmi-
nation of these legends, for the stories which it contains became, subject to refinement in details, the official version of Ch'an, repeated in all
the later histories. In arriving at the version it presents, the *Pao-lin
chuan* itself drew upon the vast body of legend current at the time.
Throughout the book there are frequent references to other works,
many of them of pre-T'ang origin, on which the *Pao-lin chuan* based
its information. Little is known of these works, for none of them sur-
vives, but presumably they provided much material concerning the
Indian Patriarchs.[172] There is, however, no indication as to what the
sources were for the information on the three new Patriarchs that the
Pao-lin chuan introduced.

[169] See Table 1.

[170] For a discussion, see Mizuno Kōgen, "Dembōge no seiritsu ni tsuite," *Shūgaku
kenkyū*, no. 2 (January, 1960), pp. 22–41, and Tanaka Ryōshō, "Dembōge ni kansuru
Tonkō shutsudo shiryō to sono kankei," *Shūgaku kenkyū*, no. 3 (March, 1961), pp.
106–11.

[171] There is no way of determining whether the verses given in the *Platform Sutra* derived from the *Pao-lin chuan* or vice versa, or if they were drawn independently from
some unknown source. The last seems the most logical assumption.

[172] These works are discussed by Tokiwa, *Shina Bukkyō no kenkyū*, II, 303–26. They
are also discussed briefly, but pertinently, in Yanagida, "Tōshi no keifu," pp. 35–36.

In addition to the stories concerning the lives of the Indian Patriarchs, this work included many legends about the Chinese Ch'an Masters. *Chüan* 7, which is missing, contained, in all probability, material on the twenty-seventh Patriarch Prajñātāra, as well as information on Bodhidharma. *Chüan* 8 deals with Bodhidharma, Hui-k'o, and Seng-ts'an. *Chüan* 9 and 10, also no longer extant, concerned Tao-hsin, Hung-jen, and Hui-neng, and may conceivably have contained information on Nan-yüeh and Ma-tsu, but this we have no way of knowing. Judging from the material supplied in *chüan* 8, however, the *Pao-lin chuan* contributed substantially to the legends concerning the Chinese Patriarchs. Two examples will serve to indicate the type of information this new work provided.

At the end of the biography of Hui-k'o is the text of an inscription attributed to the priest Fa-lin (572–640).[173] The text does not add much new information, but it contains a reference to the "Teaching of the East Mountain." Since this term did not come into common usage until the time of Hung-jen (d. 674), it would seem likely that the inscription itself is spurious, and merely another example of the growth of the Ch'an legend. Again, we do not know from what source the *Pao-lin chuan* drew its information.

Under the biography of Seng-ts'an we are told that a certain Li Ch'ang went to the Ho-tse Temple in 745 or 746[174] to ask Shen-hui about the truth of the story that the Third Patriarch had gone to Lo-fu and never returned. Shen-hui replied that his tomb was located to the north of the Shan-ku Temple in Shu-chou.[175] Later, we are told, Li Ch'ang was demoted and assigned to a lesser position in Shu-chou, where, three days after he had taken up his post, a priest paid a call on him, and he had an opportunity to ask about the temple. Verifying its existence, he went with several officials and there discovered the grave of Seng-ts'an, in which he found the sacred relics of the Patriarch. There were some three hundred pieces in all. One hundred were enshrined in a pagoda Li Ch'ang erected at the grave; another one hundred were sent to Shen-hui at the Ho-tse Temple, where they were

[173] *Pao-lin chuan,* III, 546–52. Fa-lin's biography is in *Hsü kao-seng chuan,* т50, pp. 636b–39a.

[174] The text gives T'ien-pao 5, with the cyclical designation *i-yu;* the correct designation is *ping-hsü. I-yu* applies to T'ien-pao 4 (745).

[175] Huai-ning hsien, Anhui.

placed in a pagoda before the bathhouse; and the other one hundred Li Ch'ang kept in his own family.[176]

Thus the most obscure of the Patriarchs is conveniently provided with a tomb and suitable relics, appropriately enshrined. It may be assumed that the missing *chüan* 9 and 10 similarly added substantially to the legend of the later Patriarchs. Much of the information concerning these men, which appears in later histories and cannot be traced, may well have originated in the *Pao-lin chuan*. This is particularly so in the case of Hui-neng.

The section on Bodhidharma in the *Tsu-t'ang chi*,[177] as has been pointed out by Yanagida,[178] contains a series of four verses which are said to have been given by Prajñātāra to Bodhidharma when he handed on his teaching. They are annotated and interpreted as predicting the appearance of Nan-yüeh and Ma-tsu.[179] We know that these verses were originally to be found in the missing *chüan* 7 of the *Pao-lin chuan*, because the *Ching-te ch'uan-teng lu* quotes the first of them,[180] and then refers its readers to both the *Pao-lin chuan* and the *Sheng-chou chi*,[181] another of the lost histories, compiled sometime between 898 and 901, for further information. Whether these works contained the annotations and interpretations given in the *Tsu-t'ang chi* is unknown.

The *Pao-lin chuan*, representing the new Ch'an which had risen in Kiangsi and Hunan, provided details for the Indian Patriarchs, established once and for all a theory of twenty-eight Patriarchs, added many details to the legend, and trumpeted the cause of Hui-neng, the Sixth Patriarch. The information that it carried served as the basis for all later

---

[176] *Pao-lin chuan*, III, 573–75.

[177] This work, completed in 952, was apparently little used in China and was first printed in Korea in 1245. A Ch'an history, based on the *Pao-lin chuan* and later works, it carries the biographies, records, and stories of famous priests up to the time of its completion. It is quite possible that it served as the source for much of the information in the *Ching-te ch'uan-teng lu*. A mimeographed edition has been published by Yanagida Seizan, *Sodō-shū*, 5 vols. A reduced-sized facsimile of the Korean edition has recently been issued: *Hyŏsong Cho Myŏng-gi Paksa Hwagap Kinyŏm Pulgyo Sahak Nonch'ong* [Buddhistic studies presented to Dr. Joh Myong-gi on his sixtieth birthday], 17, 129 pp. For a study of the work, see Shishiyama Kōdō, "Kōrai-ban Sodō-shū to Zenshū koten-seki," *Tōyō gakuen*, no. 2 (April, 1933), pp. 23–50.

[178] Yanagida, "Tōshi no keifu," p. 37.

[179] *Tsu-t'ang chi*, I, 65–66.

[180] T51, p. 217a.

[181] A fragment of this work (S4478) has been identified and published. See Yanagida Seizan, "Gemmon 'Shōchū shū' ni tsuite," *Bukkyō shigaku*, VII (no. 3, October, 1958), 44–57.

Ch'an histories, as it virtually swept away the laboriously compiled
works of the eighth century, and rewrote the history of Ch'an as a
whole. Later works perpetuated and refined the material it contained;
the work itself, however, did not survive as successfully as the legends
it helped to create. It is mentioned in the catalogues of books brought
back to Japan: Ennin's lists of 839,[182] 840,[183] and 847,[184] and Eichō's
list of 1094 [185] all include it, and describe the work as being in 10
chüan, so that we may assume that at these times it was still complete.
But other works came along to supplant it, and to supplement it with
accounts and stories of later priests, so that by the time the *Pao-lin chuan*
was admitted to the Northern Sung Tripitaka in 998,[186] *chüan* 2 and
10 were already missing. For *chüan* 2, information derived from the
Sheng-chou chi was substituted, but no comparable material was available for *chüan* 10. Notices inserted by the compilers of the Northern
Sung Tripitaka indicate that other sections of the work were incomplete and had to be supplemented.[187] Later, during the reign of Emperor Tao-tsung (1032–1101) of Liao, the *Pao-lin chuan* and the *Platform Sutra* were both burned as spurious works.[188] Thus, when the
compilers of the Chin Tripitaka came to reprint it, sometime between
1149 and 1173,[189] only *chüan* 1–5 and 8 were left. The work was excluded from all later editions of the Tripitaka, as well as from the
Korean printings.

The school which this work represented became one of the two important branches of Ch'an to continue after the fall of the T'ang dynasty. Its origins are obscure, and there are no reliable sources through
which we can trace its history. Traditionally, the founder is given as

---

[182] *Nihon koku Shōwa gonen nittō guhō mokuroku,* T55, p. 1075c.

[183] *Jikaku daishi zai-Tō sōshin roku,* T55, p. 1077c.

[184] *Nittō shin gushōgyō mokuroku,* T55, p. 1086c.

[185] *Tōiki dentō mokuroku,* T55, p. 1163c.

[186] The date and notice about the missing volumes appears as a note at the end of
chüan 2. *Pao-lin chuan,* I, 132.

[187] See Tokiwa, *Shina Bukkyō no kenkyū,* II, 217–18; 303–36, for a detailed discussion. The books used to supplement the *Pao-lin chuan* are all lost works, and may in
some instances have been the original source for the material in the missing portions.

[188] *Shih-men cheng-t'ung,* zz2B, 3, 5, 451b. This notice appears in the biography of
Uich'ŏn, a Korean priest of the T'ien-t'ai school, who deplored what he felt to be the
false teachings of the Ch'an sect of the time. It was through his agency that these and
other unnamed works were excluded when the emperor ordered a new edition of the
Tripitaka compiled.

[189] Tsukamoto, "Kinkoku Daizōkyō no hakken to sono kankō," p. 175.

Nan-yüeh Huai-jang (677–744),[190] who is known as a disciple of Hui-neng. Information about him is based on sources composed much later than his death; no mention is made of him in any eighth-century work, and with the last volume of the *Pao-lin chuan* missing, we cannot seek for material there. He is said to have been a native of An-k'ang in Chin-chou,[191] and, after becoming a monk, to have studied under Hui-an, the disciple of the Fifth Patriarch, remarkable for the great age to which he attained. Later he went to study under Hui-neng at Ts'ao-ch'i, but how long he stayed under the Sixth Patriarch is not clear: the *Tsu-t'ang chi*[192] says he left in 711, which would account for the fact that he is not included in the list of the ten disciples present at Hui-neng's death, as reported in the *Platform Sutra* (sec. 45). He probably traveled about, before assuming a teaching career at Mount Nan-yüeh. Our information is so scanty that it might well justify Hu Shih's assertion that his name was "exhumed from obscurity," in order that a relationship between his school and that of the Sixth Patriarch might be established.[193] His school is, however, one of the seven recognized by Tsung-mi.[194]

Nan-yüeh Huai-jang's disciple was the famous Ma-tsu Tao-i (709–788),[195] who was largely responsible for the development of this new Ch'an sect in Kiangsi. A native of Shih-fang in Han-chou,[196] his family name was Ma, from which the appellation Ma-tsu, or "Ancestor Ma," [197] is derived. He became a monk while young, taking the precepts under T'ang ho-shang.[198] Later he went to Nan-yüeh, be-

---

[190] His inscription by Chang Cheng-fu, *Heng-chou Pan-jo ssu Kuan-yin ta-shih pei-ming*, CTW, ch. 619 (XIII, 7935–36), provides his dates, but was probably written some fifty years after his death. Early biographies appear in *Tsu-t'ang chi*, I, 142–45, and *Sung kao-seng chuan*, T50, p. 761a–b.

[191] An-k'ang hsien, Shensi.

[192] *Tsu-t'ang chi*, I, 143.

[193] Hu Shih, "Ch'an (Zen) Buddhism in China . . . ," p. 12.

[194] *Yüan-chüeh ching ta-shu ch'ao*, ZZ1, 14, 3, 279a.

[195] His inscription is by Ch'üan Te-yü, *T'ang ku Hung-chou K'ai-yüan ssu Shih-wen Tao-i ch'an-shih t'a-ming*, CTW, ch. 501 (XI, 6466–67). Early biographies appear in *Tsu-t'ang chi*, IV, 33–44, and *Sung kao-seng chuan*, T50, p. 766a–c.

[196] Kuang-han hsien, Szechuan.

[197] This name has created a certain amount of confusion in the biographical records. The Oxhead priest Ho-lin Hsüan-su was also of a Ma family, and the *Sung Kao-seng chuan*, T50, p. 762b, refers to him as Ma-tsu and Ma-su. It is possible that the biographies of the two men have been confused here.

[198] Ch'u-chi, the heir of Chih-hsien, founder of the Szechuan school of Ch'an, described in the *Li-tai fa-pao chi*. The *Yüan-chüeh ching ta-shu ch'ao*, ZZ1, 14, 3, 279a,

came his disciple, and studied under him for several years, eventually becoming his heir. Ma-tsu then traveled about in Kiangsi and eventually settled at the K'ai-yüan Temple in Hung-chou,[199] where he began his teaching career, gaining a wide following. He is said to have had 139 disciples, and he died in 788 at the age of eighty. In 813 the Emperor Hsien-tsung awarded him the posthumous title "Ta-chi ch'an-shih." [200]

The origin of the other Ch'an sect that was destined to survive is even more obscure. It traces itself to Ch'ing-yüan Hsing-ssu (d. 740),[201] who is also said to have been a disciple of the Sixth Patriarch. Here again, there are no contemporary works that mention his name, and the period in which he studied under Hui-neng is completely unknown. The *Tsu-t'ang chi* records a conversation that he held with Shen-hui,[202] but when or if such a meeting actually took place cannot be determined. After his death he was given the posthumous title "Hung-chi ta-shih" by the Emperor Hsi-tsung (r. 873–888).[203]

For the biography of his heir, Shih-t'ou Hsi-ch'ien (700–790), we must again rely on late sources.[204] A native of Tuan-chou,[205] he is said to have spent some time with Hui-neng while still a youth, and after the latter's death is said to have gone to Lo-fu. Later he became the disciple and heir of Ch'ing-yüan, and, moving to Nan-yüeh, carried on his teachings there. He died in 790 at the age of ninety, and received the posthumous title "Wu-chi ta-shih."

Many legends grew up around Ma-tsu and Shih-t'ou. Both produced many disciples, and their schools developed into flourishing establishments; indeed, all the famous Masters of the late T'ang dynasty de-

gives Ma-tsu's first teacher as Chin ho-shang (Wu-hsiang), Ch'u-chi's heir. This is probably an error.

[199]Nan-ch'ang hsien, Kiangsi.

[200] *Sung kao-seng chuan*, T50, p. 766c.

[201] There is a brief notice of him in the *Sung kao-seng chuan*, T50, p. 760c, attached at the end of the biography of the Northern Ch'an Master, I-fu, but whether there was any connection between them is unknown. The *Tsu-t'ang chi*, I, 111–12, provides an extremely short notice which contains little information. The date of his death is given in both works.

[202] *Tsu-t'ang chi*, I, 111–12.

[203] *Ching-te ch'uan-teng lu*, T51, p. 240a.

[204] His biography in *Sung kao-seng chuan*, T50, 763c–64a, is based, in all likelihood, on an inscription by Liu K'o, which is no longer extant. The earliest biography is in *Tsu-t'ang chi*, I, 147–55.

[205] Kao-yao hsien, Kwantung.

rived from them. An often-quoted passage describes their fame: "In Kiangsi the Master was Ta-chi [Ma-tsu]; in Hunan the Master was Shih-t'ou. People went back and forth between them all the time, and those who never met these two great Masters were completely ignorant."[206] Their connection with the Sixth Patriarch is obscure; but there is no doubt that they adopted him as their Patriarch. By the beginning of the ninth century Hui-neng had become the father of Chinese Ch'an, the most revered of all the Patriarchs. Ch'an had an established tradition, a descent in an unbroken line from the historical Buddha himself, down through the twenty-eight Indian transmitters of the Dharma to Bodhidharma; from Bodhidharma it passed to Hui-neng, and from Hui-neng down through the centuries, as the names of more and more Patriarchs were added to the lists.

The pages of the later Ch'an histories are filled with stories of these eminent priests. The teachings of the schools that claimed descent from Hui-neng gained numerous converts, and great monastic establishments arose on isolated mountain tops. But for the Buddhism in the capital cities, the story was somewhat different. Even though the rebellion of An Lu-shan had been subdued, the vitality of the T'ang court remained a feeble shadow of the glories of the first half of the eighth century. But Buddhism, at least in terms of its esteem and prosperity, did not suffer at first; indeed it received an almost overwhelming patronage. The temples enjoyed ever greater luxury and riches; their priests participated freely in the lavish surroundings of court life. The great masters of the various sects received the highest reverence and a plentitude of temporal rewards. Men such as the renowned Chen-yen master Amoghavajra, as well as the leaders of the T'ien-t'ai, Pure Land, Hua-yen, and Ch'an schools all were accorded the honors of the imperial court. Rather than compete for favors and position, these groups showed a tendency to advocate a basic harmony among the teachings; the elements in common among the various branches of Buddhism were stressed.[207] The Oxhead school of Ch'an maintained close relationships with T'ien-t'ai. The similarity between the mantric features of Chen-yen and the Pure Land invocation of Amitābha Bud-

---

[206] *Sung kao-seng chuan*, ⊤50, p. 764a (under the biography of Shih-t'ou).
[207] For an excellent discussion of this tendency, see Tsukamoto Zenryū, *Tō chūki no Jōdokyō*, pp. 51–80.

dha's name was emphasized. Hua-yen and Ch'an found much in each
other's teachings. Such tendencies can be seen clearly in such a man as
Tsung-mi, who at the same time that he is listed among the heirs of
Shen-hui, is honored as a Patriarch of the Hua-yen sect. While this
rapprochement strengthened the scholastic aspects of Buddhism, it
made also for a conservatism centered on the Buddhists' desire to preserve their own prerogatives and position. The lines of distinction between the various groups began to be obliterated. This, coupled with
a fantastic wealth and power, the great store of precious metals hoarded
in their statues and implements, and the vast holdings of tax-free land,
provoked the inevitable reactions.[208] Eventually, under Emperor Wu-
tsung, a systematic persecution was undertaken. Temples were destroyed, monks and nuns returned to lay life, and properties were con-
fiscated. Ch'an did not emerge unscathed from the great disaster of
the Hui-ch'ang persecution, but it managed to survive with its vitality
unimpaired. Many reasons have been given: the isolation and simplic-
ity of the temple compounds; the maintenance of the community
through the labors of the priests and monks themselves; the very characteristics of the teaching. Perhaps, though, the most significant reasons for its survival were political and geographic. The Buddhism that
centered around the capitals and larger cities could not readily escape
the stringent measures taken against it; thus the Ch'an schools in these
areas were virtually destroyed. In the North, particularly in Hupeh,
however, the situation was different. The military leaders there were
at this time almost autonomous. Mostly of non-Chinese origin, they
were treated with an offhandedness bordering on contempt by the Chinese elite, and had no particular affinity with the weak and ineffectual
central government. Thus, in Hupeh particularly, the stringent provi-
sions of the persecution were scarcely put into effect. The military gov-
ernors numbered themselves among the followers of the great Ch'an
priests of the area, and they did not feel inclined to follow the dictates
of a government from which they themselves were alienated.[209] Thus,

[208] See Kenneth Ch'en, "Economic Background of the Hui-ch'ang Persecution," *HJAS*,
XIX (1956), 67–105.

[209] For a discussion of the historical and social background of Ch'an in Hupeh at this
time, see Yanagida Seizan, "Tō-matsu Godai no Kahoku chihō ni okeru Zenshū kōki no
rekishiteki shakaiteki jijō ni tsuite," *Nihon Bukkyō Gakkai nempō*, no. 25 (March,
1960), pp. 171–86.

when the persecutions were lifted under the reign of the new emperor in 846, Ch'an found itself the dominant sect of Chinese Buddhism. Although the teaching itself underwent numerous changes through the course of its later history, Ch'an, in one form or another, has remained the principal school of Chinese Buddhism.

II. The Birth of a Patriarch: Biography of Hui-neng

WE HAVE SEEN how Ch'an in the eighth century began with a school that emphasized the Laṅkāvatāra Sutra, under the direction of an illustrious and learned priest, Shen-hsiu. He was revered as few were in his time, and honors were heaped upon him; gradually his power and position grew. Among his disciples were priests of no less fame, who carried on his teachings. To assure its newly acquired position among other Buddhist sects, this Ch'an school was in need of historical records to prove its legitimacy and to attest to the antiquity of its teaching. To this end records of the sect were devised; but so scanty was the available information that the compilers of the first histories were compelled to rely on a non-Ch'an work, the *Hsü kao-seng chuan,* to piece out their story. To this they added various legends, established a line of transmission, and arrived eventually at a theory of the succession of six Patriarchs, from Bodhidharma through Shen-hsiu. This was the tradition that was known at the court and among high officials, the literati, and the populace in general, in the third decade of the eighth century. The Ch'an priests who represented this tradition were honored men; when they passed away elaborate funerals were held, and distinguished stylists composed their epitaphs. But in the hinterlands, in the provincial capitals removed from Loyang and Ch'ang-an, were other Ch'an teachers whose teachings derived from the same Hung-jen, who had been Shen-hsiu's Master. We know that they existed, but there was no one to record their teachings, no one to commemorate their deaths with elegantly inscribed stone inscriptions, no one to gather their stories or those of their spiritual ancestors.

But in 732 a hitherto unknown priest, Shen-hui, rose to challenge the powerful Ch'an in the capital cities. He accused P'u-chi, then the Northern Ch'an leader, of having falsely usurped the title of Seventh Patriarch and of having made his own teacher, Shen-hsiu, the Sixth. The real Sixth Patriarch, said Shen-hui, was Hui-neng. He told of Hui-neng's teachings, damned the doctrines of the Northern School, and claimed that his was the true Ch'an. Gradually he gained a following; his disciples recorded his sermons and disseminated the history of his school. Eventually his claims came to be accepted. The great leaders of Northern Ch'an died off, and their followers, because they were men of lesser stature, though not without power, were ultimately unable to cope with the attacks against them. The capital cities in a declining dynasty were not the appropriate environment for this new doctrine, nor were Shen-hui's followers men of talent, and after his death in 762 his teachings declined along with those of Northern Ch'an.

Meanwhile other Ch'an Masters arose in outlying areas, claiming Hui-neng as their teacher, spreading their own teachings, writing their own histories, perpetuating their own legends. Some fell into oblivion; others thrived, and from these arose the two schools from which all later Ch'an derived.

It is against this background that we must try to place Hui-neng, the Sixth Patriarch, the hero of Chinese Ch'an. His legend grows from a single mention in a single text to an elaborate biography, filled with details and dates, seeming facts and patent legends. The careers of the men of Northern Ch'an are documented, yet they fade from the pages of the later histories of Ch'an. For Hui-neng we have no facts, yet later history records his life in much detail. How much of this material are we prepared to accept; how much must we reject as unfounded fancy? Or must we conclude by saying that we can never know, that fact and legend are so inseparably intertwined that they cannot be set apart?

Among the numerous works which purport to tell of Hui-neng there are some which can be rejected at the outset as obviously spurious. All of these may be found in the *Ch'üan T'ang wen*, that vast collection of documents relating to the T'ang dynasty, compiled in 1814. Since they have been regarded as authentic by a number of scholars, their contents will be analyzed in detail.

The first of these is Fa-hai's "Brief Preface"[1] to the *Platform Sutra*. Because of its attribution to Fa-hai, who is known as the compiler of the *Platform Sutra*, many writers have accepted it and its contents as reliable.[2] Let us see what it says.[3]

[1] CTW, ch. 915 (XIX, 12032–33). It is entitled *Liu-tsu ta-shih fa-pao t'an-ching lüeh-hsü.*

[2] Ui, *Zenshū shi kenkyū*, II, 174, dates it at "around 714." W. T. Chan, *The Platform Scripture*, p. 158, n. 13, gives a similar date, and lists it first among the sources for Hui-neng's biography.

[3] The full translation from the *Ch'üan T'ang wen* is given below. The reader is re-

The Master's name was Hui-neng. His father was Lu Hsing-t'ao and his mother was of the Li family. He was born between 11 p.m. and 1 a.m. on the eighth day of the second month of Chen-kuan 12 [= February 27 or March 28, 638].[4] When he was born beams of light rose into the air and the room was filled with a strange fragrance. At dawn two mysterious monks visited the Master's father and said: "The child born last night requires an auspicious name; the first character should be 'Hui,' and the second, 'Neng.'"

"What do 'Hui' and 'Neng' mean?" inquired the father.

The priest answered: "'Hui' means to bestow beneficence on sentient beings; 'Neng' means the capacity to carry out the affairs of the Buddha." When they had finished speaking they left, and there is no one who knows where they went.

The Master would not drink his mother's milk and at night a heavenly being brought nectar for him. When he was twenty-four years of age he heard a sutra and was awakened to the Way. Going to Huang-mei, he sought sanction [for his understanding]. The Fifth Patriarch, recognizing his ability, bestowed on him the robe and Dharma and made him his heir. This was in the year 661. He returned to the south where he remained in hiding for sixteen years. On the eighth day of the first month of I-feng 1 [= February 26, 676] he met the Dharma-master Yin-tsung, who became enlightened and awakened to the Master's teaching. On the fifteenth day of the same month, before a gathering of the whole assemblage, Hui-neng had his head shaven. On the eighth day of the second month various illustrious priests gathered together and ordained him.[5] The Vinaya-master Chih-kuang of Hsi-ching sponsored his ordination; Vinaya-master Hui-ching of Su-chou supervised the functions; Vinaya-master T'ung-ying of Ching-chou served as teacher; Vinaya-master Ch'i-to-lo of India was in charge of reading the precepts; and the Indian Tripitaka Master Mi-to testified to the precepts.

The ordination platform had been set up in the Sung dynasty by the Tripitaka Master Gunabhadra, who at the same time erected a stone

---

ferred to secs. 2–11 of the translation of the *Platform Sutra* for an account of events not detailed in Fa-hai's preface.

[4] There are two second months in Chen-kuan 12. The text does not indicate which one is referred to here.

[5] The following names are those of the three superior priests and two of the priests of lesser rank whose presence was required at an official ordination.

tablet with the inscription: "In the future a living Bodhisattva will receive ordination here." In the year 502 of the Liang dynasty the Tripitaka Master Chih-yao arrived by sea from India, bringing a bo tree, which he planted beside the platform. He made the prediction: "Some 170 years from now a living Bodhisattva will preach the Supreme Vehicle from beneath this tree, and will bring salvation to countless persons. Possessing the Dharma, he will truly transmit the seal of the Buddha mind." [6]

Thereupon, the Master's head was shaven and he received the precepts, and for the sake of the assemblage, he expounded the doctrine of the single transmission [from mind to mind], just as had been predicted in the past (from the year 502 of the Liang dynasty to the year 676 of the T'ang dynasty was some 175 years). [7]

In the spring of the following year the Master took leave of the assembly to go to the Pao-lin Temple, and Yin-tsung and over a thousand monks and laymen saw him off. Soon he arrived at Ts'ao-ch'i. At that time the Vinaya-master, T'ung-ying, accompanied by several hundred students, went to the Pao-lin Temple at Ts'ao-ch'i because the Master was there.

Seeing that the temple buildings were too small for the assembly, Hui-neng wanted to enlarge them. Thereupon he asked a native of the village, Ch'en Ya-hsien: "I seek a donation from you of a piece of land on which to spread my sitting cloth (*niṣīdana*). Can you supply it for me?"

"How large is your cloth?" asked Ch'en Ya-hsien.

The Master took it out and showed it to him, and Ya-hsien agreed to his proposal, but when the Patriarch spread out his cloth it covered the whole of Ts'ao-ch'i. The Four Deva Kings materialized bodily and, squatting down, took up guard at each of the four directions, and because of this a hill within the temple precincts is known as the Deva King Peak.

[Ch'en Ya]-hsien said: "I well recognize the breadth of the power of your Dharma; however the grave of my ancestors is in this area, so that if in the future you construct a grave here, I would ask that you save a place for it. The remaining buildings you may discard as

[6] The version in the *Ching-te ch'uan-teng lu,* T51, p. 235c, differs: the Tripitaka Master is given as Paramārtha (Chen-ti); he is said to have planted two trees; and to have predicted that Hui-neng's appearance would be 120 years in the future.

[7] Note in the original text.

you wish to make this place into a treasure temple for all eternity. This is a mountain range to which the living dragon and the white elephant repair, so although you make the tops of the buildings level with the sky, do not level off the ground beneath." Later, when the temple buildings were constructed, these instructions were followed explicitly.

The Master wandered about the scenic spots within the temple precincts, stopping to rest [here and there], and eventually thirteen buildings were erected [at these resting places]. Hua-kuo Temple was one of them, and [the Master] hung a tablet at the temple gate.

The history of the Pao-lin Temple is this: the Indian Tripitaka Master, Chih-yao, on his way from Nan-hai, passed by the gateway to Ts'ao-ch'i. Drinking some of the local water, he found its fragrance delightful and, thinking this strange, he said to his followers: "This water is no different from that of India. Its source must lie at some wondrous place which would be a suitable site for erecting a temple." Following the stream to its source, he found everywhere mountains and brooks circling about, and peaks of extraordinary beauty. In admiration he exclaimed: "It is just like the treasure forest (Pao-lin) mountains of India!" Then he said to the people of Ts'ao-ch'i village: "You must erect a temple in these mountains. One hundred and seventy years from now the unsurpassed Dharma-treasure will be expounded and propagated here, and those who gain enlightenment will be as numerous as the trees in the forest. It would be good to give the temple the name Pao-lin." At that time the magistrate of Shao-chou, Hou Ching-chung, reported what [the Tripitaka Master] had said to the throne, and the emperor complied with the request and presented a tablet inscribed Pao-lin, and the temple was built. It was completed in the year 504 of the Liang dynasty.

In front of the Buddha Hall was a pool from which a dragon used always to emerge, wrecking havoc in the surrounding trees. One day it appeared in an especially large form, whipping up the waves in the pool, raising clouds and mists which obscured the skies, and terrifying all the assembled monks. The Master scolded the dragon: "You can appear only in a large form, but not in a small one. If you were a real divine dragon, you would be able to change easily; when you have a small body you should be able to make yourself large, and when your body is large, you should be able to appear in a small form." The dragon immediately vanished, and after a little while appeared again, this time in a small form, and came dancing from the surface of the lake. The Master held out his bowl and said: "Are you brave enough to get into the bottom of my bowl?" The dragon then skipped forward, and the Master scooped it up with his bowl, so that the dragon was unable to move. The Master then took the bowl to the hall, where he preached to the dragon, which promptly shed its body and departed. Its body was only seven inches long, and was equipped with a head, neck, horns, and a tail, and this was kept at the temple. Later the Master filled the pond with earth and stones and erected a stupa of iron, that stands today on the left side, in front of the Buddha Hall.

The only other place where Fa-hai's preface may be found is in the Yüan edition of the *Platform Sutra,* where it appears under the title *Liu-tsu ta-shih yüan-ch'i wai-chi.*[8] This text varies only slightly from the version translated above.[9] Not only is this preface not found in any source prior to the Yüan dynasty, but there is also no reference whatsoever to it in any of the earlier editions of the *Platform Sutra,* or in any of the literature relating to Hui-neng. Its contents, as will be seen, often parallel that of other works, but such similarities cannot serve to relate it to them chronologically. There are, however, several stories about Hui-neng's career that appear only in this preface. That they were not copied, enlarged upon, or alluded to in other works indicates that these stories are of extremely late origin, for one of the major characteristics of the literature relating to Hui-neng is the borrowing of biographical details from earlier sources. In this instance the details are too striking to enable us to entertain the possibility that this is an early work, and that the stories it contains were arbitrarily rejected by later writers.

The preface gives the exact hour and day on which the Sixth Patriarch was born. No other work provides this information. It tells of the arrival of mysterious monks who gave the newborn child a name. This

[8] T48, pp. 362b–63a. This edition places the preface at the end of the work. The Yüan edition compiled by Te-i (see below, p. 107) contains the same preface with identical title, but places it at the head of the text, following Te-i's own preface. See *Gen Enyū Kōrai kokubon Rokuso daishi hōbō dankyō, Zengaku kenkyū,* no. 23 (July, 1935), pp. 1–63.

[9] The variants are discussed in Ui, *Zenshū shi kenkyū,* II, 175–76. He notes some fourteen textual differences, mostly of an insignificant nature.

pleasant little tale is also an invention of the preface. The story of the
acquisition of land for temple-building and the appearance of the Four
Deva Kings is likewise found for the first time here. This is true, too,
of the description of the Master stopping at scenic spots to select
suitable sites for the temple buildings. The concluding story about the
dragon is mentioned only in the *Sung kao-seng chuan*.[10]

Of Fa-hai himself we know almost nothing. Other than the mention
in the *Platform Sutra* (sec. 55), which states: "This *Platform Sutra*
was compiled by the head monk Fa-hai, who on his death entrusted
it to his fellow teacher Tao-ts'an," and the notice in section 57, where
it is stated: "This priest was originally a native of Ch'ü-chiang hsien
in Shao-chou," we have no information whatsoever. Presumably the
priest mentioned in section 57 is Fa-hai; at least the compiler of the
Ching-te ch'uan-teng lu seems to have thought so, for the information
concerning Fa-hai's place of origin is repeated in that work.[11] The
notice in the *Ch'üan T'ang wen,* preceding the text of the preface,
which gives a biographical note on Fa-hai, is clearly in error.[12] It may
be possible that Fa-hai can be identified with Chih-hai, mentioned in
the *Li-tai fa-pao chi,*[13] as a disciple of the Sixth Patriarch, but there
exists no corroborating evidence.

In addition to the contents of the work, which appears to be of a
very late date, this preface is suspect because of the complete lack of any
earlier versions, or even indications that there ever were any. It is
substantially the same as its Yüan dynasty counterpart, and may best
be considered as a variant version of the text found in the Yüan
edition of the *Platform Sutra.* That it is included in the *Ch'üan T'ang
wen* is accounted for by the uncritical attitude of its compilers, who
while making an exhaustive search for T'ang materials, included much
of dubious authenticity. Fa-hai's preface would appear to have no historical validity whatsoever as a source for Hui-neng's biography.

[10] T50, p. 755a.

[11] T51, p. 237a. Chan, *The Platform Scripture,* p. 22, assumes that the priest mentioned in section 57 is Hui-neng, and that there is thus a contradiction in the text between this section and section 2, which describes Hui-neng's origins. Sections 55–57,
however, seem clearly to be additions to the text, designed to promote the authenticity
of Fa-hai's particular school, or of the priests who succeeded him. I can see no justifica-
tion for Chan's assumption.

[12] CTW, ch. 915 (XIX, 12032). The editors of *Ch'üan T'ang wen* have mistakenly
followed information concerning the Fa-hai mentioned in the *Sung kao-seng chuan,* T50,
pp. 736c–37a, but this is clearly a different person. See Ui, *Zenshū shi kenkyū,* II, 253.

[13] T51, p. 182c.

Another inscription which can be placed in the same category is the *Kuang-hsiao ssu i-fa t'a-chi*,[14] attributed to the priest Fa-ts'ai and dated 676. It commemorates the burial of Hui-neng's hair after he had received tonsure at the hands of Yin-tsung at the Fa-hsing Temple[15] in Canton. The text details the history of the establishment of an ordination platform at the Fa-hsing Temple by Gunabhadra, the planting in 502 of a bo tree by Chih-yao, and his prediction that 160 years[16] later some one would come to preach the doctrine before countless people. All this information is found in Fa-hai's preface. The text then tells how Yin-tsung was impressed by Hui-neng's ability, how the latter's head was shaven, and goes on to recount that an eight-sided seven-story pagoda was erected on the site where the hair was buried. There is no mention of this inscription in early sources, and it is not given in the *Sung kao-seng chuan,* which relied on such inscriptions for a large part of its information. The original inscription is said to have been destroyed, and a new one erected in 1612.[17] Its contents and the fact that it is not mentioned elsewhere, lead one to conclude that it is of late origin, and not of sufficient historical validity to be used as a source for Hui-neng's biography.

One item from the *Ch'üan T'ang wen* requires further mention. This is the request, previously discussed, for Hui-neng to appear at the imperial court.[18] Here it is attributed to the Emperor Chung-tsung, and relates how Shen-hsiu and Hui-an, while at court, stated: "In the south is the Ch'an Master [Hui]-neng, who was in secret given the robe and Dharma by the Master [Hung]-jen," and suggested that he be called to court. The text then reports that the envoy Hsieh Chien was dispatched to tender the invitation. The notice here is untitled and bears no date.

In the biographies of Hui-neng this invitation is frequently mentioned, but there is absolutely no corroborating evidence to show that such a request was issued by the court. Indeed, the fact that it is undated here, and that there are inconsistencies in the attribution of the invitation itself, make one hesitate to accept it as valid.[19] Furthermore,

[14] CTW, ch. 912 (XIX, 11996). The text is also found in *Kuang-hsiao ssu chih,* ch. 10, pp. 11b–12a.
[15] An old name for the Kuang-hsiao Temple.
[16] Fa-hai's preface gives 170 years.
[17] Tokiwa Daijō, *Shina Bukkyō shiseki ki'nenshū hyōkai,* p. 34.
[18] CTW, ch. 17 (I, 241). See above, p. 31.
[19] See above, p. 31.

the very nature of the request, in which two of the great Ch'an Masters of the day demean their teaching to such an extent as to acknowledge the precedence of another's doctrines, would indicate that this text is merely a fabrication on the part of the adherents of Southern Ch'an. This story has been lent dignity by the fact that it is included in the biography of Shen-hsiu in the *Chiu T'ang shu.*[20] Here the request for Hui-neng's attendance at court is attributed to the Empress Wu. The notice also describes the distinction made between Northern and Southern Ch'an; but since this distinction did not exist during Shen-hsiu's time, its inclusion in the *Chiu T'ang shu* indicates that the compilers of this history were relying on late sources for their information.

The first record of Hui-neng to which any degree of authenticity can be attached is the passage in the *Leng-chia shih-tzu chi* which includes his name along with those of ten other disciples of the Fifth Patriarch.[21] Although only his name is mentioned, there is not much reason to doubt its authenticity, since it is recorded in a history compiled by a priest of the sect that was to become the rival school to that of Shen-hui and Hui-neng.

For our next information about Hui-neng we must turn to the inscription composed by the poet Wang Wei.[22] Written at the request of Shen-hui, it mentions incidents in the life of Hui-neng as they were known to Wang Wei. Unfortunately, the inscription is not dated, so that the exact year in which it was written cannot be determined.[23] In summary, its contents are as follows:

The Ch'an Master of Ts'ao-ch'i was surnamed Lu, and the place of his origin is unknown. He lived in a barbarian village and, while still young, went to Master Jen at Huang-mei. Here his genius was recognized and he was transmitted the robe symbolic of the teaching and

[20] CTS 191, p. 14a.
[21] See above, p. 17.
[22] *Wang Yu-ch'eng chi-chien-chu,* pp. 446–49. The inscription is entitled *Neng ch'an-shih pei.*
[23] Hu Shih, "Ch'an (Zen) Buddhism in China, Its History and Method," *Philosophy East and West,* III (no. 1, April, 1953), in the same article gives two different dates for the inscription: p. 10, "about 734"; p. 13, "at the time of Shen-hui's exile" (i.e., 753–56). Gernet, "Biographie du Maître Chen-houei de Ho-tsö," *Journal Asiatique,* 249 (1951), 48, gives the probable date as 740. He reasons that since Wang Wei was made Censor of General Affairs in 739, and because he is given this title in the text of the *Shen-hui yü-lu* (Hu Shih, *Shen-hui ho-shang i-chi,* p. 137; Gernet, *Entretiens du Maître de Dhyāna Chen-houei du Ho-tsö,* p. 63), it was probably written after this date.

told to leave. For sixteen years he stayed among merchants and laborers, and then met the Dharma-master Yin-tsung, a lecturer on the Nirvāṇa Sutra. Yin-tsung was impressed, shaved Hui-neng's head, and ordained him as a priest. Hui-neng then "loosed the rain of his Dharma." He preached that "he who forbears is without birth and therefore without self," that "meditation is to enter without a place to enter; wisdom is to depend on nothing." He remarked how difficult it was "to enter the sudden teaching," and stated that "to give in donation the seven treasures as numerous as the sands in the Ganges, to practice for innumerable kalpas, to exhaust all the ink in the world, is not the equivalent of spending one's life with nothing more to do (*wu-wei*) and having a compassion unfettered by anything." We are then told that the Empress Wu summoned him to court, but that he declined the invitation, and that she then sent him cloth for garments and silks in offering. At an unknown date he told his disciples that he was about to die, and at once a mysterious fragrance permeated the room and a bright rainbow appeared. When he had finished eating, he spread his sitting-cloth and passed away. Mountains tumbled, we are told, rivers ran dry, and the birds and monkeys cried in anguish. Again, on an unknown date, his sacred coffin was moved to Ts'ao-ch'i, and his body was placed, seated, in an unidentified place. In addition, we are informed, it was in his middle age that Shen-hui first met Hui-neng.

This, then, is what Wang Wei knew of Hui-neng when he composed his inscription. Although no precise dating is possible, it was made sometime between 732, when the meeting at Hua-t'ai took place, and Wang Wei's death in 759. Roughly during this same period Shen-hui's speeches were being recorded by his disciples and a work detailing the biographies of the Chinese Patriarchs was in circulation.[24] Thus,

---

[24] In addition to the biographies contained in the *Shen-hui yü-lu* (Suzuki text), pp. 53–64, we have reference to a lost work, the *Shih-tzu hsieh-mo chuan*, which is mentioned in the *P'u-t'i-ta-mo Nan-tsung ting shih-fei lun* (Hu Shih, *Shen-hui ho-shang i-chi*, p. 159; Gernet, *Entretiens . . . .*, p. 81; Hu Shih, "Hsin-chiao-ting te Tun-huang hsieh-pen Shen-hui ho-shang i-chu liang-chung," CYLYYC, XXIX [no. 2, February, 1958], 838), and which also contained biographies of the Patriarchs. The title of this lost work is the same as an alternate title to the *Li-tai fa-pao chi* (see above, p. 40) and there is a very close resemblance between the biographical material in the *Li-tai fa-pao chi* and the *Shen-hui yü-lu* (Suzuki text). Therefore, we may be justified in assuming that there may have been a close relationship between these three works, and that a fairly detailed biography of Hui-neng was in use in Shen-hui's school at the time that Wang Wei's inscription was being written.

The problem of the dating of Shen-hui's works remains. If we knew accurately when

68   *Introduction*

at the same time that Wang Wei's vague and imprecise inscription
was being composed there probably existed a much more detailed version of the biography of Hui-neng. This version was quite similar in
content to the autobiographical section of the *Platform Sutra.*[25]

they were written, they would serve to pinpoint certain elements in the development of
the story of Hui-neng's biography. The only work for which we have an exact date, however, is the *Shen-hui yü-lu* (Suzuki text). The year the manuscript was transcribed is
given as 791 (the year of the era and the cyclical designation do not correspond. See
Gernet, "Complément aux entretiens du Maître de Dhyāna Chen-houei," *BEFEO*, XLIV
[no. 2, 1954], 454). The *Li-tai fa-pao chi* may be dated at around 780. Hu Shih, "Hsin-
chiao-ting . . . ," p. 873, estimates that the Tun-huang manuscript of the *P'u-t'i-ta-mo
Nan-tsung ting shih-fei lun* (which contains mention of the lost *Shih-tzu hsieh-mo
chuan*) was made sometime during the T'ien-pao era (742–756). This does not provide
us with a particularly precise date; however, the contents of Shen-hui's works furnish
certain clues to the approximate date of certain events. Contained are accounts of Shen-
hui's meetings with various officials; and when the biographies of these officials are con-
sulted, it is possible to date approximately when these meetings took place. For example,
a conversation between Shen-hui and the Minister Chang Yüeh is recorded (Hu Shih,
Shen-hui ho-shang i-chi, p. 115; Gernet, *Entretiens* . . . , p. 31), and since Chang
Yüeh died in 731, we know that the meeting took place prior to this date. Again Fang
Kuan (697–763), as Gernet points out (see Gernet, "Complément . . . ," p. 455, fn. 1),
is mentioned as holding the rank of Grand Secretary of the Imperial Chancellery (*Shen-
hui yü-lu* [Suzuki text], p. 42) at the time he questioned Shen-hui. Since Fang Kuan
(Biography in CTS 111, pp. 2a–6b) held this rank between 744 and 755, and later
achieved a higher rank, it would indicate that the conversation took place some time
during this period, and furthermore that the text was compiled at the same time, since
Fang Kuan would have been referred to by the highest rank he achieved if it had been
compiled later. It would thus appear safe to place Shen-hui's writings between 732, when
the meeting at Hua-t'ai took place, and the end of the T'ien-pao era, 756.

    There remains, however, one further problem: because Shen-hui's works were recorded
by his disciples and we have a manuscript made as late as 791, we might be justified in
questioning to what degree the texts have been altered, emended, or refined. There is
no way of arriving at a definite conclusion to this problem, but there seems to be no particular
reason to assume that the texts do nòt represent Shen-hui's own words, or a close approximation of them. These works did not persist in China; it is only through their
preservation at Tun-huang that we have knowledge of them. Several copies did make
their way to Japan around the middle of the ninth century (the *P'u-t'i-ta-mo Nan-tsung
ting shih-fei lun* is included in Engyō's list of 839 (*Reiganji oshō shōrai hōmon dōgu
mokuroku*, T55, p. 1073b); the *Nan-yang Wen-ta tsa-cheng i* (apparently the correct
title for what has come to be called *Shen-hui yü-lu*) is found in Ennin's list of 847
(*Nittō shin gushōgyō mokuroku*, T55, p. 1084a), Enchin's list of 857 (*Nihon biku
Enchin nittō guhō mokuroku*, T55, p. 1101a), as well as his list of 859 (*Chishō
daishi shōrai mokuroku*, T55, 1106c), and in Eichō's list of 1094 (*Tōiki dentō
mokuroku*, T55, p. 1164b); a work known as *Ho-tse ho-shang ch'an-yao* is found
in Enchin's list of 857 (T55, p. 1101a), as well as his list of 859 (T55, p. 1106c),
but these works are no longer extant. The failure of Shen-hui's works to persist in the
Ch'an tradition may justify our assumption that they were not subjected to any great
degree of textual tampering.

    The above considerations lead us to believe that at the time that Wang Wei's inscrip-
tion was made there was also in current use in Shen-hui's school a fairly detailed biographical account of the careers of the Chinese Patriarchs, including one descriptive of
Hui-neng.

[25] See above, p. 32.

From the text of Wang Wei's inscription, it is evident that he knew neither the place of Hui-neng's origin nor the date of his death, neither his age nor any of the details of his life that Shen-hui's school describes, other than that he had received the robe from the Fifth Patriarch. Wang Wei, however, knew several stories which are found neither in Shen-hui's works nor in the *Platform Sutra*. These are the stories concerning the period between the time Hui-neng left the temple of the Fifth Patriarch and the time he arrived at Ts'ao-ch'i. Wang Wei mentions that Hui-neng spent sixteen years[26] among merchants and laborers, then met Yin-tsung, the preacher of the Nirvāṇa Sutra, under whom he took tonsure and became a priest. This story appears in greatly expanded form in later accounts, but not directly in any associated with Shen-hui and his school.[27]

It would seem then, that in the third, fourth, and fifth decades of the eighth century there were two unrelated groups of legends about Hui-neng, one centering about his experiences from birth until the time that he left the Fifth Patriarch, and the other concerned with the time after he had left Huang-mei until he became a priest and started teaching at Ts'ao-ch'i. Eventually these legends were brought together, rationalized, and presented as one cohesive story.

There is no way of telling, in any of these accounts, where facts stop and legends begin. No evidence exists to corroborate any of the details of the story. The biography of a Patriarch was evolving, slowly, by trial and error, just as the legends of the Indian Patriarchs and their Chinese descendants gradually evolved during the eighth century. If we consider all the available material, and eliminate patiently all the inconsistencies by picking the most likely legends, we can arrive at a fairly credible biography of Hui-neng.[28] If, on the other hand, we eliminate the legends and the undocumented references to the Sixth Patriarch, we may only conclude that there is, in fact, almost nothing that we can really say about him. We may speculate that perhaps the answer lies somewhere between the two. We know that a man named Hui-neng existed, and that he must have had some renown, if only in the area of southern China in which he lived. Obviously many legends

---

[26] The *Li-tai fa-pao chi*, T51, p. 183c, gives seventeen years.

[27] It is included in the *Li-tai fa-pao chi* in considerable detail. It is not found under the biography of Hui-neng, which closely resembles the *Shen-hui yü-lu* (Suzuki text), but in the supplementary material which follows the biography.

[28] For such an attempt, see Ui, *Zenshū shi kenkyū*, II, 173–248.

grew up about him, legends which conceivably contain within them a certain amount of fact; but what these facts are can in no way be determined. Much of the legend may well have been devised by Shen-hui; again we have no way of knowing to what extent it represents Shen-hui's invention. As the story of Hui-neng grows, as material such as is found in Fa-hai's "Preface" is added, it develops far beyond the rather simple version current at the middle of the eighth century. But by stressing the role of Hui-neng the Patriarch, Shen-hui was, perhaps unconsciously, helping to change the whole character of Ch'an. A process of humanization was taking place, a shift in emphasis from the Buddha to the man, from the words of the Buddha to the words of the Patriarchs. This tendency became more noticeable in the following century, with the veneration that the new Ch'an schools of Kiangsi and Hunan bestowed on their priests and the words that they had spoken.

Among the books brought to Japan by Saichō is a curious work, the *Sōkei daishi betsuden*,[29] which is no longer extant in China. A biography of Hui-neng, it amalgamates the many legends and also adds a considerable body of new material, much of it demonstrably unreliable.[30] It is the product of an entirely different school of Ch'an, that of Hsing-t'ao,[31] a disciple of the Sixth Patriarch, who was the keeper of the Master's pagoda at Ts'ao-ch'i. Some of the stories parallel those already seen in the *Shen-hui yü-lu*, others are mentioned but not elaborated upon by Wang Wei, and still others are entirely new. Obviously, though, it is the source for many of the stories on which later works based their biographies. The *Tsu-t'ang chi, Sung kao-seng chuan, Ching-te ch'uan-teng lu*, and the "Preface" by Fa-hai use much of the material it contains, and it is quite probable that the missing books of the *Pao-lin chuan* included some of the material found here.

[29] zz2B, 19, 5, 483a–88a. It has a lengthy original title descriptive of its contents. The title *Sōkei daishi betsuden* was given the work by its Japanese editor Sohō in 1762. The existing manuscript was written in 803 and obtained by Saichō on his trip in 804. For a discussion of the work, see Hu Shih, "T'an-ching k'ao chih i," *Hu Shih wen-ts'un*, IV, 292–301, and Matsumoto Bunzaburō, *Bukkyō shi zakkō*, pp. 94–98. A word of caution in regard to the use of the *Zokuzōkyō* edition is required. There are apparently a considerable number of misprints in the text. A facsimile reproduction in scroll form exists, but I have been unable to locate a copy. Thus, in the summary of the work given in the following pages, what appears to be an error on the part of the *Sōkei daishi betsuden* itself may in fact be an error on the part of the editors of the *Zokuzōkyō*.

[30] Hu Shih, "T'an-ching k'ao chih-i," pp. 299–300, discusses eight errors he has discovered in the work.

[31] The *Sung kao-seng chuan*, T50, p. 755b, and the *Ching-te ch'uan-teng lu*, T51, p. 236c, give his name as Ling-t'ao.

The work can be dated approximately to 782 or 783 by virtue of a statement within the text itself to the effect that seventy-one years have elapsed between Hsien-t'ien 2 (713), the date of Hui-neng's death, and Chien-chung 2 (782).[32] This represents a miscalculation: actually it is only sixty-eight years; however, it is safe to say that this work was composed around 782. Because of the new elements and variant stories contained, it is illustrative of the process whereby the legend of Hui-neng was formed. Material of a pseudofactual character was introduced, precise dates were given, names cited, and the texts of manufactured imperial proclamations presented. Later works used this material, eliminating the obvious errors, but retaining the basic stories. A detailed summary of its contents will be given to indicate the sudden expansion of the legend of Hui-neng.

The work begins with a description of the history of the Pao-lin Temple at Ts'ao-ch'i, and includes the prediction by Chih-yao that 170 years in the future the Supreme Dharma Treasure would be propagated here. The account of Hui-neng's life follows: he is surnamed Lu, is a native of Hsin-chou, and lost both his father and his mother at the age of three.[33] Coming to Ts'ao-ch'i in 670 at the age of thirty,[34] he meets a villager, Liu Chih-lüeh, whose relative, the nun Wu-chin-ts'ang, had left home to go to the Shan-chien Temple to devote herself to the recitation of the Nirvāṇa Sutra. Hui-neng hears her, and the next morning asks her to recite it to him, explaining that he is unable to read.[35] "If you are illiterate, how can you understand its meaning?" he is asked. Hui-neng's reply is: "What has the principle of the Buddha nature to do with understanding written words? What's so strange about not knowing written words?" All present admire his response and suggest that he become a monk, which he does,[36] staying at the Pao-lin Temple for three years, thus fulfilling the prediction that 170

[32] See p. 75.

[33] This is the only source that says that Hui-neng's mother and father both died when he was young.

[34] This work gives his death date as 713, at the age of seventy-six. He would thus be thirty-three, by Chinese reckoning, not thirty, in 670.

[35] The legend of Hui-neng's illiteracy, found in section 8 of the *Platform Sutra*, and constantly repeated in later works, makes its first appearance here. It is a convenient means to emphasize that Ch'an is a teaching which must be transmitted silently from mind to mind, without recourse to written words. The frequency with which Hui-neng quotes the sutras in the *Platform Sutra* would seem to belie the legend of his illiteracy, unless he learned to read in later life. The question is academic; we do not know enough about Hui-neng to determine whether he could or could not read.

[36] He is not, however, ordained at this time.

years in the future someone would come to preach there. At this time, we are informed, Hui-neng is thirty-three years of age.[37]

At the west stone grotto, a place in the area, was a certain Yüan ch'an-shih, who practiced meditation, as well as another priest, Hui-chi by name. The Master encounters both these men and is impressed by their wisdom. From Hui-chi he hears of the Master Jen at Huang-mei, and on the third day of the first month of Hsien-heng 5 (= February 14, 674), when he is thirty-four,[38] he leaves Ts'ao-ch'i to attend on Hung-jen at Huang-mei, traversing wild and desolate areas, and passing alone and unafraid parts where fierce tigers abound. His meeting with Hung-jen is recounted: "Where are you from?" the Fifth Patriarch asks. "From Hsin-chou in Ling-nan," is the reply. "How can a person from Hsin-chou in Ling-nan expect to become a Buddha?" Hung-jen asks. Hui-neng replies: "What is the difference in Buddha-nature between someone from Hsin-chou in Ling-nan and you?"[39] Hung-jen is impressed, and recognizes Hui-neng's talent, but puts him to work for eight months pounding rice. Because his body is too light, he ties a large rock around his waist in order to give himself added weight. Later the Fifth Patriarch goes to the threshing room and talks with Hui-neng, and afterwards calls him to his room, where he expounds the Dharma, and tells of the transmission from Kāśyapa to Ānanda to Śaṇavāsa to Upagupta, and "then on through the twenty-eight Indian Patriarchs to Dharmatrāta,"[40] and then through the Chinese Patriarchs, until it reached Hung-jen, who is the Fifth. Then he transmits the Law to Hui-neng, explains how it was not cut off with Siṁha bhikṣu, the twenty-fourth Patriarch, and sends Hui-neng off, bearing the robe and bowl symbolic of the transmission. He is accompanied by Hung-jen as far as Chiu-chiang station, from where he sets out for the south.

Meanwhile the Fifth Patriarch returns to his mountain, where he keeps silent and does not preach. When asked the reason, he requests that the assemblage at the temple disperse, as he has nothing more to say, since the Law is no longer at his place. Three days after explain-

---

[37] Another miscalculation; he would be thirty-six.

[38] This too is an error; he would have been thirty-seven in 674.

[39] See Translation, sec. 3.

[40] The *Sōkei daishi betsuden* seems to have followed a tradition similar to the *Li-tai fa-pao chi*, but omitting the third Indian Patriarch. It does not, however, change the name of Dharmatrāta to Bodhidharmatrāta. It would seem that even at this late date the name of Bodhidharma had not gained full currency among all the schools of Ch'an.

ing that Hui-neng has gone south, taking the Law with him, Hung-jen passes away. His funeral is held to the accompaniment of lamentations of birds and beasts and the forces of nature. A certain ex-general of the fourth rank, Ch'en Hui-ming,[41] goes in pursuit, catches up with Hui-neng at Ta-yü Peak, and, after indicating that he is not after the robe and the bowl, receives the teaching from Hui-neng. Several hundred others are following behind, but Hui-ming manages to turn them away. Of Hui-ming we are told that he did not gain enlightenment at this time, but later, going to the top of Mount Lu-shan, attained it after three years of effort, and afterwards spent his time teaching at Meng-shan.[42] Hui-neng now returns south to Ts'ao-ch'i, but, under the pressure of men of evil intent, goes into hiding on the borders between Ssu-hui[43] and Huai-chi[44] in Kuang-chou, living for five years among hunters.

When he is thirty-nine, in the first year of I-feng,[45] he arrives at the Chih-chih Temple,[46] which is presided over by Yin-tsung, an authority on the Nirvāṇa Sutra. He participates in an argument among several monks as to whether the banner on the staff is moving or whether the wind is moving, declaring that it is neither; it is the mind that moves. Impressed, Yin-tsung talks with Hui-neng on the following day and discovers that he is the heir of the Fifth Patriarch. Eventually, on the seventeenth day of the first month of I-feng 1 (= February 6, 676) his head is shaved by Yin-tsung, and on the twenty-eighth day of the second month (= March 17, 676) he is ordained. The names and titles of several participating priests are mentioned, and the prediction made by Paramārtha when he planted two bo trees by the ordination platform is described. Later Hui-neng preaches to the assembly and engages in a question-and-answer session with the thirteen-year-old acolyte from the Ho-tse Temple, Shen-hui.[47] Hui-neng is asked to remain at the Chih-

[41] His biography is given in *Sung kao-seng chuan*, ⊤50, p. 756b–c. See Translation, p. 134, n. 47.

[42] I-ch'un hsien, Kiangsi.

[43] Ssu-hui hsien, Kwangtung.

[44] Huai-chi hsien, Kwangsi.

[45] Again a mistake in dating. Hsien-heng 5 is 674; I-feng 1 is 676. Yet he is said to have spent five years in hiding. Note that Wang Wei gives the period of time as sixteen years and the *Li-tai fa-pao chi* as seventeen years.

[46] Another name for the Fa-hsing Temple. See Ui, *Zenshū shi kenkyū*, II, 205–6, for a discussion of the changes of name of this temple.

[47] Here Shen-hui is called a young boy at the time he visits Hui-neng; he appears once as a youth in the *Platform Sutra* (sec. 48). At any rate, Shen-hui, who was born in 670, would have been seven, not thirteen, if the *Sōkei daishi betsuden* is to be believed.

chih Temple, but he expresses the desire to return to the Pao-lin Temple in Ts'ao-ch'i, and is seen off by Yin-tsung and some 3,000 followers. On the fifteenth day of the first month of Shen-lung 1 (= February 13, 705) the Emperor Kao-tsung[48] requests Hui-neng to come to court. The proclamation states that famous priests from all over the country have assembled at court, and that Shen-hsiu and Hui-an have recommended that Hui-neng be called, since he in secret received the teaching from Hung-jen and possesses the robe and bowl of Bodhidharma. It goes on to say that the court is dispatching the vice-commissioner Hsieh Chien to greet the Master, and that it is hoped that he will comply at once. Hui-neng declines, pleading illness, and says that he desires to remain at his own temple to regain his health. Here follows a passage in which Hsieh Chien asks Hui-neng questions concerning the teaching, to which Hui-neng makes reply. Hsieh Chien then returns to the capital. On the second day of the fourth month of Shen-lung 3 (= May 7, 707) a proclamation praising Hui-neng, accompanied by a gift of a priest's gown and 500 bolts of cloth, is sent to Hui-neng. On the eighteenth day of the eleventh month (= December 16, 707) a tablet entitled Fa-ch'üan Temple is sent, along with orders to repair the Buddha-hall and the sutra storehouse at the Master's temple, and also to convert the Master's old house in Hsin-chou into a temple called Kuo-en.[49] In 712[50] the Master goes to the Kuo-en Temple to see about the repairs. In 711 he has a pagoda for his coffin built at Ts'ao-ch'i. In the seventh month of 713 he urges the hurried completion of the building, but his disciples do not understand the import of his words. In the eighth month of this year, in answer to Shen-hui,[51] who asks to whom the robe is to be handed down, Hui-neng replies that it is to be given to no one, but that seventy years after his death two Bodhisattvas will appear, one a layman who will restore his temple, and the other a priest who will propagate his teachings.[52] The Master passes away on the

[48] Kao-tsung died December 28, 683; thus the attribution is obviously in error. For this proclamation, see pp. 30, 65.
[49] Both of these proclamations are erroneously attributed to Kao-tsung. They appear (as one proclamation) in the *Sung kao-seng chuan*, T50, pp. 755b–c; in the *Tsu-t'ang chi*, I, 94–96; the *Ching-te ch'uan-teng lu*, T51, p. 236c; and the Yüan edition of the *Platform Sutra*, T48, p. 360a.
[50] This date is suspicious; it is later than the next one mentioned.
[51] In the *Platform Sutra* it is Fa-hai who asks this question.
[52] We have seen this prediction before as twenty years. It so appears in the *Platform Sutra* (sec. 49). The reason for seventy years is unclear, but it may very well refer to

third day of the eighth month of this year (= August 28, 713), while in a sitting position. His age at death is seventy-six. The reactions of nature and the supernatural phenomena which occurred are described. We now hear that a metal band was fitted about his neck, his body was lacquered completely, and on the thirteenth day of the eleventh month (= December 5, 713) he was placed in a coffin.

In 739 someone dragged the Master's body out into the garden and attempted to cut off the head, but one of the monks, hearing the sound of grating metal, rushed out, and the intruder fled.[53] The text then goes on to explain that it has been seventy-one years from the Master's death in 713 until the present (782). Next we are presented with an utter confusion in dates. We are told that in 713 one of the Master's leading disciples, Hsing-t'ao, was charged with guarding the Master's robe, and that thirty-five years after this date Wei Ch'ü[54] wrote an inscription for the Master, which was effaced in 719 by a lay disciple of Northern Ch'an, Wu P'ing-i, who wrote a text of his own. Then follows a story about a certain Huang ch'an-shih, who had studied under the Fifth Patriarch and then had returned to his home temple, where he practiced meditation sitting. Ta-jung, who had spent thirty years under Hui-neng, happened to pass by Huang's temple, and, as a result of a conversation between the two priests, Huang discovered that he had been sitting thirty years in vain, went to the Sixth Patriarch, and gained enlightenment in 711.[55]

Next we have the text of a mandate by the Emperor Su-tsung, dated the seventeenth day of the twelfth month of Shang-yüan 2 (= January 16, 762),[56] in which Hsing-t'ao, together with his lay disciple Wei Li-chien,[57] is requested to accompany the imperial commissioner, Liu Ch'u-chiang,[58] to court, bearing the Sixth Patriarch's robe. On the first day of the first month of Ch'ien-yüan 2 (= February 3, 759), Hsing-

the compilers of the *Sōkei daishi betsuden*, which was made about seventy years after Hui-neng's death.

[53] This story, first introduced by Shen-hui (see p. 28), is greatly enlarged in later works. See *Sung kao-seng chuan*, т50, p. 755b, and *Ching-te ch'uan-teng lu*, т51, p. 236c.

[54] See Translation, p. 125, n. 5.

[55] This story is found, under the names of the individual priests concerned, in the *Ching-te ch'uan-teng lu*, т51, p. 237c (under Chih-huang); p. 243c (under Hsüan-su). See Ui, *Zenshū shi kenkyū*, II, 262–63, for the variations of these priest's names.

[56] Another dating error. The year is probably Ch'ien-yüan 1 (= January 20, 759).

[57] Unknown.

[58] Unknown.

t'ao declines this invitation, pleading illness, and sends in his stead his disciple Hui-hsiang,[59] who takes the robe with him. On the seventeenth day of the first month (= February 19, 759), Hsing-t'ao passes away at the age of sixty-nine.[60] Hui-hsiang is awarded a purple robe by the emperor, and a layman who accompanies him is made a priest. There follow several imperial mandates, bestowing names on temples and changing temple names.[61] Next we have a lengthy request, undated, in which Hui-hsiang asks permission to leave the court, and a statement by the emperor in which Hui-hsiang's accomplishments are praised. Then on the twentieth day of the eleventh month of Ch'ien-yüan 3 (= December 31, 760) Emperor Su-tsung sends the imperial commissioner Ch'eng Ching-ch'i [62] to offer incense before the grave of the Sixth Patriarch, whereupon from within the grave a white light leaps forth, soaring straight up to a remarkable height.

The *Sōkei daishi betsuden* then concludes its story by quoting a mandate sent by the emperor when he returned the robe to Ts'ao-ch'i in Pao-ying 2 (763).[63] The emperor states that in a dream the Sixth Patriarch had asked him to return the robe to Ts'ao-ch'i, and therefore he is sending the General Yang Ch'ung-ching[64] with the robe, which is a National Treasure, and should be installed in the temple and guarded from loss. Here follows the mention of six miraculous occurrences which happened during the Master's life and after his death.

This, then, is the legend as it appears in one particular school of Ch'an, that of Hsing-t'ao and his followers, in 782. Despite its numerous inaccuracies, this book is the source for much of the legend relating to Hui-neng. It should be noted that Shen-hui is mentioned but once, and then as a thirteen-year-old acolyte, and that no mention of a *Plat-*

---

[59] Biography unknown. The *Sung kao-seng chuan*, T50, p. 755c, gives his name as Ming-hsiang.

[60] The *Ching-te ch'uan-teng lu*, T51, p. 244a, gives his age at death as ninety-five, but does not give the year. He is said to have received the posthumous title "Ta-hsiao ch'an-shih."

[61] It is not quite clear to which temple or buildings these apply. Presumably they refer to specific buildings at Ts'ao-ch'i, or to the temple built at the Master's old home in Hsin-chou.

[62] Unknown.

[63] Although Pao-ying 2 is mentioned in the text, the mandate itself is dated the seventh day of the fifth month of Yung-t'ai 1 (= May 31, 765). Since a textual note remarks that the robe had been kept for seven years at the Tsung-ch'ih Temple, the latter date is more likely. The emperor was Tai-tsung. The text of this mandate is also found in CTW, ch. 48 (II, 646).

[64] Unknown.

form Sutra or of its compiler, Fa-hai, is made. The work, in fact, is occupied with extolling the career of Hui-neng and establishing the validity of Hsing-t'ao and his line. It lays great emphasis on the transmission of the robe, and takes pains to indicate that it is still at Ts'ao-ch'i. This was perhaps necessary to counteract the claims of the *Li-tai fa-pao chi,* which informs us that this garment had been taken to Szechuan. The school of Northern Ch'an is virtually ignored; other than one mention of Shen-hsiu and a reference to Wu P'ing-i, we are unaware of a struggle between the two rival sects. It may well be that there was no longer much need to discuss the conflict at this time; at any rate, this work represents a local school of Ch'an, far removed from the capital cities, and the rivalry was of no particular concern to it.

Unfortunately, the two concluding volumes of the *Pao-lin chuan,* the work which would contribute most to our understanding of the Hui-neng legend, are missing. We may assume, however, that the *Pao-lin chuan* contained a lengthy biography of Hui-neng, enlarged greatly on the legend, and may well have incorporated much of the material found in the *Sōkei daishi betsuden.* Later historical works relied on the *Pao-lin chuan,* as we have seen, followed its theory of the twenty-eight Indian Patriarchs, and in all likelihood based their biographies of Hui-neng on material found there.

There are two further sources for Hui-neng's biography, which are of interest because they provide conflicting information on the date of his death, given as 713 in most sources. One is the inscription by Liu Tsung-yüan,[65] written in 815 [66] to commemorate the award of the posthumous title Ta-chien to the Sixth Patriarch. The other is the inscription by Liu Yü-hsi,[67] made in the following year. Both inscriptions state that they were composed 106 years after Hui-neng's death. This would date the event at either 709 or 710. These inscriptions are important, if only to indicate that there was a lack of unanimity even in regard to the date Hui-neng is said to have died.

Tsung-mi provides a brief biographical sketch of the Sixth Patriarch in his *Yüan-chüeh ching ta-shu ch'ao,*[68] but adds no significant infor-

---

[65] *Ts'ao-ch'i ti-liu-tsu tz'u-shih Ta-chien ch'an-shih pei,* CTW, ch. 587 (XII, 7535).

[66] Ui, *Zenshū shi kenkyū,* II, 179, believes that this date should be corrected to 816.

[67] *Ts'ao-ch'i liu-tsu Ta-chien ch'an-shih ti-erh pei ping-hsü,* CTW, ch. 610 (XIII, 7824–25).

[68] ZZ1, 14, 3, p. 277a.

mation which has not been seen before. The *Sung k̟ao-seng chuan,*
while it does not add much to the knowledge of the legend, provides
information on the posthumous honors done Hui-neng by a number
of prominent officials.[69] It does not shed much light on Hui-neng himself, but does indicate the prominence to which he had been lifted by
Shen-hui's campaign. We have no corroborative sources for many of
the statements made, and we do not know on what this work based its
information. We are informed that the vice-president of the Army Ministry, Sung Ting, made an inscription concerning Hui-neng to accompany some paintings made in a new building that Shen-hui built for
the Sixth Patriarch at the Ho-tse Temple. These paintings told the
lineage of the school, starting from the Tathāgatha, running through
the Indian Patriarchs, and including the six Patriarchs in China.[70] Fang
Kuan[71] wrote a preface for the pictures which represented the six generations in China. Sung Chih-wen[72] paid a call on Hui-neng and wrote
a long piece about it.[73] Chang Yüeh (667–731)[74] offered incense and
presented a poem, presumably at Hui-neng's tomb. Wu P'ing-i wrote
a poem for the Sixth Patriarch, and since Nan-yüeh Huai-jang was
casting a giant bell at the time, the verse was inscribed on it, in Sung
Chih-wen's hand. Sung Ching (662–737)[75] paid his respects at the
pagoda and questioned Hui-neng's disciple Ling-t'ao[76] about points of
doctrine, and was pleased with the answers he received.

The authority for all this information is not known. It is significant,
however, that three of the men mentioned, Sung Chih-wen, Chang
Yüeh, and Wu P'ing-i, are known to have been connected with North-

---

[69] T50, pp. 755b–c.

[70] We are not told when these paintings were made, but it was presumably before 745,
when Shen-hui went to Loyang. One may assume that there were thirteen patriarchs represented, conforming with Shen-hui's theories of the transmission of the Dharma.

[71] For his biography see cts 111, pp. 2b–6b and hts 139, pp. 1a–2b. He rose to be
grand secretary of the Imperial Chancellery, vice-president of the Bureau of Justice, and
president of the Grand Secretariat of the Left. He died in 763 at the age of sixty-seven.

[72] His biography is in cts 190, pp. 9b–10b. A famed poet, he was recognized at court
by the Empress Wu, but was in frequent difficulties and was exiled from time to time.
He was allowed to commit suicide in the Hsien-t'ien era (712–713). He was at one time
exiled to Ling-nan, so that it is possible that he visited the Sixth Patriarch at the time.
See H. A. Giles, *Chinese Biographical Dictionary,* no. 1829.

[73] Not preserved.

[74] Biography in cts 97, pp. 7a–13b; hts 125, pp. 5a–9a. Biographical notice in Giles,
Chinese Biographical Dictionary, no. 134.

[75] Biography in cts 96, pp. 6a–10b; hts 124, 5b–9a. Biographical notice in Giles, *Chinese Biographical Dictionary,* no. 1830.

[76] He appears in the *Sōkei daishi betsuden* as Hsing-t'ao.

ern Ch'an. We are now informed that all these men had to with the Sixth Patriarch. Because this information is not recorded in other sources, much of it must be regarded as of fairly dubious authenticity.

Let us close this "biography" of Hui-neng with a translation of one of the later sources, the section in the *Ching-te ch'uan-teng lu* devoted to Hui-neng. It is dated at 1004 and is illustrative of the legend in its full-blown form.

Master Hui-neng, the thirty-third Patriarch, was surnamed Lu, and his ancestors were natives of Fan-yang. During the Wu-te period [618–626] his father Hsing-tao served as a provincial official at Hsin-chou in Nan-hai, where he later became a resident. When Hui-neng was three years old his father died and his mother, who was faithful to her husband and did not remarry, brought him up. The older he got the more poverty-stricken did his home become, and he worked as a wood-cutter to earn a living.

One day when he was taking wood to market, he heard a man reciting the Diamond Sutra. Startled, he inquired: "What Dharma is this? From where did you get it?"

The man replied: "It is called the Diamond Sutra; I got it from Master Hung-jen at Huang-mei."

Hui-neng told his mother at once what had happened and expressed his determination to visit this teacher for the sake of the Dharma. Going directly to Shao-chou, he met there Liu Chih-lüeh, a man of noble conduct, with whom he became friendly. Liu Chih-lüeh had an aunt, the nun Wu-chin-ts'ang, who constantly recited the Nirvāṇa Sutra. Hui-neng listened for a while and then explained its meaning to her. Thereupon the nun brought one roll of the text to him and asked the meaning of certain words. Hui-neng said: "I don't know written words, but if you want to know the Sutra's meaning, then just ask me."

"If you can't read the words, then how can you understand their meaning?" the nun asked.

"The mysterious principle of all the Buddhas has nothing to do with words," he replied.

Amazed, the nun reported this to the village elders: "Hui-neng is a man of Tao. We should ask his favor and make offerings to him." Those who were about vied with each other to render him homage. Nearby was the site of an old temple, Pao-lin, and the populace decided to repair it so that Hui-neng might live there. People came from all over and soon the temple building was completed.

One day Hui-neng suddenly thought to himself: "I am seeking the great Dharma. Why should I stop halfway?" The next day he went to the stone caves at the West Mountain in Ch'ang-lo hsien, where he met the Ch'an Master Chih-yüan. Hui-neng requested permission to study with him.

Chih-yüan said: "You look to be of noble manner and obviously are a superior person, scarcely like an ordinary man. I understand that the seal of the mind of the Indian Bodhidharma has been transmitted to Huang-mei [the Fifth Patriarch, Hung-jen]. You should go there and settle your doubts with him." Hui-neng left and at once became a student of the Ch'an of the East Mountain at Huang-mei. This was in the second year of Hsien-heng [670]. The moment that Master Hung-jen saw him coming, without a word being spoken, he acknowledged his capacity. Later he transmitted the robe and the Dharma to Hui-neng and then had him remain in hiding in the area between Huai-chi and Ssu-hui. On the eighth day of the first month of the first year of I-feng [= January 28, 676] Hui-neng arrived in Nan-hai, and at the Fa-hsing Temple he met the Dharma-master Yin-tsung, who lectured on the Nirvāṇa Sutra. Here he found shelter under the eaves of the temple. One evening when the wind was stirring the temple banner, he heard two monks arguing. One said that it was the flag that was moving, the other that it was the wind. Back and forth they argued, but they were unable to realize the true principle.

Hui-neng said: "Pardon a common layman for intruding into your lofty discussion, but it is neither the banner nor the wind that is moving; it is only your own mind that moves." Yin-tsung overheard this remark and his flesh crept at the strangeness of it. The next day he invited Hui-neng to his room, and in response to his intense questions about the meaning of [his remark about] the banner and the wind, Hui-neng explained the principle in detail. Yin-tsung involuntarily arose, saying: "You are no ordinary man. Who was your teacher?" Hui-neng, hiding nothing, at once told him of how he had obtained the Dharma. Then Yin-tsung assumed the position of a disciple and begged for instruction in the essentials of Ch'an. He announced to the assembly:

"I am a common man who has received the precepts, but now let us meet a living Bodhisattva," and he pointed to the lay disciple Lu [Hui-neng] who was seated with the assembly and said: "This is he." He asked Hui-neng to show the robe which served as proof of the transmission and had the assembly pay reverence to it. On the fifteenth day of the first month Yin-tsung, before a gathering of eminent Buddhists, shaved Hui-neng's head. On the eighth day of the second month Hui-neng received the full precepts from the Vinaya-master Chih-kuang. The ordination platform had been set up by the Tripitaka Master Gunabhadra during the Sung dynasty and he had predicted that later a living Bodhisattva would receive the precepts there. And again, when the Tripitaka Master Paramārtha planted two bo trees beside the platform towards the end of the Liang dynasty, he had announced to the assemblage: "Some hundred and twenty years from now an enlightened man will preach the Supreme Vehicle beneath these bo trees and will bring salvation to countless multitudes." When Hui-neng finished receiving the precepts he revealed the teaching of the East Mountain under these very trees, just as had been predicted.

On the eighth day of the second month of the next year [= March 16, 677] Hui-neng told the assembly: "I no longer wish to stay here but would like to return to my old temple." Yin-tsung and some thousand monks and laymen saw him off on his return to the Pao-lin Temple.

Wei Ch'ü, the prefect of Shao-chou, invited him to turn the wheel of the Wondrous Law at the Ta-fan Temple and to teach the precepts of the formless mind-ground. His disciples recorded his sermons and they have been given the name *T'an ching,* and have been widely circulated throughout the country.

The Master returned to Ts'ao-ch'i and let fall the rain of the Great Dharma, and at no time were there ever fewer than a thousand students under him. In the first year of Shen-lung [705] Emperor Chung-tsung issued a proclamation:

"I have invited the two Masters Hui-an and Shen-hsiu to make offerings within the palace, and have studied the One Vehicle every moment that I can spare from the affairs of state. The two Masters have recommended you, saying: 'In the south is the Ch'an Master Hui-neng, who in secret received the robe and the Dharma from Hung-jen. He is the one who should be questioned [concerning the teaching].' I am dispatching the chief palace attendant Hsüeh Chien to extend my invitation. It is hoped that you will consider this [invitation] kindly and will come quickly to the capital."

Hui-neng declined, pleading illness, saying that he desired to spend what was left of his life among the forests [of the Pao-lin Temple].

Hsüeh Chien said: "All the Ch'an Masters in the capital say that if one wants to gain an understanding of the Way one must practice sitting in meditation. Without Ch'an meditation there is as yet no one who has gained emancipation. I wonder what your opinion of this is?"

The Master answered: "The Way is realized through the mind. What should it have to do with a sitting posture! The sutra says: 'If you think of the Tathāgata as sitting or lying down you are treading the path of heresy. Why? Because the Tathāgata comes from nowhere and goes nowhere.' [77] When there is no birth and no death this is the pure *dhyāna* of the Tathāgata; when all things are empty, this is the pure sitting (*tso*) of the Tathāgata. Ultimately there is nothing to prove. So why bother with a sitting posture?"

Hsüeh Chien said: "When I return the emperor will be sure to question me. I beg of you to be so compassionate as to indicate to me the essentials of your teaching."

The Master said: "There is no light and darkness in Tao. Light and darkness suggest alternation. Light cannot be exhausted and then again it is exhausted."

Hsüeh Chien said: "Light symbolizes wisdom and darkness symbolizes the passions. If the practicer does not destroy the passions by illuminating them with wisdom, how can he escape from the endless cycle of birth and death?"

The Master said: "To illumine the passions with wisdom is the shallow view of the *Śrāvaka* and *Pratyekabuddha,* the technique of the sheep and deer.[78] No one with superior wisdom and great capacity (the Mahāyāna believer) is like this."

"What is the viewpoint of Mahāyāna?" asked Hsüeh Chien.

The Master replied: "The nature of light and darkness is not two. The nondual nature is thus the real nature. The real nature does not

---

[77] The exact quotation has not been located. It paraphrases a passage in the Diamond Sutra: "If someone says that the Tathāgata comes and goes, sits or lies down, that person does not understand what I teach" (T8, p. 752b).

[78] Reference is to the parable of the burning house in the Lotus Sutra (T9, p. 76a).

decrease in the ignorant man, nor does it increase in the wise man. It stays in the midst of passions but is not disturbed; it exists in the state of *samādhi* but is not quieted. Not cut off, not persisting, not coming, not going, it exists neither in the middle, nor in the inside, nor on the outside. It is not born nor is it destroyed. Real nature and its form are in the absolute. It is always abiding and changeless. Given a name, it is the Tao."

Hsüeh Chien asked: "You talk about nonbirth and nondestruction. How do they differ from those of the heretics?"

The Master replied: "When the heretics speak of nonbirth and nondestruction, they mean to put an end to birth with destruction and make destruction apparent with birth. Destruction, thus, is not destroyed, and birth bespeaks birthlessness. When I speak of nonbirth and nondestruction, I mean that from the outset there is no birth of itself, and again, there is no destruction. Therefore it is not the same [as the nonbirth and nondestruction] of the heretics. If you want to know the essentials of the mind, you must stop thinking about all distinctions of good and evil. When naturally you gain entrance to the pure mind, in the profound and eternal quietude, the miraculous activities are [as numberless] as the grains of sand in the Ganges."

Hsüeh Chien, while hearing these teachings, suddenly attained a great awakening. Taking leave with profound reverence, he returned to the capital and reported what the Master had said in a memorial. An edict was issued thanking Hui-neng, and a special robe, five hundred bolts of silk, and a jeweled bowl were presented to him.

On the nineteenth day of the twelfth month a proclamation was issued changing the name of the old Pao-lin Temple to Chung-hsing Temple. On the eighteenth day of the eleventh month [of Shen-lung] 3 [= December 16, 707] imperial orders were issued the prefect of Shao-chou to redecorate the temple, and a tablet, inscribed Fa-ch'üan Temple, was presented. The Master's old home in Hsin-chou was converted into the Kuo-en Temple.

One day the Master said to the assembly: "All of you good friends! Each one of you purify your mind and listen to my sermon. The mind of each one of you is itself the Buddha. Do not have any doubts about it. Outside the mind there is not one thing that can be established. It is your own mind that produces the ten thousand things. That is why the sutra says: 'If mind is produced all things are produced; if mind is destroyed all things are destroyed.' [79] If you wish to attain omniscient wisdom, you must penetrate the *samādhi* of one form and the *samādhi* of oneness. If, under all circumstances, you do not abide in form, if within that form neither hatred nor love is produced, if there is no taking and no casting away, if you do not think of gain and loss, then you will be calm and quiet, empty and unconcerned. This is called the *samādhi* of one form. If under all circumstances—walking, staying, sitting, lying—you possess pure direct mind, the place where you sit in meditation becomes, without moving, the Pure Land. This is called the *samādhi* of oneness.

"If a person is endowed with these two *samādhis,* he is like a seed within the ground which has been retained and nourished well, and then has been brought to fruit. These two *samādhis* are just like this.

"The sermon that I have just preached is like the rain that waters the great earth, and your Buddha natures are like the many seeds that sprout when they encounter the wetness. Those who embrace my teachings will without fail gain enlightenment (*bodhi*) and those who follow my practices will surely realize the wondrous fruit."

In the first year of Hsien-t'ien [712] the Master announced to the assembly: "Although unworthy, I received the robe and the Dharma from Master Hung-jen, and now I am preaching to you. The robe will not be handed down, for the root of your faith is deep, you are firm and without doubts, and you are fit for the one great causal event (the appearance of a Buddha in this world). Listen then to my verse:

> The mind-ground contains the various seeds,
> With the all-prevading rain each and every one sprouts.
> When one has suddenly awakened to the sentiency of the flower,
> The fruit of enlightenment matures of itself.

After finishing his verse the Master said: "This Dharma is not dual; neither is the mind. This Tao is pure and has no form at all. Take care not to contemplate purity or to make the mind empty. The mind is from the outset pure; there is nothing you must grasp or throw away. Each one of you must exert himself. Leave now and go to wherever circumstances lead you."

For forty years the Master preached the Dharma for the benefit of

---

[79] Unidentified.

living beings. On the sixth day of the seventh month of the same year [712] he ordered his disciples to go to the Kuo-en Temple and to erect there a pagoda, called Pao-en, and he had them hurry its construction.

There was a monk from Szechuan, Fang-pien by name, who came to visit the Master. "I am good at modeling clay figures," he said.

Keeping a straight face, the Master replied: "Try making one then."

Fang-pien did not understand the Master's intent and made a clay figure of the Master, about seven inches high, on which he expended all his ingenuity. Examining it, the Master said: "Your modeling nature is good, but your Buddha nature does not come out so well. But I'll give you some clothing in payment." The monk bowed in thanks and left.

On the first day of the second month of the second year of Hsien-t'ien [= March 1, 713] the Master said to his disciples: "I wish to return to Hsin-chou. Get me a boat and some oars at once."

The assembly was struck with grief and they begged the Master to remain a while longer. The Master said: "All Buddhas who appear in this world reveal their Nirvāna. It is always true that those who come must go. There must always be a place to which my body will return."

The assembly said: "Master, you are going away from here; you will come back soon again?"

The Master replied: "When leaves fall they return to the root; for when I return there is no date." [80]

Someone asked: "To whom are you transmitting your Dharma eye?"

The Master answered: "The possessor of Tao will get it and the one with no-mind will penetrate it."

Again someone asked: "Will there be any difficulties later?"

The Master replied: "Some five or six years after I die someone will come to get my head. Listen to my prediction:

> Atop the head offerings to parents,
> In the mouth food is sought.
> When the trouble with Man occurs,
> Yang and Liu will be officials. [81]

[80] Translation uncertain. The text reads: *lai-shih wu-jih*. The Yüan edition of the *Platform Sutra* substitutes *k'ou* (mouth) for *jih* (day) (т48, p. 361b): "When leaves return they have no mouth (speak no words)" or "When I come I will have no mouth."

[81] This verse predicts the events detailed at the end of this selection. A man in need of food was hired by a Korean monk to cut off the Sixth Patriarch's head and to take it to Korea so that it might be venerated there. The man was named Man and the officials concerned with the thief's punishment were Yang and Liu.

The Master continued: "Seventy years after I die two Bodhisattvas will come from the East, one a layman, the other a monk. Simultaneously they will gain many converts and establish my teachings. They will restore and found temples and produce numerous heirs to my Dharma."

When he had finished his talk, he went to the Kuo-en Temple in Hsin-chou, and after taking a bath, seated himself in the lotus posture and passed away. A strange fragrance impressed itself on those who were there and a bright rainbow curved over the earth. This was on the third day of the eighth month of the same year [= August 28, 713].

At this time at both Shao-chou and Hsin-chou sacred pagodas were erected and none of the monks or laymen could decide [where the body was to be enshrined]. The prefects of each county burned incense together and offered an invocation: "Wherever the smoke from the incense leads will be the place to which the Master wishes to return." The smoke from the incense burner rose and moved straight in the direction of Ts'ao-ch'i. On the thirteenth day of the eleventh month the Master's body was enshrined in its pagoda. He was seventy-six years old. Wei Ch'ü, the prefect of Ts'ao-ch'i, wrote the text for his monument.

His disciples, recalling the Master's prediction that someone would take his head, put an iron band and a lacquered cloth about his neck to protect it. Inside the pagoda was placed the "robe of faith" handed down by Bodhidharma, the robe and bowl presented by Emperor Chung-tsung, the figure of the Master modeled by Fang-pien, and various Buddhist implements. The pagoda attendant was placed in charge of these.

On the third day of the eighth month of K'ai-yüan 10 [= September 18, 722], in the middle of the night a sound like the dragging of iron chains was heard coming from the pagoda. The monks leaped up in surprise in time to see a man in mourning clothes running out from the pagoda. Later on they found that the Master's neck had been injured. The attempt at robbery was reported to county and prefectural officials. The prefectural authorities ordered Yang K'an and the prefect to obtain a warrant and to arrest the culprit at once. Five days later the thief was seized at Shih-chüeh village and was sent to Shao-chou for examination. He stated that his name was Chang Ching-man, that he was a native of Liang hsien in Ju-chou, and that he had received twenty thousand cash from a Korean monk, Chin Ta-pei of the K'ai-yüan Temple in Hung-chou, to steal the Sixth Patriarch's head and take it to Korea so that it might be venerated there.

The magistrate Liu heard the case, but did not immediately pronounce sentence, first going himself to Ts'ao-ch'i. There he asked Ling-t'ao, one of the Master's higher disciples, what sentence he should pass.

Ling-t'ao replied: "If you follow the laws of the nation then he should be executed. But the compassion of Buddhism treats enemy and friend alike. After all, he was motivated by the desire to venerate [the head]. His crime should be forgiven."

The magistrate Liu responded in admiration: "For the first time I realize the breadth and greatness of the Buddhist teaching." Then the criminal was set free.

In the first year of Shang-yüan (760) the Emperor Su-tsung sent an envoy asking for the Master's robe and bowl so that they might be brought to court for veneration.

On the fifth day of the fifth month of the first year of Yung-t'ai [= May 29, 765] the Emperor Tai-tsung had a dream in which the Sixth Patriarch asked for [the return of] the robe and bowl. On the seventh day an imperial order was issued to the prefect Yang Chien:

"I have had a dream in which the Ch'an Master Hui-neng requested that the robe which represents the transmission of the Dharma be returned to Ts'ao-ch'i. I have now ordered Liu Ch'ung-ching, the Grand General of Defense, to return it to you with due reverence. I regard it as a National Treasure. Let it be installed properly at the head temple, and be strictly guarded by special priests, who have been recipients of the main tenets of the teaching. Great care must be taken so that it is not lost."

Although in later years people did steal the robe, they did not get far with it, and it was always retrieved. This happened several times.

Emperor Hsien-tsung conferred on the Master the posthumous title of "Ta-chien" and his pagoda was named Yüan-ho Ling-chao.

In the beginning of the K'ai-pao period [968–975] of the Sung, when the imperial army subjugated the Liu family of Nan-hai, the defeated soldiers made a stand [at the temple], and the pagoda-mausoleum was completely destroyed by fire. But the Master's body was protected by the monk in charge of the pagoda and suffered no injury whatsoever.

Later an imperial order to repair the building was issued, and before it was finished it happened that Ta'i-tsung ascended the throne. He was much interested in Ch'an and contributed greatly to the splendor of the pagoda.

It has been 292 years from the Master's death in the second year of Hsien-t'ien [713] until now, the first year of Ching-te [1004].

Excluding the thirty-three heirs, among them Yin-tsung and others, who each propagated Ch'an somewhere, made their marks, and were true heirs [of the Sixth Patriarch], there were others who concealed their fame and all traces of themselves. They are listed, but no records are given; of them we list about ten men from the biographical records of other schools.[82] These represent collateral branches.[83]

We have reviewed and discussed the biographical material relating to Hui-neng. But with all this information can a biography really be written? Can we select from this material what is most probable; can we determine which account is reliable, which represents the true story? Some of the elements of some of the biographies can be rejected outright, yet what we have seen does not represent the compilation of a biography. It is no more than the development of a legend, one part of the story of the gradual rise of Ch'an in the eighth century. And when we come to the *Platform Sutra,* the work which purports to convey Hui-neng's life and describe his teachings, we find ourselves faced with the same insoluble problems.

[82] The table of contents to *chüan* five lists Hui-neng and forty-three heirs. For nineteen some sort of information is provided; the others are given by name only. Of the remaining twenty-four men, then, fourteen can be considered "true heirs," and the other ten should be assigned to "collateral branches."

[83] T51, pp. 235b–37a.

III. The Making of a Book: The Platform Sutra

BY THE END of the eighth century the Ch'an legend that was to persist had been established. The *Pao-lin chuan,* written in 801, had adjusted the list of the twenty-eight Patriarchs, presenting them in an acceptable form, and had helped to solidify the legend of Hui-neng. The version of Ch'an it furnished was, of course, not adopted at once, nor did variant legends simply die out when the *Pao-lin chuan* was written, but because the later Ch'an histories followed its theories, the story it presented came eventually to be the official one. But while the legend was, by the beginning of the ninth century, cast in a form that was destined to endure, the *Platform Sutra of the Sixth Patriarch* was still in the initial stages of its evolution.

The earliest version extant is the manuscript text discovered at Tun-huang.[1] Concerning this manuscript several obvious generalizations can be made: it is highly corrupt, filled with errors, miscopyings, lacunae, superfluous passages and repetitions, inconsistencies, almost every conceivable kind of mistake. The manuscript itself, then, must be a copy, written hurriedly, perhaps even taken down by ear, of an earlier, probably itself imperfect, version of the *Platform Sutra.* What this earlier version was like we have no way of knowing. There have been two major theories concerning it. One, maintained by Professor Ui and followed by a great number of writers in Japan, presupposes an original version of the *Platform Sutra,* completed about 714, the year following Hui-neng's death, consisting of the Master's sayings, as recorded by his disciple Fa-hai. Through the years this version was added to, probably by men of Shen-hui's school, until the text as we have it today was completed, probably around the year 820. The other interpretation, advanced by Hu Shih, while recognizing that the Tun-huang text is a copy of an earlier version, asserts that it is a product of

---

[1] S5475. It was first reproduced in facsimile form in Yabuki Keiki, *Meisha yoin,* plates 102–103. The text also appears in printed form in *Taishō Shinshū Daizōkyō,* T48, pp. 377a–45b; however, the large number of errors contained make it unsuitable for purposes of citation. An edited text was published by D. T. Suzuki and Kuda Rentarō, *Tonkō shutsudo Rokuso Dankyō.* This text was divided by the compilers into 57 sections, and for convenience this division has been maintained in the translation and text given here. Another edited version was published by Ui Hakuju, *Zenshū shi kenkyū,* II, 117–72. A translation with text, was made by W. T. Chan, *The Platform Scripture.*

Shen-hui's school, and that any attribution to Hui-neng or Fa-hai cannot be justified. There is no way of resolving these two conflicting opinions, for the *Platform Sutra,* as we have it, does not furnish sufficient information on which to base a conclusive judgment. We can, however, make certain observations about the text itself which, although they do not solve the problems created by the obscurity of its origin, may indicate why these problems cannot be solved.

The Tun-huang manuscript is not dated, but judging from its calligraphic style, it was written sometime between 830 and 860.[2] On the basis of the kinds of errors present in the manuscript itself, there can be no question that the work is a copy of an earlier version, written probably around 820. Section 55 of the present text contains a list of priests in the temple at Ts'ao-ch'i. It reads: "The *Platform Sutra* was compiled by the head monk Fa-hai, who at his death entrusted it to his fellow student Tao-ts'an. After Tao-ts'an died it was assigned to his disciple Wu-chen. Wu-chen resides at the Fa-hsing Temple at Mt. Ts'ao-ch'i in Ling-nan, and as of now he is transmitting the Dharma." If we are to trust this statement, it would indicate that Wu-chen was at least two generations after Hui-neng. However, the two Northern Sung versions of the *Platform Sutra*[3] contain similar lists which indi-

---

[2] Professor Akira Fujieda of the Research Institute for Humanistic Studies, Kyoto University, the leading expert on Tun-huang calligraphy, has been kind enough to examine the photographs of the original manuscript, and in his judgment it dates to this period. While a study of the document itself would produce more conclusive evidence, the style of writing indicates the possibility that in certain portions of the text a pen was used to simulate brush strokes. This is a peculiarity found in the Tun-huang writing style of this period.

[3] A printed version, probably a reprinting of the "Gozan" copy (see Ui, *Zenshū shi kenkyū,* II, 113) of the Sung text was discovered at Kōshōji in Kyoto. This was reproduced photolithographically by D. T. Suzuki, *Rokuso dankyō.* A printed edition of the same work was published by D. T. Suzuki and Kuda Rentarō, *Kōshōji-bon Rokuso dankyō* (hereinafter referred to as *Kōshōji*). Another version of this text was recently discovered at the Kokubunji in Sendai. Known as the Murayama edition, after the name of the head priest of the temple, it quite possibly is the "Gozan" copy of the Sung text, of which the *Kōshōji* is a later printing. It is of particular importance because it contains one leaf which is missing from the *Kōshōji* edition. A manuscript copy, also based on a Sung edition, was found at the Daijōji in Kaga. This was first published as *Kaga Daijōji shozō Shōshū Sōkeizan Rokusoshi dankyō, Komazawa Daigaku Bukkyō gakkai gakuhō,* no. 8 (April, 1938), pp. 1–56 (hereinafter referred to as *Daijōji*). An edited and indexed edition was later published: D. T. Suzuki, *Shōshū Sōkeizan Rokusoshi dankyō.* It is discussed by D. T. Suzuki, "Kaga Daijōji shozō no 'Rokuso dankyō' to 'Ichiya Hekigan' ni tsuite," *Shina Bukkyō shigaku,* I (no. 3, October, 1937), 1–23 and Ōkubo Dōshū, "Daijōji-bon o chūshin to seru Rokuso dankyō no kenkyū," *Komazawa Daigaku Bukkyō gakkai gakuhō,* no. 8 (April, 1938), pp. 57–84.

cate that Wu-chen was actually four generations after Hui-neng.[4] Thus we are immediately faced with a contradiction between the two versions of the text. These Northern Sung editions of the *Platform Sutra* will be discussed later, but all indications show that they are more reliable and represent more accurate versions of the text than does the Tun-huang manuscript. It is difficult to approximate the length of a generation in the Ch'an priesthood, but if we compare the lineage of other schools who claim Hui-neng as their Patriarch, we find that the fourth generation flourished during the second decade of the ninth century.[5] One further item serves to confirm the year 820 as a fair approximation of the date of the *Platform Sutra*. This is the inscription by Wei Ch'u-hou, discussed below,[6] which mentions the *Platform Sutra* by name. This inscription dates, in all probability, somewhere between 818 and 828.

The manuscript itself represents a transmitted text; in other words, as seen from section 47, possession of a written copy of the text served as an indication that the possessor had satisfied his teacher as to his understanding of the teaching. Whether the *Platform Sutra* was used in this way among Ch'an schools other than the one that claimed descent from Fa-hai and had its headquarters at the Fa-hsing Temple, cannot be determined. Just as the transmission of the robe and bowl was symbolic of the handing down of the teaching up to the time of Hui-neng, and later in the *Pao-lin chuan* the transmission verse was emphasized, so we have here the use of the work itself to serve as proof that a person was a legitimate possessor of the teaching. It is therefore possible to assume that several copies of a text similar to the Tun-huang manuscript were at one time in circulation. Further evidence that other copies were extant at this time can be seen from the lists of books brought back by Japanese priests: it is found in Ennin's catalog of

---

[4] The *Kōshōji* (p. 71) and *Daijōji* (p. 56) give the succession of priests as: Fa-hai—Chih-tao—Pi-an—Wu-chen—Yüan-hui. A well-known priest by the name of Wu-chen flourished in the Tun-huang area during the latter half of the ninth century. Whether there is any connection with the Wu-chen mentioned here is unknown. See Chikusa Masaaki, "Tonkō no sōkan seido," *Tōhō gakuhō*, no. 31 (March, 1961), pp. 127–32.

[5] Under Nan-yüeh Huai-jang, we have, in the fourth generation from Hui-neng, Po-chang Huai-hai (d. 814) and Nan-ch'üan P'u-yüan (d. 834); under Ch'ing-yüan Hsing-ssu we have Yao-shan Wei-yen (d. 834); under Shen-hui, we have Feng-kuo Shen-chao (d. 838).

[6] See below, p. 98.

847,[7] and in Enchin's lists of 854,[8] 857,[9] and 859.[10] In addition, the contemporary Chinese scholar, Hsiang Ta, mentions having seen a copy of the work in the hands of a private collector during a visit to Tun-huang.[11]

The title of the Tun-huang text of the *Platform Sutra*: "Southern School Doctrine, Supreme Mahāyāna Great Perfection of Wisdom: the Platform Sutra preached by the Sixth Patriarch Hui-neng at the Ta-fan Temple in Shao-chou," is highly elaborate, as is the title to the text brought back by Ennin in 847. It would indicate that at the time these two copies were made the text had yet to attain to the sophistication of a succinct and uninvolved title, or else that they were copied from primitive versions of the text.

An analysis of the contents of the Tun-huang text, in an attempt to determine which sections might represent a presumed original version, leads to rather inconclusive results.[12] The most that can be hoped for is a characterization of some of the material contained. It may be classified roughly into five types: (1) the autobiographical material, (2) sermons, (3) material designed to condemn Northern Ch'an and elevate the Southern school,[13] (4) those sections relating to Fa-hai and his school and those emphasizing that the *Platform Sutra* was a transmitted text, and (5) verses, miscellaneous stories, and other materials not included in the previous classifications.

---

[7] *Nittō shin gushōgyō mokuroku*, T55, p. 1083b. It appears here under the title: *Ts'ao-ch'i-shan ti-liu-tsu Hui-neng ta-shih shuo chien-hsing tun-chiao chih-liao cheng-fo chüeh-ting wu-i fa-pao-chi t'an-ching*. Hu Shih, "An Appeal for a Systematic Search in Japan for Long-hidden T'ang Dynasty Source Materials of the Early History of Zen Buddhism," *Bukkyō to bunka*, p. 16, translates: "The Dana sutra of the Treasure of the Law, preached by Hui-neng, the Sixth Patriarch, the Great Master of Ts'ao-hsi Hill, teaching the religion of sudden enlightenment through seeing one's own nature, that Buddhahood can be achieved by direct apprehension without the slightest doubt."

[8] *Fukushū Onshū Daishū gutoku kyōritsu ronshoki gesho tō mokuroku*, T55, p. 1095a. The title here is simplified to: *Ts'ao-ch'i-shan ti-liu-tsu Neng ta-shih t'an-ching*.

[9] *Nihon biku Enchin nittō guhō mokuroku*, T55, p. 1100c. The title here is: *Ts'ao-ch'i Neng ta-shih t'an-ching*.

[10] *Chishō daishi shōrai mokuroku*, T55, p. 1106b. The title is identical with that of the list of 857.

[11] See Hsiang Ta, *T'ang-tai Ch'ang-an yü Hsi-yü wen-ming*, p. 368. The title here is *Nan-tsung tun-chiao tsui-shang ta-ch'eng t'an-ching*, reminiscent of the first part of the title of the Tun-huang text.

[12] Ui, operating on the assumption that an original version, recorded about 714 by Fa-hai, shortly after Hui-neng's death, existed, has designated those portions of the text which he considers to be authentic. See Ui, *Zenshū shi kenkyū*, II, 76–100. Hu Shih, believing the work to be a product of Shen-hui's school, finds that the autobiographical part (secs. 2–11) and the sermon (secs. 12–31 and 34–37) formed the core of the original work. See Hu Shih, "An Appeal . . . ," p. 20.

[13] The autobiographical sections might well be included under this category.

Sections 2 to 11 contain the fictionalized autobiography of Hui-neng, and tell how the understanding of the illiterate Hui-neng triumphed over the Ch'an accomplishments of the head monk Shen-hsiu. The autobiography deals with the period from Hui-neng's birth until shortly after he was made the Sixth Patriarch and returned to the south. Contained are the famous verses of Shen-hsiu and Hui-neng, indicative of the degree of understanding each had attained (secs. 6–8). These sections, while recounting Hui-neng's life, also represent an attack on Shen-hsiu, as representative of Northern Ch'an.

Sections 12–31 and 34–37 contain sermons supposedly preached by Hui-neng at the Ta-fan Temple. This temple, however, has never been identified.[14] In examining the sermons one is struck at once by the obvious parallels with the works of Shen-hui.[15] Not only is there a similarity in the thought and concepts, but the wording is in some instances almost identical. The identity of meditation and wisdom found in section 13 is discussed in virtually the same terms in the works of Shen-hui; section 14 contains a reference to Vimalakīrti and Śāriputra, which is also found in Shen-hui's writings; section 15 includes a passage on the lamp and its light, similarly included in Shen-hui's sayings. The discussion of the concept of no-thought in section 17, the passage concerning the Mahāprajñāpāramitā in section 26, and parts of sections 30 and 31 all are paralleled in the works of Shen-hui. This is also true of the story of Bodhidharma and Emperor Wu of Liang found in section 34.

Because of the above similarities any attempt to define the "thought" of Hui-neng in the light of these sermons would not appear possible. We have seen, in addition, that Shen-hui, in his recorded sayings, at no time quotes from Hui-neng. Thus, even if we refrain from declaring that the thought of the *Platform Sutra* is derivative from the works of Shen-hui, we are at least obliged to admit that they parallel each other closely. The *Platform Sutra* contains much that can be described as

[14] The *Ch'ü-chiang hsien chih,* ch. 16, p. 10b, states: "The Pao-en kuang-hsiao Temple lies west of the river and was founded by the monk Tsung-hsi in K'ai-yüan 2 (714). It is also called K'ai-yüan Temple, and another name is the Ta-fan Temple. This is the place where the envoy Wei Chou [sic] asked the Sixth Patriarch to preach the Platform Sutra." Other than this, no mention of the temple can be found. The present identification can scarcely be regarded as reliable in view of the lack of confirming sources, the date 714, which is after Hui-neng's death, and the error in the identification of Wei Chou (see Translation, sec. 1). Wei Chou (HTS, 197, pp. 15b–16b) died between 860 and 873. Ui, *Zenshū shi kenkyū,* II, 214, surmises that the temple was located within the walls of Shao-chou.

[15] Precise references to the points of similarity are indicated in the notes to the translation.

general Buddhist teaching, such as discourses on the threefold body and
the four vows; it has much material which, as with Shen-hui's sayings,
is based on the Prajñāpāramitā concept of mind. Quotations from various sutras show the influence that these works had on the *Platform
Sutra,* but the same sutras are used by Shen-hui. The emphasis on such
concepts as the identity of *prajñā* and *dhyāna,* sudden awakening, seeing into one's own nature, of no-thought and no-mind, which are of
fundamental importance in Ch'an, are to a degree new, but they are still
to be found in Shen-hui's writings. Through the agency of later editions
of the *Platform Sutra,* some of these concepts are strengthened and developed; in a sense they are traceable to the Tun-huang edition, but
several writers who have attempted to discuss the "thought" of Hui-
neng lay particular emphasis on concepts which are not to be found
in the earliest edition of the *Platform Sutra.* Thus Suzuki states: "What
distinguishes Hui-neng most conspicuously and characteristically from
his predecessors as well as from his contemporaries is his doctrine of
'hon-rai mu-ichi-motsu' (pen-lai wu-i-wu) . . . 'from the first not a
thing is'—this was the first proclamation made by Hui-neng. It is a
bomb thrown into the camp of Shen-hsiu and his predecessors."[16] Yet
it is quite certain that this doctrine was never pronounced by Hui-neng,
for it is not found in the Tun-huang edition, and does not make its
appearance until the Sung dynasty version.[17] Other writers have laid
emphasis on a passage from the Diamond Sutra, which is said to have
occasioned Hui-neng's enlightenment; but this passage, too, is not contained in the Tun-huang version of the *Platform Sutra,* appearing first
in the Sung versions.[18] For this reason, it would appear best to consider

[16] D. T. Suzuki, *Zen Doctrine of No-mind,* p. 22.

[17] "From the first not a thing is" appears as the third line of Hui-neng's verse, given
in answer to Shen-hsiu, in the *Kōshōji,* p. 14, and *Daijōji,* p. 10. In the Tun-huang
text (see sec. 8) it is found as "Buddha nature is always clean and pure." The line,
in its altered version, is contained also in Huang-po's *Ch'uan-hsin fa-yao,* T48, p. 385b.
Since Huang-po died around 850, this is probably the first instance in which the phrase
is to be found. Caution, however, must be used when citing the "discourses" of the
famous Ch'an priests of the T'ang dynasty, for their works, as recorded by their disciples,
were not published until the Sung period or later, and if they received, even to a
limited extent, the editing, revision, and emendation to which the *Platform Sutra* was
subjected, certain reservations as to how well they reflect the exact sayings of the
Patriarch in question must be entertained.

[18] The *Kōshōji* (p. 15) and *Daijōji* (p. 11) say that Hui-neng's enlightenment came
when he heard the passage from the Diamond Sutra: "Must produce a mind which stays
in no place" (T8, p. 749c). See Itō Kokan, "Rokuso Enō Daishi no chūshin shisō,"
Nihon Bukkyō gakkai nempō, no. 7 (1934), p. 214.

the Ch'an thought found in these sermons of Hui-neng as representing, together with Shen-hui's writings, middle and late eighth-century concepts, which later Ch'an Masters organized, adjusted, clarified, and enlarged upon. But as the *Platform Sutra* was edited and corrected, its contents were still interpreted as representing the true sayings of the Sixth Patriarch. In other words, the legend is still at work, still developing, this time within the framework of the later versions of the book which purports to convey the sayings of the Sixth Patriarch.

Among those sections which are concerned with extolling the Southern school at the expense of the Northern, we find, in addition to the autobiographical sections, section 37 which, although it does not specifically mention Northern Ch'an, details a bit of Hui-neng's biography, and describes the awe in which he was held by the assembled monks. Section 39 is a direct attack on the gradual teaching of Northern Ch'an. Sections 40–41 tell the story of Chih-ch'eng, who came as a spy from Shen-hsiu, of his conversion, and of his explanation of the Northern teaching and Hui-neng's answer to it. Section 48 extols the understanding of Shen-hui, at the expense of the Master's other disciples, including Fa-hai. Section 49 includes the prediction: "twenty years after I die some one will come forward to fix the correct and false in Buddhism." This is a direct reference to Shen-hui's attacks on Northern Ch'an, and proves that this section of the work was added by men of Shen-hui's school.

The sections which are attributable to Fa-hai and his followers are chiefly those which insist that proof of the understanding of the teaching lies in the possession of a copy of the *Platform Sutra,* namely sections 1, 32, 38, 47, and 55 through 57.[19] Of these sections, only section 1 fits in to any extent with the rest of the text, and it may well be that the last few phrases, which speak of the transmission of the teaching and the need to take the *Platform Sutra* as the authority, are later additions. Section 32 cautions against the reckless spreading of the teaching, especially among those who are not ready to receive it. It does not specifically mention the transmission of the text, however, and it may well be that the attribution of this section to Fa-hai's school is inappro-

[19] The view has been advanced that Fa-hai transcribed an original text and that Shen-hui made it into a "transmitted" one, to show the errors of Northern Ch'an and to establish it in the tradition of his school, and that later sections were added by Shen-hui's followers. See Nakagawa Taka, "Dankyō no shisōshiteki kenkyū," *IBK,* no. 5 (September, 1954), p. 284.

priate. Sections 38 and 47 deal specifically with the transmission of the
text and section 55 with the handing down of the teaching, enumerat-
ing the names of the priests who have inherited it. Sections 56 and 57
are so corrupt that they are virtually unintelligible: they deal with the
transmission and refer specifically to Fa-hai. These two sections are not
to be found in any of the later editions of the text.

The remaining sections, which represent miscellaneous additions to
the text, contribute little to our knowledge of the work. Section 32,
containing the "formless verse," is in all probability a later accretion.
The verse, purportedly by Hui-neng, contains the term "ta-shih," which
certainly would not be used by a person speaking of himself, and therefore may be presumed to be the product of a later hand, or at the least
to have been revised by one. Sections 42 to 44 detail stories of Hui-neng
and various priests who come to question him, and can be classified as
late additions to the legend of Hui-neng. Sections 45 and 46 detail the
theory of the thirty-six confrontations. This theory is not found elsewhere, and its origin is completely unknown. One does not hear of it
in other Ch'an works, although it is retained in all later versions of the
text. The fact that it has been retained, although never discussed or
enlarged upon elsewhere, points to the esteem in which Hui-neng was
held. In that these sections were believed to represent the teachings of
Hui-neng, they were preserved regardless of the fact that their import
is obscure. In section 49, which contains the prediction concerning the
appearance of Shen-hui, are included the transmission verses of the six
Chinese Patriarchs. As has been seen, these verses seem to have gained
a considerable importance in the eighth century as a part of the legend,
and they play a significant role in the *Pao-lin chuan*. Their inclusion
here represents one stage in their development, probably earlier than
those to be found in the latter work. Section 50 contains two additional
transmission verses, attributed to Hui-neng; these are not found in
later versions of the *Platform Sutra*. Section 51 furnishes the list of the
Indian and Chinese Patriarchs, and, as noted before, can be dated sometime between the completion of the *Li-tai fa-pao chi* and the compilation of the *Pao-lin chuan*. Sections 52 to 54 contain verses attributed to
Hui-neng, which can be assigned a late origin, as well as a description
of the Master's death.

What conclusions can now be drawn about the Tun-huang edition
of the *Platform Sutra*? Obviously, it is composed of two basic parts:

the sermons at the Ta-fan Temple, including the autobiographical section, which if not a later addition, has undoubtedly been revised; and other material, added at a later date. The problem of the authenticity of the early section cannot be resolved. The lack of a text in any earlier form, the haziness surrounding Fa-hai, the alleged compiler, the similarity of many parts of the sermon to Shen-hui's works, the fact that no mention of the *Platform Sutra* is found among the works of Shen-hui, the lack of any reliable information concerning the Ta-fan Temple where Hui-neng's sermons are said to have been delivered, all contribute to the conviction that the *Platform Sutra* was purely a product of Shen-hui's school. Yet we cannot explicitly state that there was no Fa-hai, that he or some other disciples did not record the sayings of Hui-neng, and that they have not been revised, augmented, and changed to form the first part of the present version of the *Platform Sutra*.

There are two references that are used to support the thesis that an original version of the *Platform Sutra* existed, and that it was compiled shortly after Hui-neng's death. One is a notice in the *Ching-te ch'uan-teng lu,* contained in the sayings of Nan-yang Hui-chung (d. 775),[20] a disciple of the Sixth Patriarch, in which he laments the condition in which the *Platform Sutra* now exists. He complains that the work has been vulgarized, changed, and added to, so that the sacred import has been distorted, that this has created confusion among students who have come later, and that therefore the teaching is threatened with destruction. Ui believes that Hui-chung, who died in 775 after having been called to the imperial court in 761, must have made this comment prior to his entrance into the palace, and that this therefore indicates that the *Platform Sutra* was already in a state of confusion at this time.[21] Since the earliest source for this comment is the *Ching-te ch'uan-teng lu,* compiled in 1004, some 280 years after Hui-chung's death, and since there is no corroborating source for the statement, considerable doubts concerning the reliability of the information may be justified.

[20] The notice is contained in *chüan* 28, т51, p. 438a. Hui-chung's biography appears in *chüan* 5, pp. 244a–45a. *Chüan* 28–30 of the *Ching-te ch'uan-teng lu* contain miscellaneous passages and writings of various priests, which are not included under their separate biographies. His biography is also in *Sung kao-seng chuan,* т50, pp. 762b–63b and *Tsu-t'ang chi,* I, 113–30. They contain conflicting information. For a discussion, see Ui, *Zenshū shi kenkyū,* II, 281–94.
[21] *Ibid.,* II, 110–11.

The second reference used by advocates of an early version of the *Platform Sutra* is an inscription by Wei Ch'u-hou (773–828) for E-hu Ta-i (d. 818),[22] a disciple of Ma-tsu. The text contains a passage that characterizes four different branches of Ch'an: the Northern school, the Southern school of Shen-hui, the Oxhead school, and the teaching of Ma-tsu Tao-i. In the description of the school of Shen-hui there is a passage whose meaning has been disputed. Ui takes it to mean that in Loyang Shen-hui, receiving the teaching of Hui-neng, alone illumined the precious jewel, but, his followers being unable to distinguish the true from the false, "the orange tree changed into the thorn bush," and the *Platform Sutra* became what it is now. Ultimately, possession of a transmitted copy of the text served to reveal the status of the transmitted teaching. This interpretation is taken to show that the followers of Shen-hui distorted the original work, and made it into what it is today, merely a symbol to prove the possession of the teaching.[23] Hu Shih, on the other hand, understands the passage to mean that the disciples of Southern Ch'an were deluded in the truth and that contradictions confused the doctrine. Finally the *Platform Sutra* was composed, and the true teaching transmitted, making clear the good and the bad in the various contradictory opinions. This, Hu Shih believed, indicated that Shen-hui composed the *Platform Sutra*.[24] The text is too obscure to determine which of these two interpretations is correct; needless to say, this inscription cannot safely be used as an argument to determine the authorship and provenance of the *Platform Sutra*. It can, however, be used to date the work. If we can assume that the reference here is to a text similar to the Tun-huang version, it would necessarily have to have been in existence prior to Wei Ch'u-hou's death in 828, and quite probably prior to Ta-i's death in 818.

We can safely say that the Tun-huang version of the *Platform Sutra* was made between 830 and 860, and represented a copy of an earlier version, some of whose material dates to around 780. There were at

[22] See *Hsing-fu-ssu nei-tao-ch'ang kung-feng ta-te Ta-i ch'an-shih pei-ming*, CTW, ch. 715 (XV, 9311–13). The problems entailed in this inscription are discussed by Takao Giken, "Futatabi Zen no Namboku ryōshū ni tsuite," *Ryūkoku gakuhō*, no. 306 (July, 1933), pp. 112–14 and Gernet, "Biographie du Maître Chen-houei du Ho-tsö," *Journal Asiatique*, CCXLIX (1951), 37–38, n. 2c.
[23] Ui, *Zenshū shi kenkyū*, II, 111–12.
[24] Hu Shih, *Shen-hui ho-shang i-chi*, pp. 75–76. He later revised his opinion to indicate that it was composed by Shen-hui's disciples. See Hu Shih, "Ch'an (Zen) Buddhism in China, Its History and Method," *Philosophy East and West*, III (no. 1, April, 1953), 11, n. 9.

one time probably a considerable number of copies extant, distributed over a fairly wide area of China. Some manuscripts, we know, made their way to Japan, although they are no longer preserved. Of the evolution of the text during the ninth century we know nothing. Examination of the lists of Buddhist scriptural works brought back to Japan by Japanese priests indicates that by the mid-ninth century the title had been considerably simplified; the text is no longer known under the cumbersome titles that the Tun-huang manuscript or the version found in Ennin's list of 847 bear. It is quite possible that these versions did not contain the vast number of errors that are to be found in the Tun-huang edition. We also do not know in what schools of Ch'an the text was used. Presumably it was venerated by the branch which made its home at Ts'ao-ch'i and by the followers of Shen-hui's line, although by the mid-ninth century these schools may have been virtually extinct. To what extent it was taken up by the new schools of Ch'an that came into prominence at this time is also unknown. If it was, these schools made no effort to eliminate elements in the text which were of no concern to them—the struggle between Northern and Southern Ch'an, the emphasis on Shen-hui, the lineage of Fa-hai's school—for these elements are retained in versions of the *Platform Sutra* produced at a considerably later period. Stories about Hui-neng, however, do appear in the records of the Ch'an Masters of the ninth century,[25] so that we know that the Sixth Patriarch was held in high regard by the Ch'an Masters of late T'ang, although we cannot say to what extent the book ascribed to him was used.

The next text of the *Platform Sutra* of which we have evidence is an edition of 967, compiled by a priest named Hui-hsin, of whom nothing is known. This text is no longer extant; our knowledge of it derives from the preface to the *Kōshōji* edition,[26] a printed text, based on a "Gozan" edition, which itself was a direct copy of a Northern Sung edition of 1153. The preface to the *Kōshōji* edition is handwritten, copied from some other source by the Japanese priest Ryōnen (1559–1619)[27] in 1599. It is apparent that the printed text in Ryōnen's possession was incomplete, and that he supplemented the missing preface by copying it by hand from another text, presumably the "Gozan" edition.

[25] See p. 94, n. 27.
[26] See p. 90, n. 3.
[27] He was the founder of the Kōshōji in Kyoto. See Matsumoto Bunzaburō, *Bukkyō shi zakkō*, p. 101.

In reproducing it, however, Ryōnen made a mistake, or reproduced a prior error; he combined what originally were two prefaces to form one. The first preface is by Hui-hsin. In it he describes how poor the condition of the "old" *Platform Sutra* was: the text was obscure, and students, first taking it up with great expectations, soon came to despise the work. Therefore he revised it, dividing it into eleven sections and two *chüan*. The preface bears only a cyclical date, but this has been identified as representing the year 967.[28]

The second preface is by Ch'ao Tzu-chien[29] and is dated 1153. In it Ch'ao describes how, on a visit to Szechuan, he found a manuscript copy of the *Platform Sutra,* in the handwriting of his ancestor, Wen-yüan, to which was affixed a note to the effect that his ancestor had seen the work now for the sixteenth time and that he was in his eighty-first year at the time. Hu Shih has demonstrated that this Wen-yüan was Ch'ao Chiung,[30] and that the year in which he was eighty-one was 1031. Thus we know that the *Kōshōji* text is based on a "Gozan" copy of the Sung printed edition of 1153, which in turn derived from a manuscript copy dated 1031, which was itself copied from Hui-hsin's version of 967. Hui-hsin's text was in turn derived from a copy of the *Platform Sutra* similar to the Tun-huang text, somewhat later in date, but covering largely the same material.

Before proceeding further, we must take notice of the other Northern Sung text, the so-called *Daijōji* edition.[31] Legend has it that the manuscript is in the hand of Dōgen, generally regarded as the founder of the Japanese Sōtō sect of Zen, but it is more likely that it was made by one of his disciples.[32] It is quite close to the *Kōshōji* version, and is similarly divided into eleven sections and two *chüan*, yet considerable

[28] This and the following information are drawn largely from Hu Shih, "T'an-ching k'ao chih erh," *Hu Shih wen-ts'un*, IV, 301–18. The preface is also discussed in D. T. Suzuki, "Kōshōji-bon Rokuso dankyō kaisetsu," contained in the separate volume of explanatory material accompanying Suzuki's texts of the Tun-huang and *Kōshōji* versions of the *Platform Sutra* and the *Shen-hui yü-lu*, pp. 44–58.
[29] Biography unknown.
[30] Biography in *Sung shu* 305, pp. 7a–9b.
[31] See p. 90, n. 3.
[32] Ui, *Zenshū shi kenkyū*, II, 61. It is of interest to note that Dōgen, in his *Shōbō genzō*, remarks: "The *Platform Sutra* is a spurious work and does not represent the transmission of the Dharma-treasure. These are not the words of the Sixth Patriarch" (T82, p. 298b). This passage has caused considerable debate, and some writers question the correctness of its attribution to Dōgen. For a discussion, see Itō Kokan, "Rokuso Enō daishi no chūshin shisō," *Nihon Bukkyōgaku kyōkai nempō*, no. 7 (February, 1935), pp. 226–29.

differences in the two texts can be noted. The *Kōshōji* edition is more polished and avoids several careless errors that are present in the *Daijōji* text, but the relationship between the two editions is not clear. The *Daijōji* text contains a preface by a certain Ts'un-chung, a priest of whom nothing is known, who lived at Chiang-chün-shan in Fu-t'ang.[33] The preface provides little information; it does, however, state that the work represents a second printing. It is dated 1116. Suzuki reasons that because of various additions to the *Kōshōji* text that are not to be found in the *Daijōji* version, such as the famous story of the banner and the wind, the former work was influenced by the *Sōkei daishi betsuden,* and represents a later version of the text. His assumption is that the *Kōshōji* text is a revised and enlarged version of the *Daijōji* edition.[34] However, as Ōkubo points out,[35] Hui-hsin states in his preface that he himself divided the work into eleven sections and two *chüan.* Unless Hui-hsin's statement is to be doubted, then the *Daijōji* edition represents a manuscript copy of a reprint of the Hui-hsin version itself. Thus, according to Ōkubo, the Hui-hsin and the *Daijōji* texts are the same. This would then indicate that Hui-hsin's version was a printed text. Ōkubo believes that Ch'ao Chiung, being a prominent figure in the literary world, edited the work, and it is this version that is represented by the *Kōshōji* edition. These theories must, however, be regarded as speculations which, at this point, cannot be verified.

I am inclined to believe, and this again is purely speculation, that both the *Daijōji* and *Kōshōji* texts represent edited versions of Hui-hsin's manuscript edition of 967. There seems no particular reason to doubt Hui-hsin's statement that he divided the *Platform Sutra* into eleven sections and two *chüan,* and since both Northern Sung editions follow this division, it would seem possible to assume that they are derived from the same work. There is, apart from the differences already alluded to, one significant place where the two texts are at variance: this is in the theory of the twenty-eight Indian Patriarchs. The *Kōshōji* text, with certain changes, follows largely the version found in the Tun-huang manuscript. The *Daijōji* version, on the other hand, is based on the *Pao-lin chuan.* Thus, for the last few Indian Patriarchs we have the names given in Table 2.

[33] Southeast of Fu-ch'ing hsien, Fukien.
[34] Suzuki, "Kaga Daijōji shozō no Rokuso dankyō . . . ," p. 6.
[35] Ōkubo, "Daijōji-bon . . . ," p. 69.

TABLE 2. THE LAST INDIAN PATRIARCHS

Tun-huang text		Pao-lin chuan		Yüan-chüeh ching ta-shu ch'ao		Kōshōji		Daijōji	
Śaṇavāsa	31	Basiasita	25	Śaṇavāsa	24	Basiasita	[31]	Basiasita	[32]
Upagupta	32	Puṇyamitra	26	Upagupta	25	Upagupta	[32]	Puṇyamitra	[33]
Saṅgharakṣa	33	Prajñātāra	27	Vasumitra	26	Vasumitra	[33]	Prajñātāra	[34]
Subhamitra	34	Bodhidharma	28	Saṅgharakṣa	27	Saṅgharakṣa	[34]	Bodhidharma	[35]
Bodhidharma	35			Dharmatrāta	28	Bodhidharma	[35]		
				(= Bodhidharma)					

From this table, I conclude that the Hui-hsin text followed the Tun-huang version of the twenty-eight Patriarch theory, in its corrected version, as found in Tsung-mi's *Yüan-chüeh ching ta-shu ch'ao,*[36] and continued to include the Seven Buddhas of the Past in the numbering scheme. This, in turn, was repeated in the *Kōshōji* text.[37] The *Daijōji* edition, on the other hand, while retaining the numbering system employed in the Tun-huang manuscript, is based entirely on the *Pao-lin chuan,* and must therefore represent a different edited version of the Hui-hsin text. The preface to the *Daijōji* text, however, clearly states that it is a second printing. I would suggest that there may be a missing first printing of the *Daijōji* text, which was itself a revision of Hui-hsin's manuscript, and that this text belonged to a school of Ch'an which had at the time already accepted the *Pao-lin chuan* version of the patriarchal tradition. In diagram form, the evolution of the text would be as follows:

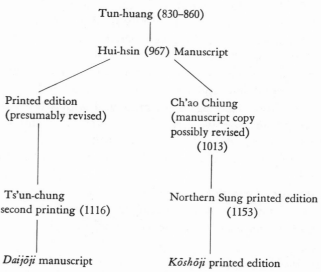

Tun-huang (830–860)

Hui-hsin (967) Manuscript

Printed edition
(presumably revised)

Ch'ao Chiung
(manuscript copy
possibly revised)
(1013)

Ts'un-chung
second printing (1116)

Northern Sung printed edition
(1153)

Daijōji manuscript

Kōshōji printed edition

Since the Tun-huang, the *Daijōji,* and the *Kōshōji* editions contain the sections relating to the transmission of the text in Fa-hai's school, it would seem permissible to assume that both the Tun-huang version and the copy on which Hui-hsin based his edition represented versions

---

[36] zz1, 14, 3, 276b.

[37] While the *Kōshōji* edition follows Tsung-mi, it changes Śaṇavāsa to Basiasita, as found in the *Pao-lin chuan.* The reason for this change cannot be determined.

of extremely limited distribution. With Hui-hsin's text of 967, however, the text most probably became available to other schools of Ch'an.
Support for this conclusion is found in the *Ching-te ch'uan-teng lu*
of 1004, which mentions the *Platform Sutra* by name, and indicates
that it was in wide use.[38] Thus what had been a text of comparatively
small distribution became available to all branches of the sect and to
the Sung literati in general by virtue of Hui-hsin's edition. The *Daijōji*
version may then represent the text as adopted by one of the Ch'an
schools which derived ultimately from the schools of Nan-yüeh and
Ch'ing-yüan, and the *Kōshōji* text may well represent the text as taken
up by the Sung literati, among whom a refined copy of the text was
more important than such details as the accuracy of the transmission
of the then accepted patriarchal tradition.

No detailed comparison of the Tun-huang text with the two Northern
Sung editions will be attempted here. The latter works have been
greatly refined, many errors have been corrected, and the texts somewhat enlarged.[39] The texts are sufficiently similar that there can be no
question that these later versions were derived from a copy similar to
the Tun-huang copy.[40]

Between the time that Hui-hsin's version was composed and the two
Northern Sung editions appeared, we hear of still another version of
the *Platform Sutra*. Here again we must deal with a text that is no
longer extant; however we have three references to this edition.[41]

1. The Ch'ü-chou edition of the *Chün-chai tu-shu chih* contains a
notice of a *Liu-tsu t'an-ching* in 16 sections and 3 *chüan,* compiled by
Hui-hsin.[42]

2. In the *Wen-hsien t'ung-k'ao, chüan* 54, there is a notice listing a
Liu-tsu t'an-ching in 3 *chüan*. No compiler is given.[43]

3. The *Hsin-chin wen-chi, chüan* 11, compiled by the famous Sung

---

[38] т51, p. 235c.
[39] See Hu Shih, "T'an-ching k'ao chih-erh," pp. 312–13. A count of the texts shows
that the Tun-huang version has 12,000 characters, the *Kōshōji* edition 14,000, and the
Yüan edition 21,000.
[40] In the translation that follows, the *Kōshōji* version has, in many instances, been
relied on to solve textual problems. References are cited in the notes to the translation.
[41] The following information is based largely on Hu Shih, "T'an-ching k'ao chih-
erh," and Matsumoto Bunzaburō, *Bukkyō shi zakkō*, p. 91.
[42] Ch'ao Kung-wu, comp., Wang Hsien-ch'ien, ed., *Chün-chai tu-shu chih,* ch. 16,
pp. 27b–28a. The Yüan-chou edition of this work lists the *Liu-tsu t'an-ching* in 2 *chüan*
and 16 sections (*Ssu-pu tsung-k'an,* ser. 3, case 19, ch. 3B, pp. 26b–37a).
[43] Ma Tuan-lin, *Wen-hsien t'ung-k'ao,* p. 1819c.

priest Ch'i-sung (1007-1072)[44] contains a preface by the *shih-lang* Lang,[45] entitled *Liu-tsu fa-pao chi hsü*.[46] Dated 1056, it relates the history of the partriarchal succession from Bodhidharma through Hui-neng, remarks on the veneration which the words of the Sixth Patri-arch are accorded, and expresses regret that common people have vulgarized and proliferated his teaching. Lang goes on to note that Ch'i-sung had written a piece in praise of the *Platform Sutra*,[47] and that two years after this was completed he had obtained a copy of an "old Ts'ao-ch'i edition," which he edited, corrected, divided into three *chüan*, and later published.

Ch'i-sung's missing edition has been the source of further contro-versy. Its importance lies in the fact that it was evidently one of the sources for the greatly expanded Yüan editions of the *Platform Sutra*, which are clearly based on an edition that differs from Hui-hsin's version. Hu Shih holds that the "old Ts'ao-ch'i edition" mentioned in Lang's preface referred to the *Sōkei daishi betsuden*, and that Ch'i-sung combined it with the Hui-hsin edition to form his new three-*chüan* work, retaining Hui-hsin's name as compiler.[48] Ui completely rejects Hu Shih's conclusions, saying that, because of differences in style be-tween the *Sōkei daishi betsuden* and the then existing texts of the *Platform Sutra*, Ch'i-sung, who had written in praise of the *Platform Sutra*, could not conceivably have considered the *Sōkei daishi betsuden* as an "old Ts'ao-ch'i edition."[49]

---

[44] Prominent also as a literary figure, Ch'i-sung was active in defending Ch'an against attacks by the T'ien-t'ai sect, which challenged the Ch'an theory of the twenty-eight Patriarchs. He wrote several histories of Ch'an, was well versed in the Classics, and was active in efforts to effect a union between Buddhism and Confucianism. His biog-raphy appears in *Hsü ch'uan-teng lu*, T51, p. 494a-b.

[45] See Ui, *Zenshū shi kenkyū*, II, 48, for a brief notice of his career.

[46] T52, p. 703b-c.

[47] The *T'an-ching tsan*, T52, pp. 662c-64b. It is also contained in the Yüan version of the *Platform Sutra* as found in the *Taishō Tripitaka* (T48, pp. 346a-47c).

[48] See Hu Shih, "T'an-ching k'ao chih-erh," pp. 306-11. Hu Shih's arguments here are not too convincing; however, his article was written before the *Pao-lin chuan* was rediscovered, and he did not have access to the *Tsu-t'ang chi*. On the basis of Ch'i-sung's Ch'an history, *Ch'uan-fa cheng-tsung-chi*, T51, pp. 715-68, Hu credits Ch'i-sung with having established the theory of the twenty-eight Patriarchs in its final form, and argues that Ch'i-sung knew the *Sōkei daishi betsuden*, because he changed the prediction made by Hui-neng that twenty years after his death someone would come forward and "raise up his essential teachings" (see translation, sec. 49), to one of seventy years, as found in the *Sōkei daishi betsuden*. This change is found, however, in the *Tsu-t'ang chi* (I, 99) and the *Ching-te ch'uan-teng lu* (T51, p. 236c), considerably before Ch'i-sung's time. The twenty-eight Patriarch theory, of course, derives from the *Pao-lin chuan*.

[49] Ui, *Zenshū shi kenkyū*, II, 49.

Here again there is no ready answer. Ch'i-sung's edition no longer exists, so that we cannot determine to what degree he enlarged or revised the text. There are, however, two Yüan editions, published independently, and apparently without reference to each other, one year apart, in 1290 and 1291. These two editions are very similar, and have obviously been based on the same work, which must be presumed to have been Ch'i-sung's missing text, or possibly a later revision of it. The two Yüan editions are greatly expanded, and include much new material not previously associated with the *Platform Sutra*. Thus Ch'i-sung's version, which is listed as being in three *chüan,* must also be presumed to have been an enlarged text.

Hu Shih has suggested that Ch'i-sung enlarged the *Platform Sutra* on the basis of the *Sōkei daishi betsuden.* There is no evidence, however, that the latter work was ever used to any significant extent in China. It has not been preserved in that country, nor do we find textual references to it. It would seem more likely that the "old Ts'ao-ch'i edition" on which Ch'i-sung depended was the *Pao-lin chuan.*[50] Although the volumes relating to Hui-neng are missing, it may be presumed that it contained a considerable body of material concerning him. At any rate, Ch'i-sung's edition must be added to the already long list of insoluble problems relating to the *Platform Sutra* and its authorship. It is perhaps significant, however, that the edition of 1036 and that of 1056 were both edited by men who had strong ties to contemporary literary circles. We do not know precisely what Ch'ao Chiung's religious commitments were, but he is said to have read the *Platform Sutra* sixteen times before making a copy of it, so that it obviously exerted a considerable influence upon him. Ch'i-sung, although a Ch'an priest, was widely associated with persons outside his clerical environment, and it may be assumed that his edition of the *Platform Sutra* was not without literary polish. Thus it is evident that this work, in its revised versions, was gaining an audience not solely confined to the priesthood. As noted before, it was also in Ch'i-sung's time, or shortly after his death, that the *Platform Sutra* and the *Pao-lin chuan* were both excluded from the Tripitaka as spurious works, which might, to a certain extent, account for the failure of Ch'i-sung's version to survive.

The history of the *Platform Sutra* during the Yüan, Ming, and Ch'ing dynasties is of enormous complexity, and a detailed study of the

[50] The full title of the *Pao-lin chuan* contains the name Ts'ao-ch'i.

various editions is quite beyond the scope of this introduction.[51] As
has been mentioned, two editions appeared, a year apart, in 1290 and
1291. They represent different printings in widely separated areas of
China, and do not appear to be based on each other, although they are
sufficiently similar that they must have been based on the same source.
The printing of 1290 was edited by Te-i.[52] In his preface he remarks:
"The *Platform Sutra* has been greatly abridged by later writers and
the complete import [of the teachings] of the Sixth Patriarch is difficult to discern. When I was young I saw a copy of an old edition, and
since then I have spent thirty years searching for it." Te-i goes on to
explain how a certain T'ung shang-jen obtained a copy for him, and
that he had it published at the Hsiu-hsiu an in Wu-chung.[53] It would
seem then that Te-i had access to a version of the Hui-hsin edition, but
that in his youth he had seen a copy of a greatly enlarged text, which
we may assume to have been the Ch'i-sung edition or a version of it.
Eventually finding another copy, he had it printed. So far from the
original Tun-huang version had the text been expanded that Te-i saw
fit to condemn what was presumably a text of the Hui-hsin version
for having been abbreviated.

In 1291 a priest by the name of Tsung-pao[54] published another edition, very similar to that of Te-i, at Nan-hai in south China. It is this
version that was incorporated into the Ming Tripitaka and is the popular edition in general use today.[55] At the time that it was added to the
Tripitaka Te-i's preface was attached to the Tsung-pao text, which
has created a certain confusion in distinguishing the two works. In his

[51] For bibliographical studies, see Ui, *Zenshū shi kenkyū*, II, 2–47; Matsumoto
Bunzaburō, *Bukkyō shi zakkō*, pp. 87–168; Nakagawa Taka, "Rokuso dankyō no ihon
ni tsuite," *IBK*, no. 3 (September, 1953), pp. 155–56. For the history of Korean editions, see Kuroda Akira, *Chōsen kyūsho kō*, pp. 93–111 and Kuroda Akira, "Rokuso
dankyō kō iho," *Sekisui sensei kakōju kinen ronsan*, pp. 153–79. A detailed listing of
all printing is found in *Shinsan zenseki mokuroku*, pp. 447–49.

[52] The Te-i edition is comparatively rare in China; see Li Chia-yen "Liu-tsu t'an-ching
Te-i pen chih fa-hsien," *Ching-hua hsüeh-pao*, X (no. 2, April, 1935), pp. 483–90.
For the text of the Te-i edition, see *Gen Enyū Kōrai kokubon Rokuso daishi hōbō
dankyō, Zengaku kenkyū*, no. 23 (July, 1935), pp. 1–63. This is the Korean edition of
1316. The Te-i edition made its way to Korea shortly after publication, and most
Korean versions stem from it. For Te-i's biography, see *Tseng-chi hsü ch'uan-teng-lu*,
zz2B, 15, 5, 416b–17a. His dates are unknown.

[53] Wu-hsien, Chiangsu.

[54] Biography unknown.

[55] T48, pp. 345–65. Translated under the title "The Dharma Treasure of the Altar
Sūtra of the Sixth Patriarch," by Lu Kuan-yü (Charles Luk), *Ch'an and Zen teachings*
(series 3), pp. 15–102.

postface Tsung-pao explains that he obtained three editions which he edited to make one volume, adding material on the relationships of various disciples with the Sixth Patriarch. This latter material is, however, also in the Te-i text. Since the Tsung-pao text was published later and the compiler claims to have added the material himself, either his statement is in error, or we must look for some other explanation. Ui suggests that Tsung-pao spoke in terms of one or two of the three editions that he used, and that these contained only a few such stories when compared with the third text of which he made use.[56] In any event, at the present state of our knowledge, it seems safe to say that the Te-i and Tsung-pao texts were produced separately, but must have been based on the same source, Ch'i-sung's missing edition of the *Platform Sutra.*

Both Yüan editions divide the text into ten sections; there are certain differences within the sections, and the titles given to each section are at variance.[57] Te-i gives Fa-hai as the compiler, placing his name at the head of the text of Fa-hai's preface. The *Kōshōji* and *Daijōji* editions mention Fa-hai as compiler only in the body of the text. Tsung-pao, on the other hand, uses his own name as the compiler of the work. The chief difference in the two Yüan texts lies in the amount of supplementary material that is attached. Te-i includes only his preface and the one attributed to Fa-hai. The Tsung-pao edition contains Te-i's preface, Ch'i-sung's words in praise of the *Platform Sutra,* Fa-hai's preface, the texts of various inscriptions, and Tsung-pao's postface.

No comparison of the Yüan editions with the Tun-huang text will be attempted. The former contain much of the same material found in the autobiographical sections and the sermon, retain many of the stories of encounters with other priests, as well as the discussion of the thirty-six confrontations and the list of the Indian Patriarchs, and some of the verses, but the text is much refined and greatly expanded throughout. The sections relating to Fa-hai and the transmission of the text have been dropped. As a result of all these alterations, the Tsung-pao text is almost twice the size of its Tun-huang counterpart.

Judging only from the great number of printings and editions, the

[56] Ui, *Zenshū shi kenkyū,* II, 49.
[57] For a comparison of the two Yüan editions, see Ōya Tokujō, "Gen Enyū Kōrai kokubon Rokuso daishi hōbō dankyō ni tsuite," *Zengaku kenkyū,* no. 23 (July, 1935), pp. 1–29.

Platform Sutra attained a tremendous circulation during the Ming and Ch'ing dynasties.[58] These editions vary slightly in arrangement and often contain additional prefatory material. What role this work played in the Ch'an teaching of the time cannot be considered without relating it to the vast changes which took place in Ch'an after the Yüan dynasty. The large number of printings would indicate that the work was widely used by lay believers as well as Ch'an priests, but an investigation of the whole range of Chinese Buddhism in the Ming and Ch'ing dynasties would be required in order to reveal its significance in the Buddhism of this time. This cannot be undertaken here.

In Japan Zen arrived as a sect during the Southern Sung and Yüan dynasties, particularly during the thirteenth and fourteenth centuries when large numbers of priests visited the continent and Chinese Masters, often refugees, came to Japan to teach or to make their homes. Various degrees and kinds of teaching were represented, but largely what was introduced was the highly organized *kōan* Zen that developed during the Sung dynasty. These priests brought with them numerous works, such as the renowned *kōan* collections *Pi-yen lu* and *Wu-men kuan,* and the "discourses" of eminent priests. Although the Yüan version of the *Platform Sutra* had yet to appear when the intercourse between Chinese and Japanese priests was at its height, there was still ample contact in the first half of the fourteenth century to have made it possible for the work to have been introduced to Japan at that time.[59] But this does not seem to have been the case, for it was not until 1634 that there was a Japanese edition of the Yüan version of the *Platform Sutra.*[60] During the Tokugawa period several printings and a number of commentaries appeared, but neither the Sung nor the Yüan versions appear to have played an important part in the Zen schools of Japan. Hui-neng is, of course, revered as the Sixth Patriarch; stories of him are known and used, and he appears prominently in *kōan* collections. The *Kattō-shū,*[61] a collection much used in Japanese Zen monasteries today, contains a story about Hui-neng's encounter with the fierce Hui-ming atop Mount Ta-yü, when the latter came in pursuit of the Dharma.[62]

[58] The *Shinsan zenseki mokuroku,* p. 448, lists some 26 different editions produced in Korea and China during Ming and Ch'ing times. How many printings were made from each set of blocks is unknown.
[59] A Korean version of the Te-i edition had already appeared in 1316.
[60] A text of the Tsung-pao edition was printed in Kyoto in Kan'ei 11. See *Shinsan zenseki mokuroku,* p. 447.
[61] First published 1689. Contained in Fujita Genro, *Zudokko,* pp. 109–97.
[62] *Ibid.,* p. 117. The same *kōan* is found in *Wu-men kuan,* T48, p. 295c.

As the account goes, Hui-ming gained enlightenment when Hui-neng asked: "Not thinking of good, not thinking of evil, just at this moment, what is your original face before your mother and father were born?" This is an important *kōan,* one of the first given the beginning student. But it is also a part of the legend, for the story is not mentioned in the Tun-huang edition, and appears only later in the Sung version of the *Platform Sutra.*[63] Thus, the *Platform Sutra* and the Patriarch it champions continue to exert their influence today.

[63] It appears first as a note at the end of the section dealing with Hui-neng's departure from the Fifth Patriarch in the *Kōshōji* edition, p. 17. The story is also found, in a slightly variant form, in the *Ch'uan-hsin fa-yao,* T48, p. 384a.

IV. Content Analysis

ALL THE DIFFICULTIES encountered in attempting to place the *Platform Sutra* in a positive historical setting repeat themselves when one attempts to deal with the thought and ideas contained in the work. One can, however, make a few remarks about the thought and structure of the *Platform Sutra* as a whole. There is a certain plan of arrangement detectable; some sections have been added by the compilers, as has been previously noted, with a specific purpose in mind. At the risk of occasional repetition, let us examine the work briefly in terms of the content of the various sections.

The *Platform Sutra* can be divided into two basic parts: the sermon at the Ta-fan Temple, which includes the autobiography (secs. 1–31, 34–37), and all the remaining portions of the work. This latter material, while largely unrelated to the sermon, does at times serve to reiterate and reinforce certain points of doctrine. The title: "Southern School Sudden Doctrine, Supreme Mahāyāna Great Perfection of Wisdom: the Platform Sutra preached by the Sixth Patriarch Hui-neng at the Ta-fan Temple in Shao-chou" applies to the sermon alone, and clearly identifies the type of Buddhism that is to be preached.

The work opens as though it proposes to launch immediately into the sermon, but the preaching has scarcely begun when it is interrupted by the story of Hui-neng's early life. By using an autobiographical format, the compilers are able to impart to the audience a sense of intimacy with Hui-neng. A simple man of humble origins, unlettered and without pretensions, he was able with his own innate capacities to achieve the highest rank in Ch'an, while yet a layman. The availability of this teaching to the populace in general is emphasized throughout the work. Not only was Hui-neng himself a layman when he first undertook his training, but the sermon is delivered at the behest of Wei Ch'ü, a government official, before a large audience of monks, nuns, and lay followers. This point is further brought out in section 36, where it is specifically stated that study as a layman is not only possible, but that it may be carried out as well outside the temple environment as within.

Hui-neng's illiteracy, much spoken of in later Ch'an, is treated here

in a rather casual manner, and serves primarily to underline the conflict with Shen-hsiu. We are told early in the autobiography (sec. 8)
that Hui-neng cannot read, and that someone with the ability to write
was needed to inscribe the verse that he had composed on the wall. In
the story of Fa-ta and the Lotus Sutra (sec. 42), we again hear of the
Sixth Patriarch's inability to read. Later Ch'an has called much attention to Hui-neng's supposed illiteracy, largely in an effort to underline
the contention that Ch'an is a silent transmission from "mind to mind,"
which does not rely on the written word. The *Platform Sutra,* however, does not seek to convey this impression: Hui-neng's first interview with the Fifth Patriarch is verbal, a written verse demonstrates
the degree of Hui-neng's understanding, and, after he has transmitted
the Patriarchship, the Fifth Patriarch spends the night expounding the
Diamond Sutra to his heir. There is no indication here that the written
word and the canonical works are in any way inimical to the teaching
of Ch'an. Indeed, when one takes into account the fairly large number
of scriptural references contained in the sermon, it is clear that the
Tun-huang version of the *Platform Sutra* was not particularly concerned with emphasizing Hui-neng's illiteracy, nor was it attempting
to assert that Ch'an was a teaching in which traditional Buddhism
played no part. It may well be that the compilers of the *Platform Sutra*
judged that a lack of knowledge of the written word on Hui-neng's
part would serve to emphasize the availability of the teaching to any
who might come to seek it.

The account of Hui-neng furnished by the autobiography stops with
his departure for the south after he has gained the Patriarchship. Of
his life until he reached Shao-chou, where he preached the sermon,
we are told nothing. In the meanwhile he has become a renowned
Ch'an Master, the recognized Sixth Patriarch, and it is as such that he
appears throughout the remainder of the *Platform Sutra.* A few
biographical details are furnished, the circumstances surrounding his
death are described, but chiefly we find him as the rather disembodied
voice represented by the phrase: "The Master said."

We do not gain from this work any precise knowledge either of the
manner in which the doctrine was transmitted or of the teaching
methods used. The transmission is described merely as the acknowledgment on the part of the teacher of his disciple's understanding. Up
to the time of Hui-neng, we are told, the robe of Bodhidharma was

handed down as a symbol of the transmission of the teaching. But the *Platform Sutra* pointedly explains that this practice ceased with the Sixth Patriarch, for in section 49 we find Hui-neng stating that the robe is no longer to be handed down. We know that the Fifth Patriarch had a large number of disciples to whom he transmitted the Law, but of this the *Platform Sutra* does not inform us, for Hui-neng alone is mentioned as heir. But of Hui-neng's disciples, some ten who were present at his death are listed (sec. 45). It would seem, then, that at this time a renowned Ch'an teacher, such as Hung-jen or Hui-neng is esteemed to have been, gathered under him a great number of disciples. Those with particular talent served the Master, attended on him, received instruction from him, and eventually became teachers on their own. We do not know precisely how these heirs were designated or which of the students whose names appear in conjunction with Hui-neng were legitimate heirs. By the time the *Ching-te ch'uan-teng lu* was completed in 1004, the number of Hui-neng's heirs had increased to forty-three.[1] The *Platform Sutra,* however, is quite specific in its insistence that a copy of the work itself be required as proof of the transmission of the teaching (sec. 38). Thus the abandonment of the robe as a symbol is compensated for, as far as this work is concerned, by the establishment of the *Platform Sutra* itself as proof of the transmission.

Exactly what teaching method was used at this time is not completely clear. We know that sermons, addressed to the monks and to people at large, played an important role. From the later sections of the work we can also gather that individual priests came, almost at will, to question the Master and to ask for an explanation of problems that bothered them. Whether these questions were put in private or before a large gathering of monks is not quite clear. We are told, in the story of Fa-ta (sec. 42), that all who were present to hear his conversation with the Master gained enlightenment, which would indicate a public assembly. It is probable that both methods were used, but we have no evidence here of the use of the private interview, a teaching technique that developed later. It would seem then that various wandering priests, the Vinaya-masters and specialists in individual sutras that we hear of, as well as monks and laymen who showed an interest, might appear as the spirit moved them. Those who felt an affinity for

[1] T51, p. 235a.

the Master's teaching would stay and become disciples, and perhaps eventually, heirs, but there seems to have been no compulsion to remain, and as yet no particular monastic establishment or order of which they were required to become members.

The *Platform Sutra* offers no clear picture of the method of study employed nor does it indicate to what extent canonical works were used. Meditation, of the type advocated by this work, was undoubtedly a major feature of the training, but the details are never spelled out. Because the need for self-realization is emphasized so greatly, it may be assumed that to a large extent the disciple was on his own. He obviously must have received some instruction from the Master, but to what degree is not explained. The method of teaching, as seen here, consisted primarily of sermons, given before both large audiences and small groups, and the elucidation of particular problems that faced the student. Other than this he seems to have been obliged to work out his own Ch'an destiny.

When one turns to the sermon one is at once struck by the fact that almost all of the basic ideas presented are drawn from canonical sources; they are by no means concepts original to the *Platform Sutra*. For the most part they are phrases, terms, and ideas taken from the context of various sutras, and discussed, to a certain extent, in terms of Ch'an. Most often these concepts are supported by canonical references; indeed the compiler makes no claim for their originality, for he quotes Hui-neng as saying: "My teaching has been handed down from the sages of the past; it is not my personal knowledge" (sec. 12). Although it is not our particular concern here, it should be reiterated that passages in the sermon are found, very frequently in almost identical form, in the works of Shen-hui. We have, then, basic ideas, drawn from a variety of sources, which, while later subjected to exhaustive elaboration and commentary by other Ch'an figures and in later editions of the *Platform Sutra,* are here presented in a rather simple form. Most often they are statements and brief descriptions of the teaching, the Sudden Doctrine of the Great Perfection of Wisdom, which the audience is exhorted to try out and realize for itself. It should be noted, too, that while at times a specific idea can be traced to a particular sutra, the same idea may very often appear in a variety of works. Thus, except where a specific book may be cited, one cannot with any degree of assurance, identify the exact source from which a certain concept derives.

Following roughly the order in which they are presented in the text, let us examine briefly the major ideas that appear. The identity of *prajñā* and meditation, a fundamental concept in the *Platform Sutra,* is described as basic to Hui-neng's teaching (sec. 13). We are told that to hold another view, to believe that one or the other comes first, or that one gives rise to the other, implies duality. The concept of the identity of the two, however, does not originate with this work, for it is to be found in the Nirvāṇa Sutra.[2] The *Platform Sutra* rejects the idea that through meditation *prajñā* can be obtained, for *prajñā* is conceived of as something possessed from the outset by everyone (sec. 12). Thus, while *prajñā* is described as the "function" of meditation, it is at the same time explained as something akin to the original nature, wisdom of which is tantamount to enlightenment. Besides representing a fundamental concept, it is probable that the identity of *prajñā* and meditation is emphasized in order to point out a basic disagreement with those sects of Buddhism that stressed one of these concepts to the exclusion of the other, or gave priority to one over the other.

The concepts of "*samādhi* of oneness," and "direct mind," a discussion of which follows in the sermon (sec. 14), are both traceable to canonical works: the former to the *Ta-ch'eng ch'i-hsin lun*[3] and the latter to the Vimalakīrti Sutra.[4] The *Platform Sutra* associates the two concepts, saying: "Just practicing direct mind only, and in all things having no attachments whatsoever, is called the "*samādhi* of oneness." Both concepts appear synonymous, and seem to be used in the sense of the ultimate meditational attitude, one in which there is no attachment to anything, including the *samādhi* of oneness itself. Implicit is a criticism of Northern Ch'an: "The deluded man clings to the characteristics of things, adheres to the *samādhi* of oneness, [thinks] that direct mind is sitting without moving and casting aside delusions without letting things arise in the mind" (sec. 14). The immediacy of the results of the practice advocated in the *Platform Sutra* is alluded to in a later passage (sec. 16), in which the Sudden Teaching is spoken

[2] T12, p. 547a.
[3] T32, p. 582b.
[4] T14, p. 538b.

of as the method used by the enlightened. Nowhere does the *Platform Sutra* spell out in detail the specific characteristics of sudden enlightenment; however, it should not be conceived of as sudden in the sense of easily obtainable, without benefit of meditation practice. A thoroughgoing experience in its methods, the practice of direct mind in contradistinction to a step-by-step process of meditation, would appear to be what is being advocated here. It is thus conceivable that the sudden method might very well, from the standpoint of time, take much longer to attain than the gradual method. The *Platform Sutra* does not specifically deal with the period after sudden enlightenment has been gained. It is possible to construe this to mean that nothing more is needed, that the student has achieved all that is necessary for him to achieve. Judging from later Ch'an practices, however, this probably was not the implication intended. Indeed, in one of the remarks attributed to Hui-neng just before his death, we find him instructing his disciples to continue to sit in meditation as if he were still present (sec. 53). Once the initial awakening was gained, more practice, more enlightenments, greater efforts, were probably called for on the part of the student. But of subsequent practice the *Platform Sutra* has nothing to say.

One of the messages most prominent in the *Platform Sutra* is the doctrine of no-thought. Here again we have a concept drawn from earlier canonical writings: it is to be found in the *Ta-ch'eng ch'i-hsin lun,*[5] among other works. In the *Platform Sutra* (sec. 17) it is referred to as the main doctrine of the teaching, and is associated with nonform as the substance, and non-abiding, as the basis. Non-abiding is defined as the "original nature of man." These terms all seem to be pointing to the same thing: the Absolute, which can never be defined in words. Thoughts are conceived of as advancing in progression from past to present to future, in an unending chain of successive thoughts. Attachment to one instant of thought leads to attachment to a succession of thoughts, and thus to bondage. But by cutting off attachment to one instant of thought, one may, by a process unexplained, cut off attachment to a succession of thoughts and thus attain to no-thought, which is the state of enlightenment. Enlightenment is gained by a meditation not inhibited by a specific formula. The *Platform Sutra* fails to explain the process, except to insist that it is something that must be ac-

[5] T32, p. 576b.

complished by the individual for himself. The *Platform Sutra* maintains that the nature of man is from the outset pure, but that his purity has no form (sec. 18). But by self-practice, by endeavoring for himself, man can gain insight into this purity. Meditation, *prajñā,* True Reality, purity, the original nature, self-nature, the Buddha nature, all these terms, which are used constantly throughout the sermon, indicate the same undefined Absolute, which when seen and experienced by the individual himself, constitutes enlightenment.

Sitting in meditation (*tso-ch'an*) is defined in words attributed to Hui-neng (sec. 19): "In this teaching 'sitting' means without any obstruction anywhere, outwardly and under all circumstances, not to activate thoughts. 'Meditation' is internally to see the original nature and not to become confused." The definition is clear but the process is not. It is a rejection of formal meditation procedures, as advocated in other schools of Buddhism and Ch'an. It is, however, by no means a rejection of meditation itself. Certainly meditation must remain one of the principal means for attaining enlightenment in any doctrine which draws its teachings from the Prajñāpāramitā. The self-practice advocated here, for which no specific details are provided, may well foreshadow the concept of a constant meditation in all the activities of daily life found in later Ch'an. But no such development is mentioned here, and it is perhaps wise not to presuppose it.

The sermon now leaves the elucidation of the various terms and concepts adopted by Ch'an and shifts its attention towards the area of Mahāyāna Buddhism in general. It turns to what appears to have been a basic concern of T'ang Buddhism in general, the conferring of the Precepts on an assemblage of monks and laymen. Here they are described as the "Formless Precepts," but no attempt to define the term is made. Formless might best be conceived of as an adjectival reference to the Absolute. Those portions of the sermon (secs. 20–26) in which Hui-neng requests the assemblage to repeat in unison what he is about to say, and in which the compiler states in a textual note that the various formulas are to be repeated three times, deal with the Precepts. We cannot tell whether any particular ceremonies were involved in this instance; however, the conferring of the Precepts seems to have had a considerable vogue at this time among a variety of Buddhist groups, so it is conceivable that it had some kind of ceremonial significance. The Precepts given here represent basic concepts that are applicable to Mahāyāna Buddhism as a whole. Based on the text, they may be divided into five categories: 1) the three-fold body of the Buddha (sec. 20); 2) the four great vows (sec. 21); 3) the formless repentance (sec. 22); 4) the three refuges (sec. 23); and 5) the preaching concerning the Prajñāpāramitā (secs. 24–30).[6] While these sections deal to some extent with what might be called peculiarly Ch'an teachings, they seem clearly to serve a wider purpose: the general initiation of a group into Buddhism as a whole.

The Prajñāpāramitā doctrine, which may be considered the last of the five Precepts mentioned above, is enlarged upon. Here the idea so widely associated with Ch'an, "seeing into one's own nature," is emphasized (sec. 29). Enlightenment is not to be sought outside, but within the mind of the practitioner himself, for "the ten thousand dharmas are all within our bodies and minds" and "unawakened, even a Buddha is a sentient being, and . . . even a sentient being, if he is awakened in an instant of thought, is a Buddha" (sec. 30). Here again the ideas should not be conceived of as original to the *Platform Sutra,* for various canonical works are invoked to lend them authority. The Diamond Sutra, particularly, is singled out for attention. Man must gain awakening for himself; if he cannot do so, he must find a good teacher to show him the way. But, in the end, the best and only teacher is oneself: "If standing upon your own nature and mind, you illumine with wisdom and make inside and outside clear, you will know your own original mind." Presumed throughout is the doctrine that holds that the Buddha nature is inherent in all sentient beings, and that to discover this nature is to see one's own original mind.

The sermon closes with a series of discourses in the form of answers given by Hui-neng to questions put by the Prefect, Wei Ch'ü. The familiar story of Bodhidharma and the Emperor Wu (sec. 34) serves to condemn the concept that good works—the making of temples, the supporting of monks, the copying of sutras—are of benefit to the attainment of salvation, and that they constitute a form of merit. Merit, we are told, is in the mind, and only by self-practice of the teachings advocated in the *Platform Sutra* can true merit be attained. The Pure

---

[6] For a discussion, see Yanagida Seizan, "Daijō kaikyō to shite no Rokuso dankyō," *IBK,* no. 23 (January, 1964), pp. 65–72. Yanagida believes that the Precepts relating to the threefold body of the Buddha derive ultimately from Tao-an (312–385) and that Hui-neng's "Formless Precepts" are stated in opposition to the gradual approach to enlightenment preached by Shen-hsiu.

Land teachings of a Western Paradise, presided over by the Buddha Amitābha, where the believer hopes to be reborn, are subjected to criticism in the final part of the sermon (secs. 35–37). To yearn for rebirth in a distant land to the west is for people of low intelligence, we are told. The superior person makes his own mind pure and finds there this Western Land; indeed, it is to be sought within the nature of man himself and never on the outside. As has been noted before, there were during the eighth century certain schools of Ch'an which emphasized the Pure Land teachings. It may well be that the *Platform Sutra* is here criticizing the type of Ch'an advocated by the Szechuan school which derived from Chih-hsien, as well as the Pure Land teaching in general.

With the completion of the sermon the text now moves into the second part, a series of miscellaneous sections containing unrelated stories, verses, and other materials, which, while distinct from the sermon, repeat to a certain extent its contents. The verse on formlessness (sec. 33) reiterates the need for the student to concern himself with a persistent effort at self-cultivation, to attach to nothing, to abide in nothing, and to achieve no-thought. The formless verse (sec. 36), which may legitimately be considered a part of the sermon, is a further exhortation on the same subject, and includes various cautionary statements regarding the correct practices to be followed. In section 48 we again have a verse which calls upon the practitioner to work for his own enlightenment. It is couched in rather general terms and contains a warning against the meditation practices attributed to Northern Ch'an. The verse in section 52 reiterates the sentiments expressed in sections 30 and 35: everyone has within him the Buddha nature, which must be sought for within oneself. The verse in section 53 deals also with self-nature and the need for self-realization. While the Sudden Doctrine is advocated as the appropriate method for this achievement, the concepts expressed relate more to the Prajñāpāramitā teaching and to Mahāyāna Buddhism in general than to any peculiarly Ch'an ideas.

When we turn to the miscellaneous stories, we find a body of material that can best be described as critical of other forms of Buddhism, and that is designed to emphasize the superiority of Hui-neng's teaching. These stories are quite similar in structure to the tale of Bodhidharma and the Emperor Wu and the criticism of the Pure Land doctrine found in the sermon. They all involve an interlocutor, who poses a question and thus enables Hui-neng to expound a particular point of doctrine. Northern Ch'an is subjected to a direct attack in the story of Chih-ch'eng (secs. 40–41), who allegedly arrives as a spy from Shen-hsiu, becomes enlightened under Hui-neng, and then chooses to remain. The story of Fa-ta and the Lotus Sutra (sec. 42) may perhaps be considered a criticism of priests who were affiliated with no particular sect, lecture-masters or specialists in one particular text or group of texts, who traveled about visiting various teachers. The Lotus doctrine itself is not a target for attack; Hui-neng is here insisting that recitation is insufficient, that the sutra's teachings must be realized in the mind of the practitioner. The wisdom of the Buddha, inherent in the minds of all sentient beings, must be awakened to. The story of Chih-ch'ang, who asks for an explanation of the Supreme Vehicle (sec. 43), serves merely to repeat the assertion that the student must practice for himself. Shen-hui appears, somewhat to his disadvantage, in the only story (sec. 44) reminiscent of the question-and-answer type so popular in later Ch'an texts. Here he is taken to task for the impudence of his remarks, and unable to reply, he bows reverently before the Master and becomes his disciple. The statement that Shen-hui never left Hui-neng and always attended on him has no basis in fact.

Among the other sections of the work we find the thoroughly obscure disquisition on the thirty-six confrontations (secs. 45–46), whose origins are quite unknown. The sections containing the transmission verses of the Chinese Ch'an Patriarchs (secs. 49–50) and the list of the Indian and Chinese Patriarchs of the sect (sec. 51) reflect the peculiar concern of Ch'an with establishing itself as a legitimate school within Buddhism as a whole. Transmission verses of this type, as has been noted, were fairly widely used at the end of the eighth century, and the *Pao-lin chuan* provided such verses for all the Patriarchs of the sect.

There are several sections whose primary concern is to attack the teachings of Northern Ch'an (secs. 37, 39, 48–49) and to extol the Sudden Doctrine at the expense of the so-called gradual teaching. These reflect the struggle for supremacy between the two schools, a problem which had resolved itself by the time that the *Platform Sutra* was composed. One last type of material must be mentioned in conclusion. There are several sections whose purpose seems merely to assert the need for the transmission of a copy of the text itself as proof of one's position as a teacher (part of sec. 1, secs. 32, 38, 47). These sections may be attributed to the particular line of transmission which stemmed from Fa-hai and made its home at Hui-neng's temple in Ts'ao-ch'i.

THE PLATFORM SUTRA
OF THE SIXTH PATRIARCH

Southern School Sudden Doctrine, Supreme Mahāyāna Great Perfection of Wisdom: The Platform Sutra[1] preached by the Sixth Patriarch Hui-neng at the Ta-fan Temple[2] in Shao-chou,[3] one roll, recorded by the spreader of the Dharma, the disciple Fa-hai,[4] who at the same time received the Precepts of Formlessness

1. The Master Hui-neng ascended the high seat at the lecture hall of the Ta-fan Temple and expounded the Dharma of the Great Perfection of Wisdom, and transmitted the precepts of formlessness. At that time over ten thousand monks, nuns, and lay followers sat before him. The prefect of Shao-chou, Wei Ch'ü,[5] some thirty officials from various

---

[1] *T'an-ching.* The precise meaning of *t'an* has been a subject of debate. Hu Shih, "An Appeal for a Systematic Search in Japan for Long-hidden T'ang Dynasty Source Materials of the Early History of Zen Buddhism," *Bukkyō to bunka,* p. 16, equates the term with the Sanskrit *dāna* (gift, donation). In the *Li-tai fa-pao chi,* T51, p. 185b, however, we find the following statement: "The monk Shen-hui of the Ho-tse Temple in the Eastern capital (Loyang) would each month construct a platform place and deliver sermons to the people." Furthermore, Ch'i-sung, in the *Chia-chu fu-chiao-pien T'an-ching yao-i,* a commentary on his own essay, the *T'an-ching tsan* (contained in ch. 10 of Ch'i-sung's commentary on his own *Fu-chiao-pien: see Kanchū Fukyō-hen,* ch. 10 [V, 1a], defines *t'an* as the piling-up of earth to make a platform.

Prior to the *Platform Sutra* we have no instance in which a work which was merely the record of the career and sermons of a certain Master is given the name Sutra. Strictly speaking, of course, it is not one. Thus Ch'i-sung took pains to justify its classification as such: "Ta-chien chih-jen [Hui-neng]," he writes, "was a Bodhisattva monk, and his preaching of the *Platform Sutra* is basically no different from the Buddha's preaching of the sutras" (*Ibid.,* p. 47b).

[2] See introduction, p. 93, n. 14.

[3] Located west of Ch'ü-chiang hsien in Kwangtung.

[4] For Fa-hai, see introduction, p. 64.

[5] His name is variously written in early texts. The *Li-tai fa-pao chi,* T51, p. 182c, states that Wei Ch'ü wrote a memorial inscription for the Sixth Patriarch, and gives his title as "Assistant in the Bureau of Imperial Sacrifices (Ta-ch'ang ssu-ch'eng)." The *Shen-hui yü-lu* (Suzuki text), p. 63, also identifies him as the author of a memorial inscription, but gives his title as "Assistant in the Imperial Household Service Department (Tien-chung-ch'eng)." The *Kuang-tung t'ung-chih* (1822 ed., ch. 12, p. 16b), however, citing a work entitled *Ho-chih,* states that Wei Ch'ü became prefect of Shao-chou in

departments, and some thirty Confucian scholars[6] all begged the Master to preach on the Dharma of the Great Perfection of Wisdom. The prefect then had the monk-disciple Fa-hai record his words so that they might become known to later generations and be of benefit to students of the Way, in order that they might receive the pivot of the teaching and transmit it among themselves, taking these words as their authority.[7]

2. The Master Hui-neng said: "Good friends,[8] purify your minds and concentrate on the Dharma of the Great Perfection of Wisdom."

The Master stopped speaking and quieted his own mind. Then after a good while he said: "Good friends, listen quietly. My father was originally an official at Fan-yang.[9] He was [later] dismissed from his post[10] and banished as a commoner to Hsin-chou[11] in Ling-nan.[12] While I was still a child,[13] my father died and my old mother and I, a solitary child, moved to Nan-hai.[14] We suffered extreme poverty and here I sold firewood in the market place. By chance a certain man bought some firewood and then took me with him to the lodging house for officials. He took the firewood and left. Having received my

713, the year of the Sixth Patriarch's death. If this statement is to be trusted, it is possible to surmise that at the time that Wei Ch'ü allegedly invited Hui-neng to preach at the Ta-fan Temple he was a minor official, but that by the time that the *Platform Sutra* was actually compiled, he had been elevated to the post of prefect, and hence is given this title, with some exceptions, throughout the text. The memorial inscription is mentioned also in section 54 of the present translation. In the *Ching-te ch'uan-teng lu,* T51, p. 235a, Wei Ch'ü is listed as an heir of the Sixth Patriarch, but no information whatsoever is given about him.

[6] Following the *Kōshōji* edition, p. 6, the number of Confucian scholars present has been supplied.

[7] There follow here two clauses which are merely repetitive of the sense of the above passage. They are not contained in the *Kōshōji* edition, and have been omitted in the translation.

[8] *Shan-chih-shih.* This term is widely used in Ch'an literature, as well as in Buddhist texts in general. Its meaning varies: here it is used as a term of address. Later in the text (sec. 12) it is used in the meaning of "a good teacher."

[9] Present-day Cho hsien in Hopeh.

[10] The *Sung kao-seng chuan,* T50, p. 754c, and the *Ch'uan-fa cheng-tsung chi,* T51, p. 747a, give the date of his dismissal as during the Wu-te era (618–626). The Tsung-pao edition of the *Platform Sutra* furnishes the exact year, 620 (T48, p. 362b).

[11] Located to the east of Hsin-hsing hsien, Kwangtung.

[12] Ling-nan indicates the areas of Kwangtung, Kwangsi, and northern Indochina.

[13] The *Ching-te ch'uan-teng lu,* T51, p. 235b, says that his father died when Hui-neng was three. The *Sōkei daishi betsuden,* zz2B, 19, 5, 483c, is alone in stating that both his father and his mother died when he was three.

[14] Located in P'an-yü hsien, Kwangtung.

money and turning towards the front gate, I happened to see another
man[15] who was reciting the Diamond Sutra. Upon hearing it my mind
became clear and I was awakened.

"I asked him: 'Where do you come from that you have brought this
sutra with you?'

"He answered: 'I have made obeisance to the Fifth Patriarch, Hung-
jen, at the East Mountain, Feng-mu shan,[16] in Huang-mei hsien in
Ch'i-chou.[17] At present there are over a thousand disciples there. While
I was there I heard the Master encourage the monks and lay followers,
saying that if they recited just the one volume, the Diamond Sutra,
they could see into their own natures and with direct apprehension
become Buddhas.'

"Hearing what he said, I realized that I was predestined to have
heard him. Then I took leave of my mother[18] and went to Feng-mu
shan in Huang-mei and made obeisance to the Fifth Patriarch, the
priest Hung-jen.

3. "The priest Hung-jen asked me: 'Where are you from that you
come to this mountain to make obeisance to me? Just what is it that
you are looking for from me?'

"I replied: 'I am from Ling-nan, a commoner from Hsin-chou. I
have come this long distance only to make obeisance to you. I am
seeking no particular thing, but only the Buddhadharma.'[19]

"The Master then reproved me, saying: 'If you're from Ling-nan
then you're a barbarian.[20] How can you become a Buddha?'

"I replied: 'Although people from the south and people from the
north differ, there is no north and south in Buddha nature. Although

[15] The *Tsu-t'ang chi*, I, 89–90, identifies this man as An Tao-ch'eng. In this account
there is only one person; An both buys the firewood and recites the Diamond Sutra.
[16] See introduction, p. 3, n. 3.
[17] Present-day Ch'i-ch'un in Hupeh.
[18] Later works see to it that Hui-neng provides properly for his mother before taking
leave of her. The *Tsu-t'ang chi*, I, 90, has An Tao-ch'eng give Hui-neng 100 *liang* to
care for her; in the *Kōshōji*, p. 7, the sum given is 10 *liang*.
[19] The text reads: *wei ch'iu Fo-fa tso*. Since we have here a series of four-character
phrases, it would seem best to regard the *tso* as an extraneous character. *Kōshōji*, p. 7,
however, renders the clause: *wei ch'iu tso Fo* (I seek only to become a Buddha), and
since later in this section of the Tun-huang text we read: "How can you become a
Buddha?" it would appear very likely that the original wording of the clause is as
found in the *Kōshōji* edition.
[20] *Ko-lao*. Term of insult, indicating that the inhabitants of southern China are bar-
barians, quite close to wild animals.

my barbarian's body and your body are not the same, what difference is there in our Buddha nature?'

"The Master wished to continue his discussion with me; however, seeing that there were other people nearby, he said no more. Then he sent me to work with the assembly. Later a lay disciple had me go to the threshing room where I spent over eight months treading the pestle.

4. "Unexpectedly one day the Fifth Patriarch called his disciples to come, and when they had assembled, he said: 'Let me preach to you. For people in this world birth and death are vital matters.[21] You disciples make offerings all day long and seek only the field of blessings,[22] but you do not seek to escape from the bitter sea of birth and death. Your own self-nature obscures the gateway to blessings; how can you be saved?[23] All of you return to your rooms and look into yourselves. Men of wisdom will of themselves grasp the original nature of their *prajñā* intuition. Each of you write a verse and bring it to me. I will read your verses, and if there is one who is awakened to the cardinal meaning, I will give him the robe and the Dharma and make him the Sixth Patriarch. Hurry, hurry!'

5. "The disciples received his instructions and returned, each to his own room. They talked it over among themselves, saying: 'There's no point in our purifying[24] our minds and making efforts to compose a verse to present to the priest. Shen-hsiu, the head monk, is our teacher. After he obtains the Dharma we can rely on him, so let's not compose verses.' They all then gave up trying and did not have the courage to present a verse.

"At that time there was a three-sectioned corridor in front of the Master's hall. On the walls were to be painted pictures of stories from

[21] *Sheng-ssu shih-ta.* The same expression is found in *Shen-hui yü-lu;* see Hu Shih, *Shen-hui ho-shang i-chi,* p. 149.
[22] *Fu-t'ien.* The term implies that by good works in this world a person prepares the ground (*t'ien*) which will produce the fruits and flowers (*fu*) of the next world. The subject is discussed in detail in Tokiwa Daijō, *Shina Bukkyō shi no kenkyū,* II, 473–98.
[23] This passage may also be interpreted as: "Your self-nature is confused by the blessings method." *Kōshōji,* p. 8, revises the text to read: "If your own self-natures are deluded, how can blessings save you?"
[24] The text has *ch'eng* [to present]; *Kōshōji,* p. 9, substitutes *ch'eng* [purify], which has been followed here. The characters are homophones.

the Laṅkāvatāra Sutra,[25] together with a picture in commemoration of the Fifth Patriarch transmitting the robe and Dharma,[26] in order to disseminate them to later generations and preserve a record of them. The artist, Lu Chen,[27] had examined the walls and was to start work the next day.

6. "The head monk Shen-hsiu thought: 'The others won't present mind-verses because I am their teacher. If I don't offer a mind-verse, how can the Fifth Patriarch estimate the degree of understanding within my mind? If I offer my mind to the Fifth Patriarch with the intention of gaining the Dharma, it is justifiable; however, if I am seeking the patriarchship, then it cannot be justified. Then it would be like a common man usurping the saintly position. But if I don't offer my mind then I cannot learn the Dharma.'[28] For a long time he thought about it and was very much perplexed.

"At midnight, without letting anyone see him, he went to write his mind-verse on the central section of the south corridor wall, hoping to gain the Dharma. 'If the Fifth Patriarch sees my verse and says that it . . . and there is a weighty obstacle in my past karma, then I cannot gain the Dharma and shall have to give up.[29] The honorable Patriarch's intention is difficult to fathom.'

[25] *Pien* and *pien-hsiang*. Reference is to paintings or sculpture which furnish a pictorial representation of the sutras and their teachings. For a detailed consideration of the various paintings of this type, see Matsumoto Eiichi, *Tonkō ga no kenkyū*, Zuzō hen, pp. 1–211. Paintings representing the Laṅkāvatāra Sutra as such are not to be found among Tun-huang materials.

[26] This passage is difficult to follow. "A picture of the Dharma" makes no sense; what is probably meant is a picture of the robe as symbolic of the Dharma. Reference may also be to the robe and bowl, which, as symbols of the transmission, would be equivalent to the robe and the Dharma. *Kōshōji*, p. 10, indicates that the reference is to some kind of genealogical chart, showing the succession of the Five Chinese Patriarchs through Hung-jen.

[27] Unknown. The Tun-huang text uses Morohashi character no. 20873 for the personal name of the artist Lu. This character may be read *lin*, *yin*, or *hsien*. *Kōshōji* and all later texts change to *Chen* (Matthews no. 301), which has been followed here.

[28] This statement does not fit into the context of the rest of the passage. The *Kōshōji* version, p. 10: "If I don't offer my verse, then I'll end up by not gaining the Dharma," makes better sense.

[29] The Tun-huang text is corrupt and scarcely readable. It also contains an obvious omission at this point. *Kōshōji*, p. 11, reads: "If the Fifth Patriarch sees the verse tomorrow and is pleased with it, then I shall come forward and say that I wrote it. If he tells me that it is not worth while, then I shall know that the homage I have received for these several years on this mountain has been in vain, and that I have no hope of learning the Tao."

"Then the head monk Shen-hsiu, at midnight, holding a candle, wrote a verse on the central section of the south corridor, without anyone else knowing about it. The verse read:

> The body is the Bodhi tree,
> The mind is like a clear mirror.
> At all times we must strive to polish it,
> And must not let the dust collect.

7. "After he had finished writing this verse, the head monk Shen-hsiu returned to his room and lay down. No one had seen him.

"At dawn the Fifth Patriarch called the painter Lu to draw illustrations from the Laṅkāvatāra Sutra on the south corridor wall. The Fifth Patriarch suddenly saw this verse and, having read it,[30] said to the painter Lu: 'I will give you thirty thousand cash. You have come a long distance to do this arduous work, but I have decided not to have the pictures painted after all. It is said in the Diamond Sutra: "All forms everywhere are unreal and false."[31] It would be best to leave this verse here and to have the deluded ones recite it. If they practice in accordance with it they will not fall into the three evil ways.[32] Those who practice by it will gain great benefit.'

"The Master then called all his disciples to come, and burned incense before the verse. The disciples came in to see and all were filled with admiration.

"The Fifth Patriarch said: 'You should all recite this verse so that you will be able to see into your own natures.[33] With this practice you will not fall into the three evil ways.'

"The disciples all recited it, and feeling great admiration, cried out: 'How excellent!'

"The Fifth Patriarch then called the head monk Shen-hsiu inside the hall and asked: 'Did you write this verse or not? If you wrote it you are qualified to attain my Dharma.'[34]

"The head monk Shen-hsiu said: 'I am ashamed to say that I ac-

---

[30] The text has *ch'ing-chi* [please record]. A copyist's error for *tu-ch'i* [finished reading]?

[31] T8, p. 749a.

[32] The three evil paths (*gati*): hell, hungry demons, beasts.

[33] Since later on in the text Hung-jen says that Shen-hsiu's verse does not show true understanding, it would perhaps be better to consider this last clause as a later interpolation, not as a part of the original version.

[34] Here again the text is contradictory; see above, n. 33.

tually did write the verse, but I do not dare to seek the patriarchship. I beg you to be so compassionate as to tell me whether I have even a small amount of wisdom and discernment of the cardinal meaning or not.'

"The Fifth Patriarch said: 'This verse you wrote shows that you still have not reached true understanding. You have merely arrived at the front of the gate but have yet to be able to enter it. If common people practice according to your verse they will not fall. But in seeking the ultimate enlightenment (*bodhi*) one will not succeed with such an understanding. You must enter the gate and see your own original nature. Go and think about it for a day or two and then make another verse and present it to me. If you have been able to enter the gate and see your own original nature, then I will give you the robe and the Dharma.' The head monk Shen-hsiu left, but after several days he was still unable to write a verse.

8. "One day an acolyte passed by the threshing room reciting this verse. As soon as I heard it I knew that the person who had written it had yet to know his own nature and to discern the cardinal meaning. I asked the boy: 'What's the name of the verse you were reciting just now?'

"The boy answered me, saying: 'Don't you know? The Master said that birth and death are vital matters, and he told his disciples each to write a verse if they wanted to inherit the robe and the Dharma, and to bring it for him to see. He who was awakened to the cardinal meaning would be given the robe and the Dharma and be made the Sixth Patriarch. There is a head monk by the name of Shen-hsiu who happened to write a verse on formlessness on the walls of the south corridor. The Fifth Patriarch had all his disciples recite the verse, [saying] that those who awakened to it would see into their own self-natures,[35] and that those who practiced according to it would attain emancipation.'

"I said: 'I've been treading the pestle for more than eight months, but haven't been to the hall yet. I beg you to take me to the south corridor so that I can see this verse and make obeisance to it. I also want to recite it so that I can establish causation for my next birth and be born in a Buddha-land.'

[35] A further contradiction; see above, nn. 33–34.

"The boy took me to the south corridor and I made obeisance before the verse. Because I was uneducated I asked someone[36] to read it to me. As soon as I had heard it I understood the cardinal meaning. I made a verse and asked someone who was able to write to put it on the wall of the west corridor, so that I might offer my own original mind. If you do not know the original mind, studying the Dharma is to no avail. If you know the mind and see its true nature, you then awaken to the cardinal meaning.[37] My verse said:

> Bodhi originally has no tree,
> The mirror also has no stand.
> Buddha nature is always clean and pure;[38]
> Where is there room for dust?

"Another verse said:

> The mind is the Bodhi tree,
> The body is the mirror stand.
> The mirror is originally clean and pure;
> Where can it be stained by dust? [39]

"The followers in the temple were all amazed when they heard my verse. Then I returned to the threshing room. The Fifth Patriarch realized that I had a splendid understanding of the cardinal meaning.[40] Being afraid lest the assembly know this, he said to them: 'This is still not complete understanding.'

[36] The *Kōshōji* edition, p. 13, identifies this man as Chang Jih-yung, vice-governor of Chiang-chou.

[37] The above four clauses scarcely fit in with the sequence of the story and would not appear to be anything that Hui-neng would have said on this occasion. The *Kōshōji* text is completely different at this point; however, the two clauses: "If you do not know the original mind, studying the Dharma is to no avail," appear later in the *Kōshōji* text, p. 15, as words addressed to Hui-neng by the Fifth Patriarch.

[38] It is only in the Tun-huang version and the Hsi-hsia translation of 1071 that the third line of this verse appears in this form (see Kawakami Tenzan, "Seikago-yaku Rokuso dankyō ni tsuite," *Shina Bukkyō shigaku,* II [no. 3, September, 1938], 64). Later works change it to the famous: "From the beginning not a thing is." See introduction, p. 94.

[39] This second verse is to be found only in the Tun-huang and the Hsi-hsia versions. Hu Shih, "An Appeal . . . ," pp. 20–21, believes that the presence of two verses indicates that the "unknown author of this fictionalized autobiography of Hui-neng was evidently experimenting with his verse writing and was not sure which verse was better."

[40] The Tun-huang text: *Tan chi shan chih shih ta i* is corrupt at this point. Both the *tan chi* and the *chih* very likely represent a copyist's error, and have been treated as superfluous characters. Compare W. T. Chan, *The Platform Scripture,* pp. 40–41.

9. "At midnight the Fifth Patriarch called me into the hall and expounded the Diamond Sutra to me. Hearing it but once,[41] I was immediately awakened, and that night I received the Dharma. None of
the others knew anything about it. Then he transmitted to me the
Dharma of Sudden Enlightenment and the robe, saying: 'I make you
the Sixth Patriarch. The robe is the proof and is to be handed down
from generation to generation.[42] My Dharma must be transmitted from
mind to mind. You must make people awaken to themselves.'

"The Fifth Patriarch told me: 'From ancient times the transmission
of the Dharma has been as tenuous as a dangling thread. If you stay
here there are people who will harm you. You must leave at once.'

10. "I set out at midnight with the robe and the Dharma. The Fifth
Patriarch saw me off as far as Chiu-chiang Station.[43] I was instantly
enlightened.[44] The Fifth Patriarch instructed me: 'Leave, work hard,
take the Dharma with you to the south. For three years do not spread
the teaching or else calamity will befall the Dharma. Later work to
convert people; you must guide deluded persons well. If you are able
to awaken another's mind, he will be no different from me.'[45] After
completing my leave-taking I set out for the south.

[41] In place of "Hearing it but once . . . ," the *Kōshōji* text, p. 15, reads: "Just when
he came to the passage, 'You must not be attached [to things], yet must produce a
mind which stays in no place . . .'" That Hui-neng was enlightened upon hearing this
passage from the Diamond Sutra (T8, p. 749c) is a celebrated story in Ch'an Buddhism,
and it is of interest that it is not included in the Tun-huang version. The identical
passage from the Diamond Sutra is quoted in *Shen-hui yü-lu* (Suzuki text, p. 18;
Hu Shih, *Shen-hui ho-shang i-chi*, p. 102; Gernet, *Entretiens du Maître de Dhyāna
Chen-houei du Ho-tsö*, p. 15).
  Strictly speaking, the Chinese translation does not follow the Sanskrit original which,
following Conze, reads: "should produce . . . a thought which is nowhere supported"
(Edward Conze, *Buddhist Wisdom Books*, p. 48).
[42] This statement is contradicted in section 49, where Hui-neng states that the robe
is not to be handed down.
[43] This station cannot be placed exactly. Ui, *Zenshū shi kenkyū*, II, 198, identifies
it with Hsin-yang Station of the Ming period, located on the south bank of the
Yangtze, near Chiu-chiang hsien, Kiangsi.
[44] This clause scarcely fits into the context of the passage. In the *Kōshōji* edition,
p. 16, there is an additional episode not contained here, and it is possible that there
is a textual omission to which the clause refers. The clause does not, however, appear
as such in the *Kōshōji* edition.
[45] *Kōshōji*, p. 17, has been followed; the Tun-huang text reads: "His enlightenment
will be no different from your own."

134   The Platform Sutra

11. "After about two months I reached Ta-yü ling.[46] Unknown to me, several hundred men were following behind, wishing to try to kill me and to steal my robe and Dharma. By the time I had gone halfway up the mountain they had all turned back. But there was one monk of the family name of Chen, whose personal name was Hui-ming.[47] Formerly he had been a general of the third rank and he was by nature and conduct coarse and violent. Reaching the top of the mountain, he caught up with me and threatened me. I handed over the dharma-robe, but he was not willing to take it.

"[He said]: 'I have come this long distance just to seek the Dharma. I have no need for the robe.' Then, on top of the mountain, I transmitted the Dharma to Hui-ming, who when he heard it, was at once enlightened.[48] I then ordered him to return to the north and to convert people there.[49]

12. "I was predestined to come to live here[50] and to preach to you officials, monks, and laymen. My teaching has been handed down from the sages of the past; it is not my own personal knowledge. If you wish to hear the teachings of the sages of the past, each of you must quiet his mind and hear me to the end. Please cast aside your own delusions; then you will be no different from the sages of the past.[51] (What follows below is the Dharma).[52]

[46] Located in Chiu-chiang hsien, Kiangsi, on the Kwangtung border.

[47] The Tun-huang text here refers to this monk by the name of Hui-hsun, but is the only text that gives this name. The Shen-hui yü-lu (Suzuki text), p. 61, Tsu-t'ang chi, V, 61, and the Kōshōji, p. 17, all give him as Hui-ming. His biography is to be found in Sung kao-seng chuan, T50, p. 756b–c, where he is identified as a native of P'o-yang in Kiangsi. Upon gaining enlightenment from the Sixth Patriarch, he changed his name, which had been Tao-ming, to Hui-ming. This account is based on the pagoda inscription by Ch'ing-chou, T'ang Hu-chou Fo-ch'uan ssu ku ta-shih t'a-ming, CTW, ch. 917 (XIX, 12062–63). His biography is also found in Ching-te ch'uan-teng lu, T51, p. 232a, under the title: Yüan-chou Meng-shan Tao-ming ch'an-shih. Here he is given as an heir of the Fifth Patriarch, and it is stated that his name was originally Hui-ming, but that he changed it in order to avoid using the same character contained in Hui-neng's name.

[48] It is on this occasion that Hui-neng is credited in later works with having uttered the famous lines: "Not thinking of good, not thinking of evil, just at this moment, what is your original face before your mother and father were born?" See introduction, p. 110.

[49] The Kōshōji edition continues with two more episodes, which are not to be found in the Tun-huang edition.

[50] Ts'ao-ch'i.

[51] The Tun-huang text is unreadable here; Kōshōji, p. 18, has been followed.

[52] This note is in the original text.

The Master Hui-neng called, saying: [53] "Good friends, enlightenment (*bodhi*) and intuitive wisdom (*prajñā*) are from the outset possessed by men of this world themselves. It is just because the mind is
deluded that men cannot attain awakening to themselves. They must
seek a good teacher to show them how to see into their own natures.
Good friends, if you meet awakening, [Buddha]-wisdom will be
achieved.

13. "Good friends, my teaching of the Dharma takes meditation (*ting*)
and wisdom (*hui*) as its basis.[54] Never under any circumstances[55] say
mistakenly that meditation and wisdom are different; they are a unity,
not two things. Meditation itself is the substance of wisdom; wisdom
itself is the function of meditation.[56] At the very moment when there
is wisdom, then meditation exists in wisdom; at the very moment when
there is meditation, then wisdom exists in meditation. Good friends,
this means that meditation and wisdom are alike. Students, be careful
not to say that meditation gives rise to wisdom, or that wisdom gives
rise to meditation, or that meditation and wisdom are different from
each other.[57] To hold this view implies that things have duality—if good
is spoken while the mind is not good, meditation and wisdom will not
be alike. If mind and speech are both good, then the internal and the

[53] Here the preaching begins.

[54] The identification of meditation and *prajñā* is found in almost identical form in
the writings of Shen-hui. See *Shen-hui yü-lu* (Suzuki text), p. 22; Hu Shih, *Shen-hui
ho-shang i-chi*, pp. 128–29, 138; Gernet, *Entretiens . . .* , pp. 50, 64; also Hu Shih,
"Hsin-chiao-ting te Tun-huang hsieh-pen Shen-hui ho-shang i-chu liang-chung,"
CYLYYC XXIX (no. 2, February, 1958), 833; also in the unpublished manuscripts
S2472 and S6977. It is also contained in *Fa-hsing lun* (S4669), cited in D. T. Suzuki,
Zen shisō shi kenkyū, II, 471. A discussion of the identification of meditation and
prajñā is found in detail in D. T. Suzuki, "Zen, a reply to Hu Shih," *Philosophy East
and West*, III (no. 1, April, 1953), 27ff. The concept is drawn from the Nirvāṇa Sutra,
т12, p. 547a, which states: "When meditation and wisdom are equal, one sees all things."

[55] *Ti-i-wu.* A very strong negative imperative in T'ang colloquial language, used to
forbid one particular thing; hence there is no need later in the text for a second or
third prohibition. It appears in a variety of forms. See Wang Chung-min, *et al., Tun-
huang pien-wen chi*, p. 468; Iriya Yoshitaka, "*Tonkō hembun shū*" *kōgo goi sakuin*,
p. 9.

[56] A passage almost identical with the above is found in *Shen-hui yü-lu*: Hu Shih,
Shen-hui ho-shang i-chi, p. 129; Gernet, *Entretiens . . .* , p. 50. The early use of the
two technical categories, *t'i* [substance] and *yung* [function] are largely, but by no
means entirely, confined to Buddhist philosophy. See Walter Liebenthal, *Book of Chao*,
pp. 18–20. For a study of the history of these terms, see Shimada Kenji, "Taiyō no
rekishi ni yosete," *Tsukamoto hakushi shōju ki'nen Bukkyō shigaku ronshū*, pp. 416–30.

[57] The holder of this deluded opinion is identified in the *Shen-hui yü-lu* (Suzuki
text), pp. 13, 31, 32, as Ch'eng ch'an-shih.

external are the same and meditation and wisdom are alike. The practice of self-awakening does not lie in verbal arguments. If you argue which comes first, meditation or wisdom, you are deluded people. You won't be able to settle the argument and instead will cling to objective things,[58] and will never escape from the four states of phenomena.[59]

14. "The *samādhi* of oneness[60] is straightforward mind at all times, walking, staying, sitting, and lying. The *Ching-ming ching* says: 'Straightforward mind is the place of practice; straightforward mind is the Pure Land.' [61] Do not with a dishonest mind speak of the straightforwardness of the Dharma. If while speaking of the *samādhi* of oneness, you fail to practice straightforward mind, you will not be disciples of the Buddha. Only practicing straightforward mind, and in all things having no attachments whatsoever, is called the *samādhi* of oneness. The deluded man clings to the characteristics of things, adheres to the *samādhi* of oneness, [thinks] that straightforward mind is sitting without moving and casting aside delusions without letting things arise in the mind. This he considers to be the *samādhi* of oneness. This kind of practice is the same as insentiency[62] and the cause of an obstruction to the Tao. Tao must be something that circulates freely; why should he impede it? If the mind does not abide in things the Tao circulates freely; if the mind abides in things, it becomes entangled.[63]

[58] *Fa-wo.* A technical term designating the false conception of an objective thing as a thing in itself.
[59] Birth, being, change, and death. This may possibly refer to four of the eight forms of misconception, beliefs in some form of ego (self, being, soul, person), mentioned in the Diamond Sutra, т8, p. 749.
[60] *I-hsing san-mei. Ekavyūha* or *ekākāra samādhi.* This term is found in the *Leng-chia shih-tzu chi,* т85, p. 1286a, which quotes a passage from the *Wen-shu-shih-li so-shou mo-ho pan-jo-po-lo-mi ching,* т8, p. 731a, in which the term is to be found. It also appears in Shen-hui's works (see Hu Shih, "Hsin-chiao-ting . . . ," p. 852), the *Ta-ch'eng ch'i-hsin lun,* т32, p. 582b, and elsewhere in Buddhist literature in a variety of meanings. A discussion of the phrase as a Ch'an technical term, its history and various uses, appears in: Kobayashi Enshō, "Ichigyō zammai shikō," *Zengaku kenkyū,* no. 51 (February, 1961), pp. 176–86. Kobayashi renders the term as "concentration on the unified oneness of the universe."
[61] *Ching-ming ching.* Another name for the Vimalakīrti Sutra, т14, pp. 537–57. The quotation here does not appear as such in the sutra; the first five characters are from the P'u-sa *p'in* (p. 542c); the second five from the Fo-kuo *p'in* (p. 538b).
[62] I.e., being like trees, rocks, etc.
[63] The Tun-huang text of this sentence is not readable: *Kōshōji,* p. 20, has been followed.

If sitting in meditation without moving is good, why did Vimalakīrti ✗
scold Śāriputra for sitting in meditation in the forest? [64]   *l*

"Good friends, some people[65] teach men to sit viewing the mind and
viewing purity, not moving and not activating the mind, and to this
they devote their efforts. Deluded people do not realize that this is
wrong, cling to this doctrine, and become confused. There are many ─
such people. Those who instruct in this way are, from the outset, greatly ‾
mistaken.

15. "Good friends, how then are meditation and wisdom alike? They
are like the lamp and the light it gives forth. If there is a lamp there
is light; if there is no lamp there is no light. The lamp is the substance
of light; the light is the function of the lamp. Thus, although they have
two names, in substance they are not two. Meditation and wisdom are
also like this.[66]

16. Good friends, in the Dharma there is no sudden or gradual, but ✗
among people some are keen and others dull. The deluded recommend
the gradual method, the enlightened practice the sudden teaching.[67] To
understand the original mind of yourself is to see into your own original nature. Once enlightened, there is from the outset no distinction
between these two methods; those who are not enlightened will for long
kalpas be caught in the cycle of transmigration.

17. "Good friends, in this teaching of mine, from ancient times up to
the present,[68] all have set up no-thought[69] as the main doctrine, non-

[64] Reference is to a passage in the Vimalakīrti Sutra, T14, p. 539c. Almost identical
passages are found in *Shen-hui yü-lu* (Suzuki text, pp. 14, 28; Hu Shih, *Shen-hui
ho-shang i-chi,* pp. 97, 117; Gernet, *Entretiens . . . ,* pp. 5, 35).
[65] The teachers of the Northern School of Ch'an.
[66] Similar passages appear in the unpublished S6977 and in Shen-hui's works. See
Hu Shih, "Hsin-chiao-ting . . . ," p. 833; the text given in D. T. Suzuki, "Jinne
oshō no 'Dango' to kangaubeki Tonkō shutsudo-bon ni tsukite," *Ōtani gakuhō,* XVI
(no. 4, December, 1935), 27; *Kōkan Shōshitsu issho oyobi kaisetsu,* pp. 66–67.
[67] There is, of course, no need for an enlightened man to practice with the aim of
gaining awakening. This may best be interpreted as a criticism of Northern Ch'an and
the advocacy of the Southern method as a means to enlightenment.
[68] The Tun-huang text has the two characters *tun-chien* [sudden and gradual] inserted here. They do not appear in the parallel passage in the *Kōshōji* edition, and have
been omitted in the translation.
[69] *Wu-nien.* Often rendered as the equivalent of *wu-hsin* [no mind]. A term widely
used in Ch'an, it is considered one of the most important and characteristic elements in

form as the substance, and non-abiding as the basis.[70] Non-form is to be separated from form even when associated with form. No-thought is not to think even when involved in thought. Non-abiding is the original nature of man.

"Successive thoughts do not stop; prior thoughts, present thoughts, and future thoughts follow one after the other without cessation. If one instant of thought is cut off, the Dharma body separates from the physical body, and in the midst of successive thoughts there will be no place for attachment to anything. If one instant of thought clings, then successive thoughts cling; this is known as being fettered. If in all things successive thoughts do not cling, then you are unfettered. Therefore, non-abiding is made the basis.

"Good friends, being outwardly separated from all forms, this is non-form. When you are separated from form, the substance of your nature is pure. Therefore, non-form is made the substance.

"To be unstained in all environments is called no-thought. If on the basis of your own thoughts you separate from environment, then, in regard to things, thoughts are not produced. If you stop thinking of the myriad things, and cast aside all thoughts, as soon as one instant of thought is cut off, you will be reborn in another realm. Students, take care! Don't rest in objective things and the subjective mind. [If you do so] it will be bad enough that you yourself are in error, yet how much worse that you encourage others in their mistakes. The deluded man, however, does not himself see[71] and slanders the teachings of the sutras.

the teaching of the Sixth Patriarch. It is discussed in Itō Kokan, "Rokuso Enō daishi no chūshin shishō," *Nihon Bukkyōgaku kyōkai nempō*, no. 7 (February, 1935), pp. 235–38. D. T. Suzuki has devoted a book to the general subject: *Zen Doctrine of No-mind*. Gernet (*Entretiens* . . . , pp. 12–13, n. 5) renders the term as "absence de pensée," and discusses its origins and implications. *Wu-nien* is used in the *Ta-ch'eng ch'i-hsin lun*, т32, p. 576b, the apocryphal *Chin-kang san-mei ching*, т9, p. 369a, and in the *Li-tai fa-pao chi*, where it is dealt with in detail (т51, pp. 185a, 192a–b, 195b–c). It is found also throughout the works of Shen-hui: in the *T'an-yü* (Hu Shih, "Hsin-chiao-ting . . . ," p. 832) we read: "True Reality is the substance of no-thought." In the *Hsien-tsung chi* (Hu Shih, *Shen-hui ho-shang i-chi*, p. 193) we find: "Thought (*nien*) is to concentrate on True Reality." This would imply that no-thought (*wu-nien*) is its reverse, and would correspond with the "no-thought is not to think even when involved in thought" of the following passage in the Tun-huang text.

[70] Here follow the four characters *ho ming wei hsiang* [What is form?]. They are out of context and are not contained in the parallel passage in the *Kōshōji* edition. They have been omitted in the translation.

[71] The text, as given in *Kōshōji*, p. 22, has been followed. Compare Chan, *The Platform Scripture*, pp. 52–53.

Therefore, no-thought is established as a doctrine. Because man in his delusion has thoughts in relation to his environment, heterodox ideas stemming from these thoughts arise, and passions and false views are produced from them. Therefore this teaching has established no-thought as a doctrine.

"Men of the world, separate yourselves from views; do not activate thoughts. If there were no thinking, then no-thought would have no place to exist. 'No' is the 'no' of what? 'Thought' means 'thinking' of what? 'No' is the separation from the dualism that produces the passions. 'Thought' means thinking of the original nature of True Reality.[72] True Reality is the substance of thoughts; thoughts are the function of True Reality. If you give rise to thoughts from your self-nature, then, although you see, hear, perceive, and know, you are not stained by the manifold environments, and are always free.[73] The Vimalakīrti Sutra says: 'Externally, while distinguishing well all the forms of the various dharmas, internally he stands firm within the First Principle.'[74]

18. "Good friends, in this teaching from the outset sitting in meditation does not concern the mind nor does it concern purity; we do not talk of steadfastness.[75] If someone speaks of 'viewing the mind,' [then I would say] that the 'mind' is of itself delusion, and as delusions are just like fantasies, there is nothing to be seen. If someone speaks of 'viewing purity,' [then I would say] that man's nature is of itself pure, but because of false thoughts True Reality is obscured. If you exclude delusions then the original nature reveals its purity. If you activate your mind to view purity without realizing that your own nature is originally pure, delusions of purity will be produced. Since this delusion has no place to exist, then you know that whatever you see is nothing but delusion. Purity has no form, but, nonetheless, some people try to postulate the form of purity and consider this to be Ch'an prac-

[72] This passage is omitted in the Tun-huang version and has been supplied from *Kōshōji*, p. 22.
[73] A passage of very similar import appears in *Shen-hui yü-lu*. See Hu Shih, *Shen-hui ho-shang i-chi*, p. 130; Gernet, *Entretiens . . .*, p. 52.
[74] T14, p. 537c. The "externally" and "internally" are not in the original text of the Vimalakīrti Sutra.
[75] The Tun-huang edition reads: *pu-yen-tung* [do not speak of motion]. *Kōshōji*, p. 22, in the parallel passage has: *i pu-shih pu-tung* [this, too, is not steadfastness]. The text has been emended to *pu-yen pu-tung* [do not speak of steadfastness] here, particularly in light of the expression *pu-tung* [stand firm] in the excerpt from the Vimalakīrti Sutra quoted above.

tice. People who hold this view obstruct their own original natures and end up by being bound by purity. One who practices steadfastness does not see the faults of people everywhere.[76] This is the steadfastness of self-nature. The deluded man, however, even if he doesn't move his own body, will talk of the good and bad of others the moment he opens his mouth, and thus behave in opposition to the Tao. Therefore, both 'viewing the mind' and 'viewing purity' will cause an obstruction to Tao.

19. "Now that we know that this is so, what is it in this teaching that we call 'sitting in meditation' (tso-ch'an)? In this teaching 'sitting' means without any obstruction anywhere, outwardly and under all circumstances, not to activate thoughts. 'Meditation' is internally to see the original nature and not become confused.[77]

"And what do we call Ch'an meditation (ch'an-ting)? [78] Outwardly to exclude form is 'ch'an'; inwardly to be unconfused is meditation (ting). Even though there is form on the outside, when internally the nature is not confused,[79] then, from the outset,[80] you are of yourself pure and of yourself in meditation. The very contact with circumstances itself causes confusion.[81] Separation from form on the outside is 'ch'an';

[76] The Tun-huang manuscript has: "see all the faults everywhere"; however, in the "Formless Verse" (sec. 36) we read:

> If you are a person who truly practices the Way,
> Do not look at the ignorance of the world.
> For if you see the wrong of people in the world,
> Being wrong yourself, you will be evil.

This would indicate that a negative has been dropped here. The same concept is found in a verse in the *Li-tai fa-pao chi*, T51, p. 192b: "You should be engaged in your own practice. Don't see the right and wrong in others." In the *Lin-chi lu*, T47, p. 498b, the same idea is expressed: "If he be a true practicer of the Way, he will not seek out the faults of the world."

[77] In the opening passage of an unpublished manuscript from Tun-huang entitled *Ta-ch'eng san-k'o*, in one roll, owned by Mr. Suzuki Shintarō of Itō, Shizuoka, the text is very similar to the *Platform Sutra* here. Quoted in Sekiguchi Shindai, *Daruma daishi no kenkyū*, p. 243.

[78] Ch'an is *dhyāna*; *ting* is its Chinese translation. The meaning is equivalent to *tso-ch'an*, above.

[79] For this passage *Kōshōji*, pp. 23–24, reads: "If outwardly you attach to form, inwardly the mind is then confused; if outwardly you exclude form, inwardly the mind is composed."

[80] *Kōshōji*, p. 24, reads here: "The original nature is in itself pure."

[81] The text is difficult to follow here. Following this sentence, the Tun-huang text has six characters which are out of context and have been omitted in the translation. The parallel passage in the *Kōshōji* edition has been changed completely.

being untouched on the inside is meditation (*ting*). Being 'ch'an' externally and meditation (*ting*) internally, it is known as ch'an meditation (*ch'an-ting*). The Vimalakīrti Sutra says: 'At once, suddenly, you regain the original mind.'[82] The *P'u-sa-chieh* says: 'From the outset your own nature is pure.'[83]

"Good friends, see for yourselves the purity of your own natures, practice and accomplish for yourselves. Your own nature is the *Dharmakāya* and self-practice is the practice of Buddha; by self-accomplishment you may achieve the Buddha Way for yourselves.

20. "Good friends, you must all with your own bodies receive the precepts of formlessness and recite in unison what I am about to say. It will make you see the threefold body of the Buddha in your own selves. 'I take refuge in the pure *Dharmakāya* Buddha in my own physical body. I take refuge in the ten thousand hundred billion *Nirmāṇakāya* Buddhas in my own physical body. I take refuge in the future perfect *Sambhogakāya* Buddha in my own physical body.' (Recite the above three times).[84] The physical body is your own home; you cannot speak of turning to it. The threefold body which I just mentioned is within your own self-natures.[85] Everyone in the world possesses it, but being deluded, he cannot see it and seeks the threefold body of the Tathāgata on the outside. Thus he cannot find the threefold Buddha body in his own physical body.

"Good friends, listen![86] I shall make you see that there is a threefold Buddha body of your own self-natures in your own physical bodies. The threefold Buddha body is produced from your own natures.

"What is the pure *Dharmakāya* Buddha? Good friends, although the nature of people in this world is from the outset pure in itself, the ten thousand things are all within their own natures. If people think of all the evil[87] things, then they will practice evil; if they think of all the good things, then they will practice good. Thus it is clear that in this way all the dharmas are within your own natures, yet your own na-

---

[82] T14, p. 541a.
[83] Another name for the *Fan-wang ching Lu-she-na fo-shuo p'u-sa hsin-ti chieh p'in ti-shih*, T24, pp. 997–1010. The quotation is from ch. 10, pt. 2 (p. 1003c).
[84] Note is in original text.
[85] The Tun-huang text has: "in your own dharma natures." *Kōshōji*, p. 29, omits the "dharma," and this has been followed in the translation.
[86] The four characters *ju shan-chih-shih* are superfluous, and have been omitted.
[87] The word "evil" is supplied from the *Kōshōji* edition, p. 30.

tures are always pure. The sun and the moon are always bright, yet if they are covered by clouds, although above they are bright, below they are darkened, and the sun, moon, stars, and planets cannot be seen clearly. But if suddenly the wind of wisdom should blow and roll away the clouds and mists, all forms in the universe appear at once. The purity of the nature of man in this world is like the blue sky; wisdom is like the sun, knowledge like the moon. Although knowledge and wisdom are always clear, if you cling to external environments, the floating clouds of false thoughts will create a cover, and your own natures cannot become clear. Therefore, if you meet a good teacher, open up the true Dharma, and waft aside your delusions and errors; inside and outside will become clear. Within your own natures the ten thousand things will all appear, for all things of themselves are within your own natures. Given a name, this is the pure *Dharmakāya* Buddha.[88] Taking refuge in oneself is to cast aside all actions that are not good; this is known as taking refuge.[89]

"What are the ten thousand hundred billion *Nirmāṇakāya* Buddhas? If you do not think, then your nature is empty; if you do think, then you yourself will change. If you think of evil things then you will change and enter hell; if you think of good things then you will change and enter heaven. [If you think of] harm you will change and become a beast; [if you think of] compassion you will change and become a Bodhisattva. [If you think of] intuitive wisdom you will change and enter the upper realms; [if you think of] ignorance you will change and enter the lower quarters. The changes of your own natures are extreme, yet the deluded person is not himself conscious of this. [Successive thoughts give rise to evil and evil ways are always practiced].[90] But if a single thought of good evolves, intuitive wisdom is born. [This is called the *Nirmāṇakāya* Buddha of your own nature. What is the perfect *Sambhogakāya* Buddha?][91] As one lamp serves to dispel a thousand years of darkness, so one flash of wisdom destroys ten thousand years of ignorance. Do not think of the past; always think

[88] The text here merely reads *dharmakāya*, but by context "Buddha" must be added. See *Kōshōji*, pp. 30–31.

[89] Here there are obvious omissions and confusions in the original text. In the *Kōshōji* edition, pp. 30–31, the explanation of the *Nirmāṇakāya* Buddhas given below in the text is used in description of the phrase "to take refuge in oneself."

[90] Here again there are omissions in the Tun-huang text; this sentence has been added following *Kōshōji*, p. 31.

[91] These two sentences have been supplied from *Kōshōji*, p. 31.

of the future; if your future thoughts are always good, you may be called the *Sambhogakāya* Buddha. An instant of thought of evil will result in the destruction[92] of good which has continued a thousand years; an instant of thought of good compensates for a thousand years of evil and destruction. If from the timeless beginning future thoughts have always been good,[93] you may be called the *Sambhogakāya* Buddha. Observed from the standpoint of the *Dharmakāya*, this is none other than the *Nirmāṇakāya*.[94] When successive thoughts are good, this then is the *Sambhogakāya*. Self-awakening and self-practice, this is 'to take refuge.' Skin and flesh form the physical body; the physical body is the home. This has nothing to do with taking refuge. If, however, you awaken to the threefold body, then you have understood the cardinal meaning.

21. "Now that you have already taken refuge in the threefold body of Buddha, I shall expound to you the four great vows. Good friends, recite in unison what I say: 'I vow to save all sentient beings everywhere. I vow to cut off all the passions everywhere. I vow to study all the Buddhist teachings everywhere. I vow to achieve the unsurpassed Buddha Way.' (Recite three times.) [95]

"Good friends, when I say 'I vow to save all sentient beings everywhere,' it is not that I will save you, but that sentient beings, each with their own natures, must save themselves.[96] What is meant by 'saving yourselves with your own natures'? Despite heterodox views, passions, ignorance, and delusions, in your own physical bodies you have in yourselves the attributes of inherent enlightenment,[97] so that with correct views you can be saved. If you are awakened to correct views, the wisdom of *prajñā* will wipe away ignorance and delusion, and you all will

---

[92] The Tun-huang text has here *hsin* [mind]. Suzuki, *Tonkō shutsudo Rokuso dankyō*, p. 19, changes the text to *wang* [destruction]. *Kōshōji*, p. 32, has *mieh* [destruction]. Suzuki's rendering has been followed.

[93] The Tun-huang text has been emended to follow Ui, *Zenshū shi kenkyū*, II, 130.

[94] The text here is difficult to follow and the translation uncertain.

[95] Note is in original text.

[96] Translation uncertain. The *hsin-chung* [within the mind], in the Tun-huang text, has been regarded as superfluous.

[97] *Pen-chüeh*. This term derives from the *Ta-ch'eng ch'i-hsin lun*, T32, p. 576b. It is used in contradistinction to *shih-chüeh*, the initial enlightenment, which is gained by means of practice, and which enables one to awaken to the ultimate reality. Since initial enlightenment exists because of original enlightenment, the two separate terms are used; however, once awakening is gained through practice, the two become the same. See *Kokuyaku daizōkyō*, Rombu, V, 14, n. 4.

save yourselves. If false views come, with correct views you will be saved; if delusion comes, with awakening you will be saved; if ignorance comes, with wisdom you will be saved; if evil comes, with good you will be saved; if the passions come, with *bodhi* you will be saved. Being saved in this way is known as true salvation.

" 'I vow to cut off all the passions everywhere' is, with your own minds to cast aside the unreal and the false. 'I vow to study all the Buddhist teachings everywhere' is to study the unsurpassed true Dharma. 'I vow to achieve the unsurpassed Buddha Way' is always to act humbly, to practice reverence for all things, to separate oneself from erroneous attachments, and to awaken to the wisdom of *prajñā*. When delusions are cast aside you are self-enlightened, achieve the Buddha Way, and put into practice the power of the vows.

22. "Now that I have finished speaking of the four vows, I shall give you the formless repentance and destroy[98] the crimes of the three realms."

The Master said: "Good friends, if in past thoughts, present thoughts, and future thoughts, if in successive thoughts, you are not stained by delusion and you at once[99] cast aside with your own natures previous bad actions, this is seeking forgiveness. If in past thoughts, future thoughts, and present thoughts, if in successive thoughts, you are not[100] stained by ignorance, and cast aside forever your previous arrogant minds, this is called seeking forgiveness with your own natures. If in past thoughts, present thoughts,[101] and future thoughts, if in successive thoughts, you are not stained by jealousy and cast aside with your own natures previous feelings of jealousy, this is seeking forgiveness.[102] (Recite the above three times.) [103]

"Good friends, what is repentance (*ch'an-hui*)? 'Seeking forgiveness' (*ch'an*)[104] is to do nothing[105] throughout your life. 'Repentance' (*hui*)

[98] This word is supplied from *Kōshōji*, p. 25.
[99] We have here a succession of seven-character clauses, the third of which is missing one character. This has been left as a lacuna. The construction and wording, however, are parallel with the last clause of the paragraph.
[100] The negative is supplied from *Kōshōji*, p. 25.
[101] This word is supplied from *Kōshōji*, p. 25.
[102] The *Kōshōji* text, p. 26, concludes with: "The above is the formless repentance."
[103] Note in original text.
[104] This word supplied from *Kōshōji*, p. 26.
[105] The translation follows the Tun-huang text here. The *Kōshōji* edition, p. 26, amplifies the text, and although containing no parallel passage, indicates that one is never

is to know the mistakes and evil actions you have perpetrated up to now, and never to let them be apart from the mind. It is useless to make a confession in words before the Buddhas. In my teaching, forever to engage in no action[106] is called repentance.

23. "Having finished repentance, I shall give you the formless precepts of the three refuges."

The Master said: "Good friends, 'take refuge in enlightenment [the Buddha], the most honored among two-legged beings; take refuge in the truth [the Dharma], the most noble [doctrine which sets people] free from the desires; take refuge in purity [the Sangha], the most honored among sentient beings.'[107] From now on you will call enlightenment[108] your master and will not rely on other teachings which are deluded and heretical. Always prove it clearly yourselves with the three treasures of your own natures.[109] Good friends, I urge you to take refuge in the three treasures in your own natures. The Buddha is enlightenment, the Dharma is truth, and the Sangha is purity. If in your own minds you take refuge in enlightenment [the Buddha], heterodoxies and delusions are not produced, you have no desires and are content with yourself as you are, and stand apart from the passions and physical wants. Therefore Buddha is called 'most honored among two-legged beings.' If in your own mind you rely on truth [the Dharma], then, because there is no falseness in successive thoughts, there will be no attachments. Since there will be no attachments, [the Dharma] is called 'the most noble [doctrine which sets people] free from the desires.' If in your own mind you rely on purity [the Sangha], although all the passions and false thoughts are within your own natures, your natures are not stained. Therefore, [the Sangha] is called 'most honored among sentient beings.' The ordinary man does not[110] understand

again to "do evil" throughout one's life. This may well have been the meaning intended by the author of the present text.

[106] Here, again, the *Kōshōji* text indicates that one "is never again to do evil."

[107] The three refuges given above are to be found, also in the same form, in *Ch'ih-hsiu Pai-chang ch'ing-kuei*, T48, p. 1137c. For other interpretations of the text see Chan, *The Platform Scripture*, p. 67, and Lu, *Ch'an and Zen Teachings*, series 3, p. 53.

[108] The Tun-huang text has: "You will call Buddha your Master." The translation follows *Kōshōji*, p. 28.

[109] The Tun-huang text is corrupt, but might be rendered: "I beg of you to illumine with compassion the three treasures of your own natures." Here, however, the *Kōshōji* version, p. 28, appears more apt and has been followed in the translation.

[110] Negative supplied from *Kōshōji*, p. 28.

146 The Platform Sutra

and from day to day receives the precepts of the three refuges. If he says he relies on the Buddha, where is that Buddha? If he doesn't see the Buddha then he has nothing on which to rely. If he has nothing on which to rely, then what he says is deluded.[111]

"Good friends, each of you must observe well for himself. Do not mistakenly use your minds! The sutras say to take refuge in the Buddha within yourselves; they do not say to rely on other Buddhas. If you do not rely upon your own natures, there is nothing else on which to rely.

24. "Now that all of you have yourselves devoutly taken refuge in the three treasures, I shall expound to you on the doctrine of the Mahā-prajñāpāramitā (Mo-ho-pan-lo-po-lo-mi). Good friends, although you recite it, you do not understand its meaning, so I shall explain. Listen every one of you! Mahāprajñāpāramitā is an Indian Sanskrit term; in Chinese it means the Great Perfection of Wisdom, reaching the other shore. This Dharma must be practiced; it has nothing to do with recitations. If you recite it and do not practice it, it will be like an illusion or a phantom. The Dharma body of the practicer is the equivalent of the Buddha.[112]

"What is Mo-ho? Mo-ho is 'great.' The capacity of the mind is broad and huge, like the vast sky.[113] Do not sit with a mind fixed on emptiness. If you do you will fall into a neutral kind of emptiness. Emptiness includes the sun, moon, stars, and planets, the great earth, mountains and rivers, all trees and grasses, bad men and good men, bad things and good things, heaven and hell; they are all in the midst of emptiness. The emptiness of human nature is also like this.

25. "Self-nature contains the ten thousand things—this is 'great.' The ten thousand things are[114] all in self-nature. Although you see all men

[111] I.e., his own statement that he "relies on the Buddha."
[112] The Kōshōji version, p. 34, of the above passage reads: "You must practice completely with the mind; it has nothing to do with recitations. If you recite and do not practice with the mind, it will be like an illusion, a phantom, the dew, or a flash of lightning. If you recite and practice with the mind, mind and mouth will correspond. Your original nature is Buddha; apart from your nature there is no other Buddha."
[113] The Kōshōji text, p. 34, is greatly enlarged at this point. In explanation of the passage following it reads: "All the many Buddha-lands are the same as the empty sky. The marvelous nature of man is basically empty; there is not one single thing to obtain. The true emptiness of self-nature is also like this. Good friends, you listen to my explanation of emptiness and then you stick to emptiness."
[114] The Kōshōji edition, at this point, is missing one leaf, containing 462 characters.

and non-men,[115] evil and good, evil things and good things, you must not throw them aside, nor must you cling to them, nor must you be stained by them, but you must regard them as being just like the empty sky. This is what is meant by 'great.' This is the practice of *mo-ho*. The deluded person merely recites; the wise man practices[116] with his mind. There are deluded men who make their minds empty and do not think, and to this they give the name of 'great.' This, too, is wrong. The capacity of the mind is vast and wide,[117] but when there is no practice it is small. Do not merely speak of emptiness with the mouth and fail to practice it. A person such as this is not a disciple of mine.

26. "What is *prajñā? Prajñā* is wisdom (*chih-hui*). When at all times successive thoughts contain no ignorance, and you always practice wisdom, this is known as the practice of *prajñā*. If but one instant of thought contains ignorance, then *prajñā* is cut off; but if one instant of thought contains wisdom, then *prajñā* is produced. Within the mind there is always ignorance. [People] themselves say: "I practice *prajñā*," but it has neither shape nor form. This, then, is the nature of wisdom.[118]

"What is *po-lo-mi-to (pāramitā)*? This is the Indian Sanskrit pronunciation and means 'other-shore-reached.' When its meaning is understood you are apart from birth and destruction. When you are attached to environment, birth and destruction arise. Take waves rising on the water—they are something that occurs on 'this' shore. Being apart from environment and putting an end to birth and destruction is like going along with the flow of the water. Thus it is called 'reaching the other shore,' in other words, *pāramitā*. The deluded person recites it; the wise man practices with the mind. If you have delusion [in

Suzuki has supplemented his text from the so-called *Kan'ei* edition of 1631, a Tokugawa reprint of the *Kōshōji* edition, which includes the missing leaf.

[115] *Amanuṣya*. Variously described as beings other than those of the human race; heavenly beings, mythical animals, etc.

[116] This word supplied from the *Kan'ei* edition. See *Kōshōji*, p. 34.

[117] This word supplied from the *Kan'ei* edition. See *Kōshōji*, p. 34.

[118] Beginning with "within the mind there is always ignorance," the text is corrupt and obviously has been miscopied. The *Kan'ei* edition (see *Kōshōji*, p. 36) reads: "People are deluded and do not see *prajñā*. They speak of *prajñā* with the mouth, but in their minds they are constantly ignorant. They themselves say: 'I am practicing *prajñā*,' and in consecutive thoughts they speak of emptiness, yet they do not know the true emptiness. *Prajñā* has no shape and form. This, then, is the mind of widsom."

your mind] when you recite it, the very existence of this delusion is not a true existence. If in successive thoughts you practice it, this is called true existence. Those who awaken to this Dharma have awakened to the Dharma of *prajñā* and are practicing the *prajñā* practice. If you do not practice it you are an ordinary person; if you practice for one instant of thought, your Dharma body[119] will be the same as the Buddha's. Good friends, the very passions are themselves enlightenment (*bodhi*).[120] When past thoughts are deluded, this is the common man; when future thoughts are awakened to, this is Buddha.[121]

"Good friends, the *Mahāprajñāpāramitā*[122] is the most honored, the supreme, the foremost. It does not stay, it does not leave, nor does it come, and all the Buddhas of the three worlds issue from it. With great wisdom it leads to the other shore and destroys the passions and the troubles of the five skandhas. Since it is the most honored, the supreme, the foremost, if you praise the supreme Dharma and practice according to it, you will certainly become Buddha. Not leaving, not staying, not going or coming, with the identity of wisdom and meditation, and unstained in all things, the various Buddhas of the three worlds issue forth from it,[123] and change the three poisons[124] into discipline, meditation, and wisdom.

27. "Good friends, this teaching of mine [derives] from the eighty-four thousand wisdoms.[125] Why is this so? Because there are eighty-four thousand passions in this world. If the passions are done away with, *prajñā* is always there, and is not apart from your own nature. If you awaken to this Dharma you will have no thoughts, no recollections, no

---

[119] The *Tsung-pao* edition, ⊤48, p. 350b, changes "Dharma body" to "your own body." The *Kan'ei* edition (*Kōshōji*, p. 36) follows the Tun-huang text.

[120] The same concept is found frequently, although often with different wording, throughout Ch'an works. It appears in the *Shih-ssu k'o-sung*, by Pao-chih ho-shang (418–514), contained in *Ching-te ch'uan-teng lu*, ⊤51, p. 451a; in the *Li-tai fa-pao chi*, ⊤51, p. 180c; and in the *Ch'uan-hsin fa-yao*, ⊤48, p. 361a, and elsewhere.

[121] The *Kan'ei* edition (*Kōshōji*, p. 36) continues the thought: "When past thoughts adhere to the environment, they are the passions; when future thoughts are apart from the environment, they are enlightenment (*bodhi*)."

[122] See *Shen-hui yü-lu* (Suzuki text, p. 31; Hu Shih, *Shen-hui ho-shang i-chi*, pp. 180–81; Gernet, *Entretiens* . . . , p. 99) where the following concepts are expressed in almost identical wording.

[123] The above passage is highly repetitive and may well represent an error on the part of the copyist. *Kōshōji*, p. 37, gives a greatly simplified version.

[124] Concupiscence, anger, and ignorance.

[125] *Kōshōji*, p. 37, reads here: "In this teaching of mine, from one [realization of] *prajñā* the eighty-four thousand wisdoms are produced."

attachments. Do not depart from deceptions and errors;[126] for they of themselves are the nature of True Reality. When all things are illumined by wisdom and there is neither grasping nor throwing away, then you can see into your own nature and gain the Buddha Way.

28. "Good friends, if you wish to enter the most profound Dharma realm of the *prajñā samādhi,* you must straightforwardly practice the *prajñāpāramitā.* With only the one volume of the Diamond Sutra you may see into your own natures and enter into the *prajñā samādhi.* You will surely understand that the merit of such a person is without bounds. In the sutras it is clearly praised and there is no need for me to elaborate. It is the Dharma of the Supreme Way that is expounded for men of great wisdom and high capacities. Should a man of small capability for knowledge hear this Dharma, faith would not be produced in his mind. Why is this so? Should a great dragon deluge the earth (Jambūdvīpa) with[127] a great rain, [then cities, towns, and villages would all be washed away] [128] like floating grass and leaves. But should this great rain fall in the great ocean, its waters would neither increase nor lessen.

"Should a person of the Mahāyāna hear the Diamond Sutra, his mind will open and he will gain awakening. Therefore we can say that in the original nature itself the wisdom of *prajñā* exists, and that by using this wisdom yourself and illuminating with it, there is no need to depend on written words.[129] It is as though the rain waters did not come from heaven,[130] but from the beginning the dragon king draws up the

[126] *Kōshōji,* p. 37, has changed the Tun-huang text "do not depart from deceptions and errors" to "do not give rise to deceptions and errors." A thought similar to the Tun-huang version, however, is to be found in the *Cheng-tao ko,* attributed to Hsüan-chüeh (665–713), contained in *Ching-te ch'uan-teng lu,* T51, p. 460a: "Do not discard deluded thoughts, do not seek the truth; the true nature of ignorance is itself the Buddha nature." Thus, the change made in the *Kōshōji* edition can, perhaps, be considered unjustified.

[127] Chan, *The Platform Scripture,* pp. 178–79, n. 114, changes *i* (= *yü,* on) to *fang* (to spread), to correspond with the *fang* in the next sentence, and translates (p. 75): "Suppose the great dragon causes a heavy rain to fall and the rain spreads over Jambūdvīpa." I prefer to read the character in both instances as *yü.* Since Jambūdvīpa is the world as known to the Indians, any rain that falls would necessarily fall *on* Jambūdvīpa. There is no need for it to spread anywhere.

[128] A textual omission. Supplied from *Kōshōji,* p. 38.

[129] The above passage is quoted in the *Tsung-ching lu,* T48, p. 498c.

[130] Following *Kōshōji,* p. 38, *wu* [not] has been changed to *t'ien* [heaven]. Chan, *The Platform Scripture,* p. 75 and 179, n. 118, sees no reason for making the change,

water from the rivers and seas and covers all beings, trees and grasses, things sentient and nonsentient, with its wetness. All these waters flow together and enter into the great sea, and the sea gathers them together and combines them into one. So it is with the *prajñā* wisdom of the original natures of sentient beings.

29. "When people of shallow capacity hear the Sudden Doctrine being preached they are like the naturally shallow-rooted plants on this earth, which, after a deluge of rain, are all beaten down and cannot continue their growth. People of shallow capacity are like such plants. Although these people have *prajñā* wisdom and are not different from men of great knowledge, why is it that even though they hear the Dharma they are not awakened? It is because the obstructions of their heterodox views are heavy and the passions deep-rooted. It is like the times when great clouds cover the sun; unless the wind blows the sun will not appear. There is no large and small in *prajñā* wisdom. Because all sentient beings have of themselves deluded minds, they seek the Buddha by external practice, and are unable to awaken to their own natures. But even these people of shallow capacity, if they hear the Sudden Doctrine, and do not place their trust in external practices, but only in their own minds always raise correct views in regard to their own original natures; even these sentient beings, filled with passions and troubles,[131] will at once gain awakening. It is like the great sea which gathers all the flowing streams, and merges together the small waters and the large waters into one. This is seeing into your own nature. [Such a person] does not abide either inside or outside; he is free to come or go. Readily he casts aside the mind that clings [to things], and there is no obstruction to his passage. If in the mind this practice is carried out, then [your own nature] is no different from the *prajñā-pāramitā.* [132]

30. "All the sutras and written words, Hīnayāna, Mahāyāna, the twelve

and translates: "It is like the rain which does not really come from nothing. Originally the Dragon King himself draws this water from the ocean . . ."

[131] The parallel passage in the *Kōshōji* edition, p. 39, reads: "Passions and troubles can never stain them."

[132] The text contains the word "sutra" following *prajñāpāramitā. Kōshōji,* p. 39, and the Tsung-pao edition, T48, p. 351a, both have here "Prajñā Sutra." Chan, *The Platform Scripture,* p. 77, believes this refers specifically to the Diamond Sutra, as does Lu, *Ch'an and Zen Teachings,* ser. 3, p. 34. Since the text is dealing specifically with the *prajñā-pāramitā* (secs. 26–29), I follow the interpretation adopted by Ui, *Zenshū shi kenkyū,* II, 140, and delete the word "sutra" from the text.

divisions of the canon,[133] all have been postulated by men. Because of the nature of wisdom [within man] it has been possible, therefore, to postulate them. If we were without this wisdom,[134] all things would, from the outset, have no existence in themselves. Therefore it is clear that all things were originally given rise to by man, and that all the sutras exist because they are spoken by man. Among men there are the stupid and the wise. The stupid are insignificant, the wise, great men.[135] Should deluded people ask the wise, the wise will expound the Dharma for the stupid and enable them to understand and gain a deep awakening. If the deluded person understands and his mind is awakened, then there is no difference between him and the man of wisdom. Therefore we know that, unawakened, even a Buddha is a sentient being,[136] and that even a sentient being, if he is awakened in an instant of thought, is[137] a Buddha.[138] And thus we know that the ten thousand dharmas are all within our own minds. Why not from your own natures make the original nature of True Reality suddenly appear? The *P'u-sa-chieh ching* says: 'From the outset our own nature is pure.'[139] If we perceive the mind[140] and see our own natures, then of ourselves we have achieved the Buddha Way. 'At once, suddenly, we regain our original mind.'[141]

31. "Good friends, when I was at Priest Jen's place, hearing it [the Diamond Sutra][142] just once, I immediately gained the great awak-

[133] The twelve varieties in which Buddhism is preached. See Leon Hurvitz, "Chih-i," *Mélanges Chinois et Bouddhiques*, XII (1962), Appendix C, pp. 337–38.

[134] *Kōshōji*, p. 39, reads here: "If there were no men in this world." The Tun-huang text scarcely makes sense at this point.

[135] "Insignificant" and "great" correspond to Hīnayāna and Mahāyāna; i.e., Hīnayāna is the teaching for men of small talent; Mahāyāna for those of great capabilities.

[136] The same concept is found in Pao-chih's *Ta-ch'eng tsan* (in *Ching-te ch'uan-teng lu*, T51, p. 449b); in the *Shen-hui yü-lu* (Suzuki text, p. 18; Hu Shih, *Shen-hui ho-shang i-chi*, p. 124; Gernet, *Entretiens . . .* , p. 45; and in the *Ch'uan-hsin fa-yao*, T48, p. 379c. The wording differs in each instance.

[137] Following *Kōshōji*, p. 39, the negative in the original text is omitted.

[138] See sec. 35, where the same thought is expressed.

[139] The same quotation appears in sec. 19, except that the *wo* [our], not in the original sutra, is added here.

[140] *Shih-hsin*. This term is found in the *Ssu-shih-erh chang ching*, T17, p. 722, where we read: "The Buddha said: 'One who bids his parents farewell and retires from the world, *perceives the mind*, penetrates the basis, and understands the Dharma of *wu-wei* is called *śramāna*.' " The term is not to be found, however, in the version of this sutra contained in the *Pao-lin chuan*, I, 6–29.

[141] Quotation from the Vimalakīrti Sutra. The identical quotation is to be found in sec. 19.

[142] The autobiography (sec. 2) states that Hui-neng was enlightened on hearing the Diamond Sutra before going to see the Fifth Patriarch.

152   *The Platform Sutra*

ening and saw suddenly that True Reality was my original nature.
Therefore, I have taken this teaching[143] and, passing it on to later generations, shall make you students of the Way suddenly awaken to enlightenment, and let each of you see into your own minds,[144] and
suddenly awaken to your own original natures. If you cannot[145] gain
enlightenment for yourselves, you must seek a great teacher to show
you the way to see into your own self-natures. What is a great teacher?
He is a man who understands at once that the Dharma of the Supreme
Vehicle is indeed the correct path. This is a great teacher. This is the
great causal event,[146] the so-called conversion which will enable you to
see Buddha. All the good dharmas are activated by a great teacher.
Therefore, although[147] the Buddhas of the three worlds and all the
twelve divisions of the canon are from the beginning within the nature
of man, if he cannot gain awakening with his own nature, he must
obtain a good teacher to show him how to see into his own self-nature.
But if you awaken by yourself, do not rely on teachers outside. If you
try to seek a teacher outside and hope to obtain deliverance, you will
find it impossible. If you have recognized the good teacher within your
own mind, you have already obtained deliverance. If you are deluded
in your own mind and harbor erroneous thoughts and contrary concepts, even though you go to an outside teacher [you will not be able
to obtain salvation].[148] If you are not able to obtain self-awakening,
you must give rise to *prajñā* and illuminate with it, and then in one
instant false thoughts will be destroyed. Once you have awakened to

[143] Here the Tun-huang text is difficult to read, and *Kōshōji*, p. 40, has been followed.
[144] *Kuan-hsin*. For this term, which may well be of Northern Ch'an origin, see *Kuan-
hsin lun*. It is contained in *Shōshitsu rokumon* under the title *P'o-hsiang lun* (T48, pp.
366c–69c). The Tun-huang manuscript version is reproduced in T85, pp. 1270–73
(S2595), and S5532 represents an additional unpublished fragment of the same work.
A collection of five different versions appears in D. T. Suzuki, *Daruma no zempō to
shisō oyobi sono ta*, pp. 184–232. Kamio Kazuharu, "Kanshin ron shikō," *Shūkyō kenkyū*, new ser., IX (no. 5, September, 1932), 102, points out that in Hui-lin's *I-ch'ieh
ching yin-i*, T54, p. 932a, the statement is made that the *Kuan-hsin lun* was written by
Shen-hsiu the leader of the Northern School of Ch'an. Suzuki in the above mentioned
work (pp. 176–77) does not feel that the evidence is sufficient to warrant this attribution. Yabuki Keiki, *Meisha yoin kaisetsu*, pp. 543–60, and Sekiguchi Shindai, *Daruma
daishi no kenkyū*, pp. 217–34, on the other hand, feel that from the contents of the
work, and other factors, the attribution of the work to Northern Ch'an is justifiable.
[145] Negative supplied from *Kōshōji*, p. 40.
[146] The great event of the appearance of a Buddha in this world. Drawn from the
Lotus Sutra, Fang-pien p'in, T8, p. 7a, where the term appears as *i-ta-shih yin-yüan*.
[147] The Tun-huang text has here *yün* [to say]. It has been taken to mean *sui-yün*
[although].
[148] This clause has been supplied from *Kōshōji*, p. 40.

the fact that you yourself are your own true good teacher, in one awakening you will know the Buddha. If, standing upon your own nature and mind, you illuminate with wisdom and make inside and outside clear, you will know your own original mind. If you know your original mind, this then is deliverance. Once you have attained deliverance this then is the *prajñā samādhi*. If you have awakened to the *prajñā samādhi*, this then is no-thought.[149] What is no-thought? The Dharma of no-thought means: even though you see all things, you do not attach to them, but, always keeping your own nature pure, cause the six thieves[150] to exit through the six gates.[151] Even though you are in the midst of the six dusts,[152] you do not stand apart from them, yet are not stained by them, and are free to come and go. This is the *prajñā samādhi,* and being free and having achieved release is known as the practice of no-thought. If you do not think of the myriad things, but always cause your thoughts to be cut off, you will be bound in the Dharma. This is known as a biased view. If you awaken to the Dharma of no-thought, you will penetrate into all things thoroughly, and will see the realm of the Buddha. If you awaken to the sudden doctrine of no-thought, you will have reached the status of the Buddha.

32. "Good friends, those in later generations who obtain my teaching[153] will always see that my Dharma body is not apart from where they are. Good friends, take this doctrine of the Sudden Teaching, look at it and practice it together, fix your resolve on it, and receive and guard it. Because it is tantamount to serving the Buddha, if for all your lives you receive and guard it and do not retrogress, you will enter into the ranks of the sacred. Now I should like to hand it on. But from the past the Dharma has been handed down in silence; only when the great resolve has been made and there has been no retrogression from enlightenment (*bodhi*),[154] then should it be passed on. When you meet people whose understanding is not the same as yours and whose resolve is not deter-

---

[149] See *Shen-hui yü-lu* (Suzuki text, pp. 16–17, 23). See also sec. 13.
[150] *Liu-tse.* The six fields of the senses (*cauras*): seeing, hearing, smelling, tasting, feeling, and discerning. The *Kōshōji,* p. 41, has *liu-shih* [six consciousnesses].
[151] *Liu-men.* The six sense organs (*indriyas*): eyes, ears, nose, tongue, body, and mind.
[152] *Liu-ch'en.* The six qualities produced by the objects and organs of sense (*gunas*): sight, sound, smell, taste, touch, and idea.
[153] Tun-huang reads: "Those in later generations who awaken to the Dharma." *Kōshōji,* p. 41, has been followed.
[154] This passage is not in the *Kōshōji* edition. "Retrogression from *bodhi*" scarcely makes sense, and may well represent a copyist's error.

mined, never recklessly demonstrate the teaching to them. If you do so you will do them harm, and in any event it will be of no value whatsoever. If you happen to meet people who do not understand and who despise this teaching, for a hundred kalpas, ten thousand kalpas, a thousand lives, Buddhism[155] will be extirpated."

33. The Master said: "Good friends, listen. I will preach to you a verse of formlessness. It will cause the destruction of the crimes of you deluded people. It is also called the verse for destroying crimes.[156]

"The verse says:

The ignorant person practices seeking future happiness,[157] and does not practice the Way,
And says that to practice seeking future happiness *is* the Way.
Though he hopes that almsgiving and offerings will bring boundless happiness,
As before, in his mind the three karmas are created.[158]
If you wish to destroy your crimes by practicing seeking future happiness,
Even though in a future life you obtain this happiness, the crime will still be left.[159]
If you can, in your mind cast aside the cause of your crimes,
Then each of you, within your own natures, will truly repent.
If you awaken to the Mahāyāna and truly repent,
Evil being removed and good achieved, you will truly attain to crimelessness.
If students of the Way observe their own selves well,[160]
They will be the same as those already awakened.

[155] Ui, *Zenshū shi kenkyū*, II, 144, considers *hsing* [nature] here to be a homophone for *hsing* [family name]. Thus, *Fo-chung hsing* means merely "Buddhists." *Kōshōji*, p. 42, and later texts all interpret this phrase as "the nature of the Buddha seed." Ui's interpretation has been followed.
[156] This phrase may well be a later interpolation.
[157] *Hsiu-fu*. The practice which seeks the rewards of the field of blessings. See p. 128, n. 22.
[158] The Tun-huang text reads for this passage: *hsin-chung san-yeh yüan-lai tsai* [as before the three karmas exist within the mind]. The *tsai*, however, is obviously in error, since it does not rhyme with the *tao* [Way], above in the verse. *Kōshōji*, p. 42, has thus been followed. See Bernhard Karlgren, *Grammata Serica Recensa, BMFEA*, XXIX (1957), 272; the T'ang rhyme is *d'âu . . . ts'âu*. The three karmas are used as a Ch'an technical term, in the sense of the three karmas of deed, word, and thought. *Kōshōji*, p. 42, changes the three karmas to the three evil ways (hell, hungry ghosts, and beasts).
[159] The Tun-huang version of this last line is again obviously in error, as the last character *tsao* [to make] does not rhyme with the *hai* [sea; a homophone for *hai* (repent)], below in the verse. *Kōshōji*, p. 42, has been followed.
[160] Compare *Kōshōji*, p. 42: "If students of the Way always observe their own self-natures."

I [161] am causing this Sudden Teaching to be transmitted,
And one who aspires to learn it will become one with me.
If in the future you wish to seek your original body,[162]
Wash out the evil causes of the three poisons from within your minds.
Work hard to practice the Way; do not be absent-minded.
If you spend your time in vain your whole life will soon be forfeited.
If you encounter the teaching of the Mahāyāna Sudden Doctrine,
Join your palms in devotion and sincerity, and strive earnestly to reach it."

When the Master had finished preaching, the Prefect[163] Wei, the government officials, and the monks and laymen uttered words of praise: "What a boundless teaching! This we have never heard before!"

34. The Prefect Wei bowed deeply and said: "Your exposition of the Dharma was certainly amazing. Right now I have some small doubts that I should like to ask you about, and hope that out of your great compassion you will resolve them for me."

The Master said: "If you have doubts, then ask. There is no need to repeat yourself." [164]

The prefect asked: "Isn't the Master's Dharma the essentials of the teaching of the First Patriarch, the Indian Bodhidharma?"

The Master said: "Yes."

[The prefect said:] "I have heard that, when Bodhidharma was converting Emperor Wu of Liang, the emperor asked Bodhidharma: 'I have spent my whole life up to now building temples, giving alms, and making offerings. Have I gained merit or not?' and that Bodhidharma answered saying: 'No merit.' Then the emperor was greatly disappointed and banished Bodhidharma across the border. I don't understand this story and beg of you to explain it."

The Sixth Patriarch said: "Indeed he gained no merit. Do not doubt the words of Bodhidharma. The emperor was attached to a heterodox way and did not know the true Dharma." [165]

---

[161] Here the term *ta-shih* [Great Master] is used in reference to Hui-neng and is an appellation which he would by no means apply to himself, indicating that this verse was written by his disciples or later followers of the school.

[162] Compare *Kōshōji*, p. 43: ". . . seek the *Dharmakāya*."

[163] Wei, in the earlier portions of the text, is identified as prefect. Here he is spoken to with the respectful form of address, *shih-chün*. For the sake of uniformity, his original title is retained in the translation.

[164] It may be assumed that out of politeness the prefect has been asking the Master numerous times for assistance in the resolution of his doubts.

[165] This story also appears in the *P'u-t'i-ta-mo Nan-tsung ting shih-fei lun*, Hu Shih,

The prefect asked: "Why did he have no merit?"

The Master said: "Building temples, giving alms, and making offerings are merely the practice of seeking after blessings. One cannot make merit with blessings. Merit[166] is in the *Dharmakāya*, not in the field of blessings. In Dharma nature itself there is merit (*kung-te*). [Seeing into your own nature is *kung*];[167] straightforward mind is *te*.[168] Inwardly, see[169] the Buddha nature; outwardly, practice reverence. If you make light of all men and do not cut off the ego, then you yourself will be without merit. If your own nature is false, the Dharma body is without merit.[170] If in successive thoughts there is virtuous practice and there is straightforward mind, merit will not be held lightly and practice will always be reverent. Your own practice with the body is *kung;* your own practice with the mind is *te*. Merit is created from the mind; blessings and merit are different. The Emperor Wu did not understand the true principle; hence the Patriarch was not in the wrong."

35. The prefect bowed deeply and asked: "I notice that some monks and laymen always invoke the Buddha Amitābha and desire to be reborn in the West. I beg of you to explain whether one can be born there or not, and thus resolve my doubts."

The Master said: "Prefect, listen and I shall explain things for you. At Śrāvastī the World-honored One preached of the Western Land in order to convert people, and it is clearly stated in the sutra, '[The Western Land] is not far.'[171] It was only for the sake of people of inferior capacity that the Buddha spoke of farness; to speak of nearness[172] is only for those of superior attainments. Although in man there are nat-

Shen-hui ho-shang i-chi, p. 160; Gernet, *Entretiens* . . . , p. 83. See Introduction, p. 27.

[166] Supplied from *Kōshōji*, p. 44.

[167] *Ibid.*

[168] The Tun-huang text is corrupt at this point. What apparently is intended is *p'ing-teng chih-hsin* [straightforward mind], as found later in this passage. See Vimalakīrti Sutra, T14, p. 542c: "Straightforward mind is the place of practice."

[169] Following Suzuki, *Tonkō shutsudo Rokuso dankyō*, p. 34, *nei chien* [within, see] has been added at the beginning of the clause.

[170] This contradicts the statement above: "Merit is in the *Dharmakāya* . . ." *Kōshōji*, p. 45, changes the passage completely: "If your own nature is false and unreal, then you yourself have no merit."

[171] *Kuan-wu-liang-shou ching*, T12, p. 341c.

[172] The farness and nearness are in reverse order in the Tun-huang text. Change based on *Kōshōji*, p. 45.

urally two types, in the Dharma there is no inequality.[173] In delusion and awakening there is a difference, as may be seen in slowness and fastness of understanding. The deluded person concentrates on Buddha and wishes to be born in the other land; the awakened person makes pure his own mind. Therefore the Buddha said: 'In accordance with the purity of the mind the Buddha land is pure.'[174]

"Prefect, people of the East [China], just by making the mind pure, are without crime; people of the West [The Pure Land of the West], if their minds are not pure, are guilty of a crime. The deluded person wishes to be born in the East[175] or West, [for the enlightened person][176] any land is just the same. If only the mind has no impurity, the Western Land is not far. If the mind gives rise to impurities, even though you invoke the Buddha and seek to be reborn [in the West], it will be difficult to reach. If you eliminate the ten evils[177] you will proceed one hundred thousand li; if you do away with the eight improper practices[178] you will pass across eight thousand li.[179] But if you practice straightforward mind, you will arrive there in an instant.

"Prefect, practice only the ten virtues. Why should you seek rebirth [in the Western Land]? If you do not cut off the ten evils, what Buddha can you ask to come welcome you? If you awaken to the sudden Dharma of birthlessness, you will see the Western Land in an instant. If you do not awaken to the Sudden Teaching of Mahāyāna, even if

---

[173] A character has been dropped in the Tun-huang version. Following Ui, *Zenshū shi kenkyū*, II, 137, *t'ung* [same] has been supplied. Suzuki, *Tonkō shutsudo Rokuso dankyō*, p. 34, inserts *i* [oneness].

[174] Vimalakīrti Sutra, T14, p. 538c.

[175] There is no logical reason why the East should be brought in at this point. It may best be regarded as merely a figure of speech, a somewhat cynical comment on the adherence to a delusion in which superficial distinctions of direction are considered important.

[176] Supplied from *Kōshōji*, p. 46. Compare Chan, *The Platform Scripture*, pp. 90–91, for a variant of both the text and the translation of this section.

[177] *Shih-o, Daśākuśala*: killing, stealing, adultery, lying, double-tonguedness, coarse language, filthy language, covetousness, anger, and perverted views.

[178] *Pa-hsieh*. The eight delusions and attachments that arise in opposition to the true form of the various dharmas: birth, destruction, oneness, differentiation, past, future, permanence, and cessation.

[179] The theory that the Western Paradise was located 108,000 li from China has not been found in any canonical work. The Sukhāvatīvyūha Sutra, T12, p. 346a, locates it "a hundred thousand Buddhalands to the West." There is a story, whose source I have not been able to trace, which states that from the west gate of Ch'ang-an to the east gate of Kapilavastu in 108,000 li. See *Hōbō dankyō kōkan*, III, 21b.

you concentrate on the Buddha and seek to be reborn, the road will be long. How can you hope to reach there?"

The Sixth Patriarch said: "I will move the Western Land in an instant and present it to you right before your eyes. Does the prefect wish to see it or not?"

The prefect bowed deeply: "If I can see it here, why should I be reborn there? I ask you in your compassion to make the Western Land appear for my sake. It would be wonderful."

The Master said: "There is no doubt that the Western Land can be seen here in China.[180] Now let us disperse." The assembly was amazed and did not know what to do.

The Master said: "You people assembled here, listen carefully. The physical body of man in this world is itself a city. The eyes, ears, nose, tongue, and body are the gates to the city. Outside there are five gates; inside there is the gate of consciousness. Mind is the ground; self-nature is the king. If there is self-nature, there is a king; if self-nature departs, there is no king. If there is self-nature, the body and mind exist; if self-nature departs, the body and mind [181] are destroyed. Since Buddha is made by your own nature, do not look for him outside[182] your body. If you are deluded in your own nature, Buddha is then a sentient being;[183] if you are awakened in your own nature, sentient beings are then Buddhas. Compassion is Avalokiteśvara; joyful giving is Mahāsthāmaprāpta; capacity for purity is Śākyamuni; straightforwardness is Maitreya. The false view of the self is Mount Sumeru; the perverted mind is the great sea and the passions are the waves. The poisoned mind is an evil dragon, troubles are fish and sea turtles, delusions are supernatural demons, the three poisons are hell; ignorance forms the realm of beasts, and the ten virtues are heaven. If there is no false view of the self, then Mount Sumeru will fall of itself. If the perverted mind is cast aside the ocean will dry up, and when the passions are gone the waves will subside. If the passions and harm are done away with then the dragons and fish will disappear. Let the Tathāgata of enlighten-

---

[180] The translation here is tentative. Chan, *The Platform Scripture*, p. 93, 182, n. 156, following Ui, *Zenshū shi kenkyū*, II, 148, translates T'ang [the Chinese dynasty] as "passageway." This would appear to be a quite dubious rendering. Later texts omit this passage.

[181] Supplied from *Kōshōji*, p. 47.

[182] *Ibid.*

[183] The same thought is expressed in sec. 30.

ment within your own mind-ground release the luminosity of great wisdom, shine upon the six gates, and with its purity destroy the six heavens of the world of desire (*kāmadhātu*). [If your own nature illuminates inwardly] [184] the three poisons will be cast aside and hell will at once be destroyed. If inside and outside are clear, this will be no different from the Western Land. If you don't carry out this practice, how will you be able to reach there?"

On hearing this sermon, the praising voices of those who sat before him rose to heaven, and all [185] the deluded people understood clearly. The prefect bowed deeply and said in praise: 'Excellent, excellent! We all hope that the sentient beings of the Dharma World who hear this will at once gain enlightenment."

36. The Master said: "Good friends, if you wish to practice, it is all right to do so as laymen;[186] you don't have to be in a temple. If you are in a temple but do not practice, you are like the evil-minded people of the West. If you are a layman but do practice, you are practicing the good of the people of the East. Only I beg of you, practice purity yourselves; this then is the Western Land."

The prefect asked: "Master, how should we practice as laymen? I wish you would instruct us."

The Master said: "Good friends, I shall make a formless verse for you monks and laymen. When all of you recite it and practice according to it, then you will always be in the same place as I am. The verse says:

Proficiency in preaching and proficiency in the mind,[187]

[184] The Tun-huang text is corrupt; *Kōshōji*, p. 48, has been followed.
[185] *Ying-shih*. T'ang colloquial term, meaning "all." Compare Chan, *The Platform Scripture*, p. 95.
[186] Wei Ch'ü and other members of the audience, it should be noted, were laymen.
[187] *Shuo-t'ung* and *hsin-t'ung*. The terms *tsung-t'ung* [proficiency in the doctrine] and *shuo-t'ung* [proficiency in preaching] appear in the Laṅkāvatāra Sutra, т16, p. 499b; in the *Cheng-tao ko*, т48, p. 396a (in a slightly different form); in the *Shen-hui yü-lu*, Hu Shih, *Shen-hui ho-shang i-chi*, p. 147, Gernet, *Entretiens* . . . , p. 77; and in the *Tsu-t'ang chi*, V, 75. Gernet renders the terms "compréhension doctrinale" and "compréhension discursive." In none of the examples that Gernet cites (see his *Entretiens* . . . , p. 77, n. 9) does the term *hsin-tsung* [proficiency in the mind] appear, and Gernet, considering it to be meaningless, believes it to be an error in the Tunhuang text of the *Platform Sutra*. In all editions of this work, however, including the Hsi-hsia version (see the text of the fragment housed at Ryūkoku University, contained in Nishida Tatsuo, "Seikago to Seika moji," *Chūō Ajia kodai bunken*, p. 458), the

Are like the sun and empty space.[188]
Handing down this sudden teaching alone,
Enter into the world and destroy erroneous doctrines.
Although in the teaching there is no sudden and gradual,
In delusion and awakening there is slowness and speed.[189]
In studying the teaching of the sudden doctrine,[190]
Ignorant persons cannot understand completely.
Although[191] explanations are made in ten thousand ways,
If you combine them with the principle, they become one.
Within the dark home of the passions,
The sun of wisdom must at all times shine.
Erroneous [thoughts] come because of the passions;
When correct [thoughts] come the passions are cast aside.
Use neither the erroneous nor the correct,
And with purity you will attain to complete nirvāṇa.[192]
Although enlightenment [bodhi] is originally pure,[193]
Creating the mind that seeks it is then delusion.
The pure nature exists in the midst of delusions,
With correct [thoughts] alone remove the three obstacles.[194]
If people in this world practice the Way,
There is nothing whatsoever to hinder them.
If they always make clear the guilt within themselves,
Then they will accord with the Way.
All living things of themselves possess the Way;
If you part from the Way and seek it elsewhere,

term *hsin-t'ung* is retained. Furthermore, in the *Pao-lin chuan*, III, 504, in the conversation between Bodhidharma and Yang Hsüan-chih, the compiler of the *Lo-yang chia-lan chi*, T51, pp. 999–1022, we find the term *Fo-hsin-tsung* [the basis of the Buddha mind]. Here "mind" and "basis" are roughly equivalent in meaning, the Buddha mind being the basis of Ch'an teaching. If this assumption is correct, it might justify leaving the text of the Tun-huang version uncorrected at this point.

[188] These two lines appear in the *P'u-t'i-ta-mo Nan-tsung shih-fei lun*, Hu Shih, *Shen-hui ho-shang i-chi*, p. 158; Gernet, *Entretiens* . . . , p. 81, as: "Proficiency in preaching, proficiency in the doctrine, are like the moon and empty space."

[189] Compare *Shen-hui yü-iu* (Suzuki text), p. 40: "In the resolve to turn to Buddhism there is the sudden and the gradual; in delusion and awakening there is slowness and speed."

[190] *Kōshōji*, p. 48, changes this phrase to: "In this teaching of seeing into one's own true nature."

[191] Here *hsü* [must] is used as a homophone for *sui* [although]. See Chang Hsiang, *Shih-tz'u-ch'ü-yü-tz'u hui-shih*, p. 36. This usage is found frequently in Tun-huang *pien-wen*. See also Iriya Yoshitaka, "*Tonkō hembun shū*" *kōgo goi sakuin*, p. 19.

[192] *Wu-ch'u;* aśeṣa. The extinction of both birth and death, where nothing more remains to be discarded.

[193] *Kōshōji*, p. 49, reads: "Although enlightenment is from the outset within your own nature."

[194] *San-chang*. The three *vighna*. There are several groups. The *Hōbō dankyō kōkan*, III, 16a, identifies them as the passions, deeds done, and retributions. They are described in the Nirvāṇa Sutra, T12, p. 428c.

Seek it you may, but you will not find it,
And in the end, indeed, you will be disappointed.
If you aspire to attain the Way,
Practice correctly; this is the Way.
If in yourselves you do not have the correct mind,
You will be walking in darkness and will not see the Way.
If you are a person who truly practices the Way,
Do not look at the ignorance of the world,
For if you see the wrong of people in the world,
Being wrong yourself, *you* will be evil.
The wrong in others is not your own crime,[195]
Your own wrong is of itself your crime.
Only remove the wrong in your own mind,
Crush the passions and destroy them.
If you wish to convert an ignorant person,
Then you must have expedients.
Do not allow him to have doubts,[196]
Then enlightenment (*bodhi*)[197] will appear.
From the outset the Dharma has been in the world;
Being in the world, it transcends the world.
Hence do not seek the transcendental world outside,
By discarding the present world itself.
Erroneous views are of this world,[198]
Correct views transcend this world.
If you smash completely the erroneous and the correct,
[Then the nature of enlightenment (*bodhi*) will be revealed as it is].[199]
Just this is the Sudden Teaching;
Another name for it is the Mahāyāna.
Having been deluded throughout a multitude of kalpas,
One gains awakening within an instant.[200]

37. The Master said: "Good friends, if all of you recite this verse and practice in accordance with it, even if you are a thousand li away from me, you will always be in my presence. If you do not practice it, even

---

[195] The Tun-huang text is in the affirmative: "The wrong of others is your own crime." *Kōshōji*, p. 49, has been followed.

[196] The Tun-huang text reads here: "Do not destroy his doubts for him," which is out of context. *Kōshōji*, p. 49, has been followed.

[197] *Kōshōji*, p. 49, substitutes "self-nature" for "enlightenment (*bodhi*)."

[198] The Tun-huang text reads: "Erroneous views transcend this world." *Kōshōji*, p. 50, has been followed.

[199] A clause has been dropped in the Tun-huang edition. Supplied from *Kōshōji*, p. 50.

[200] Compare *Shen-hui yü-lu* (Hu Shih, *Shen-hui ho-shang i-chi*, p. 120; Gernet, *Entretiens . . .* , p. 40): "In delusion the kalpas accumulate, but awakening is gained in an instant."

if we are face to face, we will always be a thousand li apart. Each of you yourselves must practice. The Dharma doesn't wait for you.

"Let us disperse for a while. I am going back to Mount Ts'ao-ch'i. If any of you have great doubt, come to that mountain and I shall resolve that doubt for you and show you the Buddha world as well."

All the officials, monks, and laymen who were sitting together bowed low before the Master, and there was none who did not sigh: "Wonderful, great awakening! These are things we have never heard before. Who would have expected[201] Ling-nan to be so fortunate as to have had a Buddha born there!" The entire assembly dispersed.

38. The Master went to Mount Ts'ao-ch'i and for over forty years converted the people in Shao-chou and Kuang-chou. If one were to talk about the number of his disciples, to say several thousand people, both monks and laymen, would not do it justice. If one were to talk about the pivot of his teaching, it lies in the transmission of the *Platform Sutra,* and this serves as the authority. Unless a person has received the *Platform Sutra,* he has not received the sanction. The place, date, and the name of the recipient must be made known, and these are attached to it when it is transmitted. Someone who does not have the *Platform Sutra* and the sanction is not a disciple of the Southern School.[202] Someone who has not yet obtained sanction, even though he preaches the doctrine of sudden enlightenment, does not know the basic teachings, and in the end will not be able to avoid disputes. Those who have the Dharma should practice it wholeheartedly, for disputations show a contentious mind and are a betrayal of the Way.

39. People in the world all say: "In the south Neng, in the north Hsiu,"[203] but they do not know the basic reason. The Ch'an Master Hsiu practiced as head priest of the Yü-ch'üan Temple in Tang-yang hsien in Ching-nan fu;[204] the Master Hui-neng lived at Mount Ts'ao-ch'i, thirty-five li east of the capital of Shao-chou. The Dharma is one teaching, but people are from the north and south, so Southern and

---

[201] Reading *chih* [wisdom] as *chih* [to know]. Compare Chan, *The Platform Scripture,* p. 103.
[202] Here and in the following section are the first mentions of the Southern School as such.
[203] See introduction, p. 29.
[204] Present-day Tang-yang hsien, Hupeh.

Northern Schools have been established. What is meant by 'gradual'
and 'sudden?' The Dharma itself is the same, but in seeing it there is
a slow way and a fast way. Seen slowly, it is the gradual; seen fast it
is the sudden [teaching]. Dharma is without sudden or gradual, but
some people are keen and others dull; hence the names 'sudden' and
'gradual.' "

40. The teacher Shen-hsiu one day[205] heard someone talking about the
swiftness of Hui-neng's Dharma and his direct pointing at the Way.
Hsiu then called his disciple, the monk Chih-ch'eng,[206] and said:
"You're bright and of wide knowledge. Go for me to Mount Ts'ao-ch'i,
and when you get to Hui-neng's place, make obeisance to him and just
listen. Don't tell him I've sent you, but just listen to the essentials of
his teaching, memorize them, and come back and tell me. Then I'll be
able to tell which of our understandings is the swifter. And at all costs
come back quickly or else I will be angry."

Chih-ch'eng was delighted to carry out this mission, and after about
half a month reached Mount Ts'ao-ch'i. He saw the priest Hui-neng,
made obeisance to him, and listened without saying from where he
had come. Chih-ch'eng heard the Dharma and was at once enlightened, and awakened to his original mind. Arising, he bowed low and
said: "Master, I come from Yü-ch'üan Temple, but under my teacher
Hsiu I have been unable to gain awakening. But now, on hearing your
sermon, I have awakened to my original mind. I wish that, in your
compassion, you would give me instruction."

Hui-neng said: "If you come from that place then you are probably a
spy."

[Chih-ch'eng answered: "No, I'm not."

The Master said: "Why not?"] [207]

Chih-ch'eng said: "When as yet you hadn't preached your sermon to
me I was a spy, but now that you have preached I am not." [208]

[205] Reading *ch'ang* [once] for *ch'ang* [always].
[206] His biography is unknown. He is described in *Ching-te ch'uan-teng lu*, T51, p.
237b, as a disciple of the Sixth Patriarch, and is identified as a native of T'ai-ho in Chi-
chou. Originally a disciple of Shen-hsiu, he was later converted to Southern Ch'an. We
have no way of knowing whether such a man actually existed, and since this section of
the *Platform Sutra* is obviously a later addition, designed to damn Northern Ch'an, there
is much room for doubt as to its historical authenticity.
[207] Supplied from *Kōshōji*, p. 52.
[208] The Tun-huang text is corrupt; *Kōshōji*, p. 52, has been followed.

The Sixth Patriarch said: " 'The very passions are enlightenment' is also like this."

41. The Master said to Chih-ch'eng: "I hear that your teacher instructs people only by handing down precepts, meditation, and wisdom.[209] What are the precepts, meditation, and wisdom that he teaches?"

Chih-ch'eng answered: "The priest Hsiu explains them in this way: Not to commit the various evils is the precepts; to practice all the many good things is wisdom; to purify one's own mind is meditation. These he calls precepts, meditation, and wisdom, and this is the kind of explanation that he gives. What is your own view, Master?"

The Master Hui-neng answered: "This explanation is wonderful, but my view is different."

Chih-ch'eng asked. "How does it differ?"

Hui-neng answered: "There is slow seeing and swift seeing."

Chih-ch'eng asked the Master to give his explanation of the precepts, wisdom, and meditation.

The master said: "Listen to my explanation and you will know my view. The mind-ground,[210] not in error, is the precept of self-nature; the mind-ground, undisturbed, is the meditation of self-nature; the mind-ground, not ignorant, is the wisdom of self-nature."

Master Hui-neng said: "Your precepts, meditation, and wisdom are to encourage people of shallow capacities, mine are for men of superior attainments. [Because] the awakening of self-nature [is the pivot of my teaching],[211] I don't even set up precepts, meditation, and wisdom."

Chih-ch'eng said: "Please explain what you mean by 'not set up.' "

[209] In the *Li-tai fa-pao chi*, T51, p. 185b, in the section on Wu-hsiang, Shen-hui of the Ho-tse Temple is described as mounting a platform each month to deliver a sermon in which he speaks of concentration, wisdom, and meditation. See Gernet, *Entretiens* . . . , p. 64, n. 9.

[210] *Hsin-ti*. It is defined in the *Tsu-t'ang chi* under the biography of Nan-yüeh Huai-jang (I, 144): "Ma-tsu made obeisance to the Master [Huai-jang] and asked: 'What should I do with my mind to attain the state of formless *samādhi*?' The Master answered: 'You should understand the doctrine of the mind-ground, which teaches that this mind-ground is as if planted with seeds. When I expound the essentials of the Dharma to you, it will be like rain falling upon that ground. Because the circumstances of your make-up join with the rain, therefore you are able to see the Way.' See the last verse in sec. 49.

[211] The Tun-huang text reads: "If you are able to awaken to self-nature, precepts, meditation, and wisdom are not set up." In this instance, however, Hui-neng is describing his own system as contrasted with that of Shen-hsiu. The translation has thus been supplemented to bring out this point.

The Master said: "Self-nature is without error, disturbance, and ignorance. Every thought puts forth the radiance of *prajñā* wisdom, and when one is always separated from the form of things, what is there that can be set up? Self-awakening to self-nature, and sudden practice with sudden awakening—there is nothing gradual in them, so that nothing at all is set up." [212]

Chih-ch'eng bowed deeply and did not leave Mount Ts'ao-ch'i. He became a disciple and never departed from the Master's side.

42. There was another priest by the name of Fa-ta,[213] who had been reciting the Lotus Sutra continuously for seven years, but his mind was still deluded and he did not know where the true Dharma lay. [Going to Mount Ts'ao-ch'i, he bowed and asked]:[214] "I have doubts about the sutra, and because the Master's wisdom is great, I beg of him to resolve my doubts."

The Master said: "Fa-ta, you are very proficient in the Dharma[215] but your mind is not proficient. You may have no doubts in so far as the sutras are concerned, [but your mind itself doubts].[216] You are searching for the true Dharma with falsehood in your mind. If your own mind were correct and fixed, you would be a man who has taken the sutra to himself.[217] "I have never in my life known written words, but if you bring a copy of the Lotus Sutra and read it to me, upon hearing it, I will understand it at once."

Fa-ta brought the Lotus Sutra and read it through to the Master. Hearing it, the Sixth Patriarch understood the Buddha's meaning, and then discoursed on the Lotus Sutra for the sake of Fa-ta.

The Sixth Patriarch said: "Fa-ta, the Lotus Sutra does not say anything more than is needed. Throughout all its seven *chüan*[218] it gives

[212] The Tun-huang text is corrupt; *Kōshōji*, p. 54, has been followed.

[213] This is the oldest known reference to this man. A more elaborate but highly unreliable account of his career appears in *Ching-te ch'uan-teng lu*, т51, pp. 237c–38b. Fa-ta must be included among the numerous Ch'an priests and monks who appear in the records but of whom nothing definite is known.

[214] Supplied from *Kōshōji*, p. 55.

[215] Here Hui-neng is playing upon Fa-ta's name.

[216] Supplied from *Kōshōji*, p. 55.

[217] *Ch'ih-ching*. This term appears in the Lotus Sutra, т9, p. 31b, in the sense of one who receives, holds, and takes to himself the teachings of the Lotus doctrine.

[218] According to the investigations of the Tun-huang Documents Research Section of the Research Institute for Humanistic Studies, Kyoto University, among the documents in the Stein Collection, there are in all some 1,050 copies of the Lotus Sutra. Of these, a little less than eighty percent represent the seven-*chüan* text, some twenty percent the

parables and tales about causation.[219] The Tathāgata's preaching of the Three Vehicles was only because of the dullness of people in the world. The words of the sutra clearly state that there is only one vehicle of Buddhism, and that there is no other vehicle."

The Master said: "Fa-ta, listen to the one Buddha vehicle and do not seek two vehicles, or your nature will be deluded. Where in the sutra do we find this one Buddha vehicle? Let me explain to you. The sutra says: 'The various Buddhas and the World-honored One appeared in this world because of the one great causal event.'[220] (The above sixteen characters are the true Dharma).[221] How do you come to understand this Dharma? How do you practice this Dharma? Listen, and I shall explain to you.

✕   "The mind has nothing to do with thinking, because its fundamental source is empty.[222] To discard false views, this is the one great causal event. If within and without you are not deluded then you are apart from duality. If on the outside you are deluded you cling to form; if on the inside you are deluded you cling to emptiness. If within form you are apart from form and within emptiness you are separated from emptiness, then within and without you are not deluded.[223] If you awaken to this Dharma, in one instant of thought your mind will open and you will go forth in the world. What is it that the mind opens? It opens Buddha's wisdom and the Buddha means enlightenment. Separately considered there are four gates: the opening of the wisdom of enlightenment, the instruction of the wisdom of enlightenment, the

eight-*chüan* text, while only a very few copies of the ten-*chüan* text are to be found. It is presumed that a similar proportion exists among the documents in the Pelliot Collection. In the parallel passage in the *Kōshōji* edition, p. 55, the Lotus Sutra in ten *chüan* is mentioned; in the *Daijōji* edition, p. 44, the seven-*chüan* text is cited. In the "Song of Twelve Hours" found in the Pelliot Collection (P2054, 2714, 3087), the following passage appears: "Śākyamuni was skilled in expediencies, and spoke the Lotus Sutra in eight rolls." See Jen Erh-pei, *Tun-huang chü hsiao lu*, p. 153.

[219] This may well refer to the "one great causal event" mentioned later in the text.
[220] Lotus Sutra, т9, p. 7a.
[221] Note is in the original text.
[222] The first part of this passage is difficult to follow and the translation uncertain. The phrase *k'ung-chi pen-yüan*, found in the Tun-huang text, makes little sense. However, in the *P'u-t'i hsin-lun*, т32, p. 573b, translated by Amoghavajra between 746 and 774, we find the phrase *hsin-yüan k'ung-chi* [the mind as the source (of the ten thousand things) is empty], and it may possibly be that this was intended here. The term *hsin-yüan* is also to be found in the *Ta-ch'eng ch'i-hsin lun*, т32, p. 576b, where we read: "It is called ultimate enlightenment because one has awakened to the source of the mind."
[223] This clause is unreadable in the Tun-huang text; *Kōshōji*, p. 56, has been followed.

awakening of the wisdom of enlightenment, and the entering into the wisdom of enlightenment. This is called opening, instructing, awakening, and entering.[224] Entering from one place,[225] this is the wisdom of enlightenment, and [with this] you see into your own nature, and succeed in transcending the world."

The Master said: "Fa-ta, it is my constant wish that all the people in the world will always themselves open the wisdom of the Buddha in their own mind-grounds. Do not cultivate the 'wisdom' of sentient beings. The people of the world have errors in their minds, create evil with stupidity and delusion, and thus cultivate the 'wisdom' of sentient beings. If people in the world are correct in their minds, they will give rise to wisdom and illuminate it, and open up for themselves the wisdom of the Buddha. Do not open up the 'wisdom' of sentient beings! Open up the wisdom of the Buddha and then transcend the world."

The Master said: "Fa-ta, this is the one-vehicle Dharma of the Lotus Sutra. Later on in the sutra[226] the Buddha's teaching is divided into three [vehicles] in order to benefit the deluded. Depend only on the one Buddha vehicle."

The Master said: "If you practice with the mind you turn the Lotus; if you do not practice with the mind, you are turned by the Lotus.[227] If your mind is correct you will turn the Lotus; if your mind is incorrect you will be turned by the Lotus. If the wisdom of the Buddha is

---

[224] In the Lotus Sutra, т9, p. 7a, we find the following passage: "Śāriputra, why did the various Buddhas and the World-honored One, just because of the one great causal event, appear in the world? The various Buddhas and the World-honored One appeared in the world because they wanted to *open* the Buddha's wisdom for sentient beings and enable them to become pure. Because they wanted to *instruct* sentient beings in the wisdom of Buddha, they appeared in the world. Because they wanted to bring the *awakening* of Buddha's wisdom to sentient beings, they appeared in the world. Because they wanted to have sentient beings *enter* into the way of Buddha's wisdom, they appeared in the world." The four stages mentioned here correspond to the four gates described in the Tun-huang text.

[225] Unclear. This may refer to "where the true Dharma lies" at the beginning of this section.

[226] As described in sec. 2, the Fang-pien *p'in,* of the sutra, т9, pp. 5–10. *Hsiang-hsia* is a T'ang colloquial expression meaning "afterwards," "behind"; here it merely means, "later on in the sutra."

[227] *Chuan Fa-hua . . . Fa-hua chan.* Actually *chuan* [to turn] here means *chuan-tu* [to cite or to read]. It also contains the meaning of "roll" or "turn," as in unrolling or unfolding a sutra roll, as well as "to control" or "to have command of." See Iriya Yoshitaka, *Kanzan,* pp. 143–44. In the *Li-tai fa-pao chi,* т51, p. 192a, we find the same concept: "No-thought, this is turning the Lotus; having thoughts, this is to be turned by the Lotus."

opened, you will turn the Lotus; if the 'wisdom' of sentient beings is opened, you will be turned by the Lotus."

The Master said: "If you practice the Dharma with great effort, this then is turning the sutra."

Fa-ta, upon hearing this, at once gained great enlightenment and broke into tears. "Master," he said, "indeed up to now I have not turned the Lotus, but for seven years I have been turned by it. From now on I shall turn the Lotus, and in consecutive thoughts practice the practice of the Buddha."

The Master said: "The very practice of Buddha, this is Buddha."

Among those in his audience at that time there was none who was not enlightened.

43. At one time a monk named Chih-ch'ang[228] came to Mount Ts'ao-ch'i and, making obeisance before Hui-neng, asked about the meaning of the Dharma of the Four Vehicles. Chih-ch'ang asked Hui-neng: "The Buddha spoke of three vehicles, but you speak of a Supreme Vehicle.[229] I don't understand and wish that you would instruct me."

The Master Hui-neng said: "Look at your own body and mind and do not cling to outer forms. From the outset there were no four vehicles, but the human mind itself has four grades,[230] therefore the Dharma has four vehicles. Seeing, hearing, reciting—this is the small vehicle.[231] Awakening to the Dharma and understanding its principle —this is the middle vehicle. Practicing according to the Dharma—this is the great vehicle. Passing through the ten thousand things completely, being fully equipped with the ten thousand practices, not separating from all things, but only from the characteristics of things, and in all actions obtaining nothing—this is the Supreme Vehicle. 'Vehicle'

---

[228] Chih-ch'ang is mentioned in the *Ching-te ch'uan-teng lu,* T51, p. 239a–b, where he is identified as a native of Kuei-hsi in Pen-chou. Originally a disciple of Shen-hsiu, he is said to have come to Hui-neng because he was unable to gain enlightenment under his first teacher. No further biographical information is available.

[229] *Tsui-shang-ch'eng.* This term is found in the Diamond Sutra, T9, p. 755a. It is also used by Shen-hui (*Shen-hui yü-lu,* Hu Shih, *Shen-hui ho-shang i-chi,* p. 112; Gernet, *Entretiens . . . ,* p. 28) in the same sense as in the paragraph below.

[230] The Tun-huang text is corrupt; *Kōshōji,* p. 57, has been followed. The four grades correspond to those who have the capacity for the attainment of each of the four vehicles described below in the text.

[231] Or the stage of Śrāvaka; similarly the middle vehicle is the stage of the Pratyeka-buddha; the great vehicle, the stage of the Bodhisattva.

means practice;[232] it is nothing that can be discussed, but is something that you yourself must do. So don't ask me."

44. There was another monk by the name of Shen-hui who was a native of Nan-yang.[233] He came to Mount Ts'ao-ch'i, made obeisance, and asked: "Master, when you are sitting in meditation, do you see or not?"

The Master got up and hit Shen-hui three times. Then he asked: "Shen-hui, when I hit you, did it hurt or didn't it?"

Shen-hui answered: "It hurt and it also didn't hurt."

The Sixth Patriarch said: "I see and I also do not see."

Then Shen-hui again asked: "Master, why do you see and not see?"

The Master answered: "My seeing is always to see my own errors; that's why I call it seeing. My non-seeing is not to see the evils of people in the world. That's why I see and also do not see.[234] What about your hurting and also not hurting?"

Shen-hui said: "If it did not hurt, I would be the same as an insentient tree or rock. If it did hurt, I would be the same as a common person, and resentments would arise."[235]

The Master said: "The seeing and non-seeing you asked about just now is dualistic; hurting and not hurting[236] are birth and destruction. You don't even see your own nature; how dare you come and toy with me!" Shen-hui bowed down and did not speak.

The Master said: "Your mind is deluded and you cannot see, so you go and ask a teacher to show you the way. You must awaken with your own mind and see for yourself, and you must practice with the Dharma. Because you yourself are deluded and you do not see your own mind, you come asking me whether I see or not. Even if I see for myself,[237] I cannot take the place of your delusion; even if you see for yourself, you cannot take the place of my delusion.[238] Why don't you practice for yourself and then ask me whether I see or not?"

[232] The characters *tsui-shang* [supreme] in the Tun-huang text are out of context and have been omitted in the translation.

[233] Located south of Loyang in Honan. Shen-hui is also known as Nan-yang ho-shang.

[234] Following *Kōshōji*, p. 58. The Tun-huang text says literally: "Your seeing is also non-seeing."

[235] *Kōshōji*, p. 58, gives this answer of Shen-hui's as a continuation of Hui-neng's speech: "If it did not hurt you . . .".

[236] Supplied from *Kōshōji*, p. 58.

[237] Following *Kōshōji*, p. 59.

[238] *Ibid.*, p. 59.

Shen-hui bowed deeply and became a disciple. He did not leave Mount Ts'ao-ch'i and always attended on the Master.

45. The Master then called his disciples Fa-hai, Chih-ch'eng, Fa-ta, Chih-ch'ang, Chih-t'ung,[239] Chih-ch'e,[240] Chih-tao,[241] Fa-chen,[242] Fa-ju,[243] and Shen-hui, and said: "You ten disciples, come clōse. You are different from other people; after I die each of you will become a teacher somewhere. I am explaining the Dharma to you so that the basic teaching will not become lost.

"I shall give you the teaching in the three categories[244] and the thirty-six confrontations[245] of activity. As things rise and sink, you must separate from dualism.[246] When you explain all things, do not stand apart

[239] It is only in the Tun-huang edition that the first character of Chih-t'ung's name is written with Matthews' no. 971. *Kōshōji*, p. 59, and later works render the *chih* with Matthews' no. 933; thus either the Tun-huang edition is in error, or one character has been used as a homophone for the other. Chih-t'ung appears in *Ching-te ch'uan-teng lu*, τ51, p. 238b–c, where he is given as a native of An-feng in Shou-chou. No further biographical information is supplied. He is described as one who read the Laṅkāvatāra Sutra, but because he did not understand the meaning of the "three bodies and the four wisdoms," came to Hui-neng to inquire concerning them. As Ui points out (*Zenshū shi kenkyū*, II, 256), the "four wisdoms" are spoken of at a later date in Ch'an Buddhism, so that Chih-t'ung's questions and Hui-neng's answers to them may be presumed to be later additions to the text.
[240] In the *Ching-te ch'uan-teng lu*, τ51, pp. 238c–39a, he is described as a native of Chiang-hsi, of the family name of Chang and personal name of Hsing-chang. The story is told that, belonging originally to Shen-hsiu's group, he came to Hui-neng with the intention of stabbing him, but instead was converted by the Master and sent on his way. Returning a second time, he gained enlightenment as a result of instruction in the Nirvāṇa Sutra. This story has no historical validity whatsoever, and was no doubt made up in an effort to discredit the Northern School.
[241] From Kuang-chou, he was a native of Nan-hai. He had been reading the Nirvāṇa Sutra for over ten years, without understanding it, until he came to Hui-neng and gained enlightenment. See *Ching-te ch'uan-teng lu*, τ51, pp. 239b–c, 240a.
[242] Unknown.
[243] Unknown.
[244] The three categories comprise the five aggregates, twelve entrances, and eighteen realms of sense, as identified below in the text. They are described in the Tun-huang manuscript, *Ta-ch'eng san-k'o* (quoted in Sekiguchi, *Daruma daishi no kenkyū*, p. 243). That these three categories were fairly commonly used at this time is evidenced by a passage in the *Tsu-t'ang chi*, biography of Pao-tz'u ho-shang (IV, 12): "As for brilliant words and marvelous meanings, they are all described in the [twelve divisions of the] teachings; now give me your instruction without concerning yourself with the three categories."
[245] Their explanation follows below in the text. No example of their use in any work other than the *Platform Sutra* has been found. The only other reference to them that I have been able to locate is in the *Tsu-t'ang chi*, V, 75, where they are mentioned without enumeration or elaboration.
[246] Translation tentative. Compare Chan, *The Platform Scripture*, p. 121.

from nature and form.[247] Should someone ask you about the Dharma, what you say should all be symmetrical and you must draw parallels for everything. Since they originate each from the other, if in the end dualisms are all completely cast aside, there will be no place for them to exist. The teaching of the three categories is that of the aggregates,[248] the realms of sense,[249] and the entrances.[250] There are five aggregates, eighteen realms of sense, and twelve entrances. What are the five aggregates? They are form, reception, conception, functioning, and ideation. What are the eighteen realms of sense? They are the six dusts, the six gates, and the six consciousnesses. What are the twelve entrances? Externally they are the six dusts; internally they are the six gates. What are the six dusts? They are sight, sound, smell, taste, touch, and idea. What are the six gates? They are the eyes, ears, nose, tongue, body, and mind. Dharma-nature gives rise to the six consciousnesses—seeing, hearing, smelling, tasting, touching, and thinking—as well as the six gates and the six dusts. All things are included in your own natures; this is known as the storehouse consciousness.[251] Thinking, consciousness is turned, the six consciousnesses produced, and the six dusts are seen emerging from the six gates.[252] The three sixes make eighteen. From the errors of your self-nature the eighteen errors arise. If your self-nature is correct, then the eighteen correct things arise.[253] If it contains evil activities, then you are a sentient being; if it contains good activities, then you are a Buddha. From what do activities stem? They stem from the confrontations that face your own nature.[254]

46. "The confrontations of the natural phenomena of the external environment are five: heaven and earth, the sun and the moon, darkness and light, Yin and Yang, and water and fire. There are twelve confrontations in language and the characteristics of things:[255] active

---

[247] I.e., the nature of something and its phenomenal form.

[248] The five *skandhas*, accumulations, substances, components of an intelligent being.

[249] The eighteen *dhātu*, or realms of sense: the six organs, their objects or conditions, and their perceptions.

[250] The twelve *āyatana*. The six organs and their objects or conditions.

[251] *Ālayavijñāna.*

[252] The text here is corrupt and the translation tentative.

[253] The Tun-huang text is again unreadable. Suzuki's collation (*Tonkō shutsudo Rokuso dankyō*, p. 49) has been followed.

[254] Translation tentative.

[255] Here again the Tun-huang text is unreadable. The parallel passage in the *Kōshōji* edition, p. 60, has been considerably revised. The translation follows Suzuki's collation,

and material and inactive and non-material, with characteristics and without characteristics, within the flow of birth and death and without that flow, matter and emptiness (*śūnyatā*), motion and stillness, purity and uncleanliness, profane and sacred, monk and layman, old and young, large and small, long and short, and high and low. In the activities to which your self-nature gives rise there are nineteen confrontations: the incorrect and the correct, ignorance and wisdom, stupidity and knowledge, confusion and *samādhi*, following the precepts and not following them, straight and crooked, real and unreal, steep and level, passions and enlightenment, compassion and doing harm, joy and anger, giving and begrudging, progressing and retrogressing, birth and destruction, permanence and impermanence, the *Dharmakāya* and the physical body, the *Nirmāṇakāya* and the *Sambhogakāya*, substance and function, nature and characteristics, and sentience and insentience.[256] In language and the characteristics of things there are twelve confrontations, in the external environment there are five confrontations of natural phenomena, [and in the functions given rise to by your self-nature there are nineteen confrontations],[257] making all together thirty-six confrontations. If you can employ the law of the thirty-six confrontations, it will apply to all the sutras, and, leaving and entering, you will stand apart from dualism. Why is it that your self-nature gives rise to activities? When you speak to others about these thirty-six confrontations, on the outside, while within form, separate from form; on the inside, while within emptiness, separate from emptiness. If you cling to emptiness then you will only be increasing your ignorance. If you cling to form, you will only increase

which is based on the *Kōshōji* revisions. In the following list of twelve confrontations, *Kōshōji* includes "existence and non-existence" and "language and Dharma." It omits "high and low" and "short and long."

[256] There are actually twenty confrontations listed in the Tun-huang version. *Kōshōji*, p. 60, places "short and long" at the head of the list of nineteen confrontations, whereas the Tun-huang text includes it among the twelve above. *Kōshōji* omits "substance and function," "nature and characteristics," and "sentience and insentience." It adds "compassion and doing injury." The order in which the confrontations are listed differs considerably in the two texts.

[257] Here again the Tun-huang text is quite confused and the translation highly tentative. *Kōshōji*, p. 61, has merely: "These are the nineteen confrontations. The Master said: 'If you employ the law of the thirty-six confrontations . . . ' " The Tun-huang text has, following the statement concerning the five confrontations, the clause *san-shen yu san-tui* [in the three bodies are three confrontations], which is completely out of context and has been omitted from the translation. The collation proposed by Suzuki (*Tonkō shutsudo Rokuso dankyō*, p. 50) has been followed.

your false views, slander the Dharma, and be quick to say that one should not use written words. Once you say one should not use written words, then people should not speak, because speech itself is written words. Even[258] if you explain emptiness from the standpoint of your own nature, this in effect, becomes language [?]. Since the original nature is not empty, you are deluded and deceive yourself, just because you have cast aside speech [?]. Darkness is not darkness by itself; because there is light there is darkness. That darkness is not darkness by itself is because light changes, becoming darkness, and with darkness light is revealed. They originate each from the other. The thirty-six confrontations are also like this."

47. The Master said: "You ten disciples, when later you transmit the Dharma, hand down the teaching of the one roll of the *Platform Sutra;* then you will not lose the basic teaching. Those who do not receive the *Platform Sutra* do not have the essentials of my teaching. As of now you have received them; hand them down and spread them among later generations. If others are able to encounter the *Platform Sutra*, it will be as if they received the teaching personally from me."

[258] The text of the Tun-huang version in the remaining discussion of the thirty-six confrontations has a great number of omissions and errors, and is difficult to follow. The translation, thus, is tentative. *Kōshōji,* pp. 61–62, renders this section in much greater detail: "The Master continued: 'Once you say, "do not set up words," the very words "do not set up" are themselves words. Hearing [the words] spoken by man, you say that words slander others and that this is clinging to words. It is bad enough to be deluded oneself, let alone to slander the sutras. Do not blaspheme against the sutras, or else you will commit numberless crimes and create obstructions. Those who on the outside cling to form and seek the truth by creating dharmas, or build large places for practice, and speak of the presence or absence of errors [on the part of others], will for numberless kalpas be unable to see into their own natures. Rather than encouraging practice according to the Dharma, merely listen to it and practice yourself. Do not think of the hundred things and impede the nature of the Way. If you hear [the Dharma] and do not practice, you will do harm to others and cause erroneous thoughts to be born. Just practicing with the Dharma is the almsgiving of the Dharma of the form of non-abiding. If you awaken, preach with this, base your activities upon this, practice with this, work according to this, and then the essentials of the teachings will not be lost. Should someone ask you its meaning, if they ask of existence, answer with non-existence; if someone asks of non-existence, answer with existence. If someone asks you of the profane, answer with the sacred; if someone asks you of the sacred, answer with the profane. From the correlation of the confrontations produce the true essential. To one question give one answer; as for other questions, treat them in the same way, and you will not lose the principle. If someone should ask you "What is darkness?" say in answer: "Light is a primary cause; darkness a secondary cause. When light disappears we have darkness, darkness is manifested by light, and with darkness light appears. They originate each from the other." Produce the essential meaning! Other questions are all like this!' "

These ten monks received the teaching, made copies of the *Platform Sutra,* handed them down, and spread them among later generations. Those who received them have without fail seen into their own true natures.

48. The Master passed away on the third day of the eighth month of the second year of Hsien-t'ien (= August 28, 713).[259] On the eighth day of the seventh month he called his disciples together and bade them farewell. In the first year of Hsien-t'ien the Master had constructed a pagoda at the Kuo-en Temple[260] in Hsin-chou, and now in the seventh month of the second year of Hsien-t'ien he was taking his leave.

The Master said: "Come close. In the eighth month I intend to leave this world. If any of you have doubts, ask about them quickly, and I shall resolve them for you. I must bring your delusions to an end and make it possible for you to gain peace. After I have gone there will be no one to teach you."

Fa-hai and the other monks heard him to the end and wept tears of sorrow. Only Shen-hui was not impressed, nor did he weep. The Sixth Patriarch said: "Shen-hui, you are a young monk, yet you have attained the [status of awakening] in which good and not good are identical, and you are not moved by judgments of praise and blame. You others have not yet understood: what have you been practicing at this temple these several years? You're crying now, but who is there who's really worried that I don't know the place to which I'm going?[261] If I didn't know where I was going then I wouldn't be leaving you. You're crying just because you don't know where I'm going. If you knew where I was going you wouldn't be crying. The nature itself is without birth and without destruction, without going and without coming. All of you sit down. I shall give you a verse, the verse of the true-false moving-quiet. All of you recite it, and if you understand its meaning,

[259] Most sources agree on the date of the Master's death. For variations, see Introduction, p. 77.
[260] The *Sōkei daishi betsuden,* zz2B, 19, 5, 486b, states that Hui-neng's old home in Hsin-chou was turned into a temple and given the name Kuo-en. The *Sung kao-seng chuan,* τ50, p. 755a, furnishes similar information.
[261] *Kōshōji,* p. 63, reads: "Whom are you worrying about? If you're worrying about my not knowing the place to which I'm going, [then let me tell you] that I *do* know the place."

you will be the same as I. If you practice with it, you will not lose the essence of the teaching."

The assembly of monks bowed down and begged: "Master, leave us your verse; we shall receive and retain it with reverent hearts." The verse said:

> Nowhere is there anything true;
> Don't try to see the True in any way.
> If you try to see the True,
> Your seeing will be in no way true.
> If you yourself would gain the True,
> Separate from the false; there the mind is true.
> If the mind itself does not separate from the false,
> There is no True. What place is there for it to be?
> Sentient beings can move,
> Non-sentient things are without motion;
> If you undertake the practices of non-motion,
> You will be identical with the non-motion of the non-sentient.
> If the true non-motion is observed,
> It is but non-motion postulated on motion.
> Non-motion is no more than no motion itself;
> Non-sentient beings contain no Buddha seed.
> Distinguishing well the forms [of the various dharmas],
> Remain firm within the First Principle.[262]
> If you awaken and come to this view,
> This then is the functioning of True Reality.
> Let me tell all you students of the Way
> That you must exert your utmost efforts.
> Do not, in the teaching of the Mahāyāna,
> Cling to the knowledge of birth and death.
> When in the future you encounter a person you are destined to meet,[263]
> Then discuss together the words of the Buddha.
> If he is really not such a person,
> Then, with palms joined, have him strive for the good.
> From the outset this teaching has never engaged in disputes;
> Disputations will betray the intention of the Way.[264]
> If you cling to delusions and argue about the teaching,
> Your own natures will enter into the cycle of birth and death.

[262] A paraphrase of the passage from the Vimalakīrti Sutra quoted in sec. 17.

[263] *Hsiang-ying.* A technical term, indicating a predestined encounter with someone who is fully responsive to the teaching.

[264] The Tun-huang edition reads: "Not engaging in dispute will betray the intention of the Way." This is out of context, and the translation has been changed to conform with *Kōshōji*, p. 65.

49. Once the assembled monks heard this verse they understood the Master's meaning. They did not dare to argue and they knew that they must practice according to the Dharma. In unison they all bowed deeply, knowing that the Master would not stay in the world forever.

The head monk Fa-hai came forward and said: "Master, after you leave, who will inherit your robe and Dharma?"

The Master said: "The Dharma has already been entrusted; that you may not ask. Some twenty years[265] after I have died evil dharmas will run rampant and becloud the essentials of my teaching. Then someone will come forward and, at the risk of his life, fix the correct and false in Buddhism,[266] and raise up the essentials of the teaching. This will be my true Dharma.

"The robe may not be handed down. In case you do not trust in me, I shall recite the verses of the preceding five patriarchs, composed when they transmitted the robe and the Dharma. If you depend on the meaning of the verse of the First Patriarch, Bodhidharma, then there is no need to hand down the robe. Hear me as I recite them to you. The verses say:

Verse of the First Patriarch, the Priest Bodhidharma

I originally came to China,
To transmit the teaching and save deluded beings.
One flower opens five petals,[267]
And the fruit ripens of itself.

Verse of the Second Patriarch, the Priest Hui-k'o

Because originally there is earth,
From this earth seeds bring forth flowers.

---

[265] This prediction refers to Shen-hui's attack on the Northern School of Ch'an in 732 at Hua-t'ai in Honan. The *Shen-hui yü-lu* (Suzuki text, p. 62), in the biography of Hui-neng, sets the prediction at forty years. It is found as twenty in the *Kōshōji* edition, p. 65, but later editions of the *Platform Sutra* have dropped the prediction altogether. We have already seen the same prediction set at seventy years in both the *Sōkei daishi betsuden* and the *Ching-te ch'uan-teng lu.*

[266] The wording of this passage brings to mind the work of Shen-hui, *P'u-t'i-ta-mo Nan-tsung ting shih-fei lun*. Together with the prediction above, it forms strong evidence to support Hu Shih's contention that the *Platform Sutra* was written by a disciple or a later member of Shen-hui's school. See Hu Shih, "Ch'an (Zen) Buddhism in China, Its History and Method," *Philosophy East and West*, III (no. 1, April, 1953), 11, n. 9.

[267] This phrase is traditionally interpreted to refer to the Five Patriarchs after Bodhidharma. Another interpretation is that it predicts the later division of Ch'an into five branches: Lin-chi, Ts'ao-tung, Yün-men, Fa-yen, and Wei-yang.

If from the outset there were no earth,[268]
From where would the flowers grow? [269]

Verse of the Third Patriarch, the Priest Seng-ts'an

Although flower seeds rely upon the earth,
It is on the earth that seeds produce flowers.
If flower seeds had no nature of growth,
On the earth nothing would be produced.[270]

Verse of the Fourth Patriarch, the Priest Tao-hsin

Flower seeds have the nature of growth;
From the earth seeds produce flowers.
If former causality is not harmonized,
Nothing at all will sprout.[271]

Verse of the Fifth Patriarch, the Priest Hung-jen

Sentient beings come and lay down the seeds,
And non-sentient flowers grow.
If there is insentiency and there are no seeds,
The mind-ground, as well, produces nothing.[272]

[268] The *Pao-lin chuan*, III, 542, *Tsu-t'ang chi*, I, 79, and *Ching-te ch'uan-teng lu*, T51, p. 220c, all give this line as: "If from the outset there were no seeds." *Kōshōji* and later editions of the *Platform Sutra* give only the verse of Bodhidharma, omitting those of the other Patriarchs.

[269] The *Pao-lin chuan*, III, 542, and *Tsu-t'ang chi*, I, 79, have here: "The flowers would not be able to sprout."

[270] Other works show considerable variation in this verse: *Pao-lin chuan*, III, 559, gives for the first line: "Flower seeds are not of the earth"; other works are identical with the Tun-huang edition. Beginning with the *Pao-lin chuan*, all other works give the second line as: "From the earth seeds and flowers sprout." The third line, also beginning with the *Pao-lin chuan*, is changed entirely to read: "If there were not men to plant the seeds." The fourth line is rendered, in the *Pao-lin chuan* and *Ching-te ch'uan-teng lu*, T51, p. 221c, as: "All the flowers would not grow in the earth." *Tsu-t'ang chi*, I, 81, reads: "Flower seeds all will not sprout."

[271] Again we find great variations in other versions of this verse. The first line is the same in all texts. The *Tsu-t'ang chi*, I, 82, renders the verse:

> Flower seeds have the nature of growth,
> From the earth flower nature is produced.
> If the great condition [?] is in harmony with the nature,
> To grow is either not to grow or to grow.

The *Ching-te ch'uan-teng lu*, T51, p. 222b, renders the verse:

> Flower seeds have the nature of growth,
> From the earth flowers grow.
> If the great condition [?] is in harmony with faith,
> To grow is either to grow or not to grow.

The volumes of the *Pao-lin chuan*, relating to Tao-hsin and later Patriarchs, are, of course, missing.

[272] The *Tsu-t'ang chi*, I, 85, and *Ching-te ch'uan-teng lu*, T51, p. 233b, give this verse as:

Verse of the Sixth Patriarch, the Priest Hui-neng

The mind-ground contains the seed of living things,
When the rain of the Dharma falls the flowers are brought forth.
When yourself you have awakened to the living seeds of the flower [?],[273]
The fruit of enlightenment matures of itself.[274]

50. The Master Hui-neng said: "All of you listen to the two verses
I have made; their import is taken from the verses of the Priest Bodhidharma. If you deluded ones practice according to these verses, you
will without fail see into your own true natures. The first verse says:

If evil flowers bloom in the mind-ground,
Five blossoms flower from the stem.
Together they will create the karma of ignorance;
Now the mind-ground is blown by the winds of karma.

The second verse says:

If correct flowers bloom in the mind-ground,
Five blossoms flower from the stem.
Together practice the *prajñā* wisdom;
In the future this will be the enlightenment of the Buddha.

After the Sixth Patriarch had finished expounding these verses, he
had the group disperse. His disciples went out, and, thinking things
over, they knew that the Master was not long for this world.[275]

Sentient beings come and lay down the seeds,
From the earth fruit is produced.
When there is no sentiency there are no seeds;
Without nature nothing is produced.

[273] The text is unreadable and the translation uncertain.
[274] Later versions of this verse also contain variations. *Tsu-t'ang chi*, I, 97, renders it:

The mind-ground contains the various seeds,
With the all-pervading rain each and everyone sprouts.
Once one has suddenly awakened to the sentiency of the flower,
The fruit of enlightenment matures of itself.

Kōshōji, p. 66, renders the first two lines:

The mind-ground contains the seed nature;
When the rain of the Dharma falls the flowers are brought forth.

The last two lines are identical with those in the *Tsu-t'ang chi*. A concept similar to
that expressed in this verse appears in the biography of Hui-neng in the *Ching-te
ch'uan-teng lu*, T51, p. 236b: "The sermon that I have just preached is like the rain that
waters the great earth, and your Buddha natures are like the many seeds that sprout
when they encounter the wetness."
[275] This section is not found in the *Kōshōji* edition.

51. And now on the third day of the eighth month, after eating, the Master said: "All of you take your positions and be seated. I am going to leave you now."

Fa-hai asked: "From the very beginning up to now, how many generations have there been in the transmission of the doctrine of the Sudden Enlightenment teaching?"

The Master said: "The first transmission was from the Seven Buddhas [of the past], and Śākyamuni was the seventh. Eighth was Kāśyapa, ninth Ānanda, tenth Madhyāntika, eleventh Śanavāsa, twelfth Upagupta, thirteenth Dhṛtaka,[276] fourteenth Buddhanandi, fifteenth Buddhamitra, sixteenth Pārśva, seventeenth Puṇyayaśas, eighteenth Aśvaghoṣa, nineteenth Kapimala, twentieth Nāgārjuna, twenty-first Kāṇadeva, twenty-second Rāhulata, twenty-third Saṅghānandi, twenty-fourth Gayaśāta, twenty-fifth Kumārata, twenty-sixth Jayata, twenty-seventh Vasubandhu, twenty-eighth Manorhita, twenty-ninth Haklenayaśas, thirtieth Siṁha bhikṣu, thirty-first Śanavāsa, thirty-second Upagupta, thirty-third Saṅgharakṣa,[277] thirty-fourth Śubhamitra,[278] thirty-fifth Bodhidharma, prince from southern India, thirty-sixth, the Chinese priest Hui-k'o, thirty-seventh Seng-ts'an, thirty-eighth Tao-hsin, thirty-ninth Hung-jen, and as of now I am the fortieth to have received the Law."

The Master said: "From today on transmit the teaching among yourselves, but be sure that you have the sanction, and do not let the essentials of the teaching become lost."

52. Fa-hai spoke again, asking: "Master, you are going now. What Dharma are you leaving behind, and how will you make it possible for those who come later to see the Buddha?"

The Sixth Patriarch replied: "Listen! If only they know sentient beings, deluded people of later generations will be able to see the Buddha. If they do not know sentient beings, even though they seek the Buddha, they will not be able to see him in ten thousand kalpas. I shall now let you see the sentient being in your own mind and let you

---

[276] Following Dhṛtaka, Miccaca, found in other lists, has been omitted in error. See Table 1.

[277] The positions of the thirty-third and thirty-fourth Patriarchs have been inverted. See Table 1.

[278] Following Shen-hui's error, "Śubhamitra" has been written for "Vasumitra." See introduction, p. 30.

see the Buddha nature in your own mind.[279] Also I shall leave you a verse on 'Seeing the true Buddha and gaining emancipation.' If you are deluded you will not see the Buddha; if you are awakened you will see him. Fa-hai, please listen. Hand the teaching down to successive generations, and do not allow it to be cut off."

The Sixth Patriarch said: "Hear me as I explain to you. If men in later generations wish to seek the Buddha, they have only to know that the Buddha mind is within sentient beings; then they will be able to know the Buddha. Because the Buddha mind[280] is possessed by sentient beings, apart from sentient beings there is no Buddha mind.[281]

> Deluded, a Buddha is a sentient being;
> Awakened, a sentient being is a Buddha.[282]
> Ignorant, a Buddha is a sentient being;
> With wisdom, a sentient being is a Buddha.
> If the mind is warped, a Buddha is a sentient being;
> If the mind is impartial, a sentient being is a Buddha.
> When once a warped mind is produced,
> Buddha is concealed within the sentient being.
> If for one instant of thought we become impartial,
> Then sentient beings are themselves Buddha.
> In our mind itself a Buddha exists,
> Our own Buddha is the true Buddha.
> If we do not have in ourselves the Buddha mind,
> Then where are we to seek Buddha?"

53. The Master said: "My disciples, farewell. I am going to leave you a verse entitled the 'Self-nature true Buddha emancipation' verse. Should deluded men in later generations grasp the purport of this verse, they will see the true Buddha of their own minds and of their own self-natures. With this verse I shall part from you. The verse says:

True reality and a pure nature—this is the true Buddha;
Evil views and the three poisons—this is the true demon.
For the person with evil views, the demon is in his home;
For the person with correct views, the Buddha will call at his home.
If from the evil views within the nature the three poisons are produced,

---

[279] The Tun-huang text reads: "I shall let you know sentient beings and see Buddha." The translation has been altered to follow *Kōshōji*, p. 68.

[280] The Tun-huang text is unreadable here. From context "Buddha mind" has been supplied.

[281] *Kōshōji* renders the following verse in prose.

[282] See secs. 30 and 35, where the same concept is given.

This means that a demon king has come to reside in the home.
If correct views of themselves cast aside the mind of the three poisons,[283]
The demon changes and becomes a Buddha, one that is true, not false.
The *Nirmāṇakāya*, the *Sambhogakāya*, the *Dharmakāya*,
These three bodies are from the outset one body.
If within your own nature[284] you seek to see for yourself,
This then is the cause of becoming Buddha and gaining enlightenment
(*bodhi*).
Since from the outset the *Nirmāṇakāya* produces the pure nature,
This pure nature is always contained within the *Nirmāṇakāya*.
If your nature activates the *Nirmāṇakāya* to practice the correct way,
In the future perfection is achieved, a perfection true and without limit.
The licentious nature is itself the cause of purity,
Outside of licentiousness there is no pure nature.
If only within your self-nature you yourself separate from the five desires,
The instant you see into your own nature—this is the True [Buddha].
If in this life you awaken to the teaching of the Sudden Doctrine.
Awakening, you will see the World-honored One before your eyes.
If you wish to practice and say you seek the Buddha,
Who knows where you will find the True [One]?
If within your own body you yourself have the True,
Where the True is, there is the means of becoming Buddha.
If you do not seek the True yourself and seek the Buddha outside,
All your seeking will be that of a highly ignorant man.
The teaching of the Sudden Doctrine has come from the West [?].[285]
To save people of the world you must practice yourself.
Now I say to all Ch'an students in this world,
If you do not rely on this Way you are leading vacant lives."

The Master, having finished his verse, then said to his disciples:
"Good-by, all of you. I shall depart from you now. After I am gone,
do not weep worldly tears, nor accept condolences, money, and silks
from people, nor wear mourning garments. If you did so it would
not accord with the sacred Dharma, nor would you be true disciples of
mine. Be the same as you would if I were here, and sit all together in
meditation. If you are only peacefully calm and quiet, without motion,
without stillness, without birth, without destruction, without coming,
without going, without judgments of right and wrong, without staying
and without going—this then is the Great Way. After I have gone
just practice according to the Dharma in the same way that you did on

---

[283] The Tun-huang text is again unreadable. *Kōshōji*, p. 69, has been followed.
[284] The Tun-huang text reads "body"; *Kōshōji*, p. 69, has been followed.
[285] The wording here is very peculiar and the translation tentative.

the days that I was with you. Even though I were still to be in this world, if you went against the teachings, there would be no use in my having stayed here."

After fiinishing speaking these words, the Master, at midnight, quietly passed away. He was seventy-six years of age.

54. On the day the Master died a strange fragrance, which did not fade for several days, filled the temple. Mountains crumbled, the earth trembled, and the forest trees turned white. The sun and moon ceased to shine and the wind and clouds lost their colors.

He died on the third day of the eighth month, and in the eleventh month his sacred coffin was received and interred on Mount Ts'ao-ch'i. From within his resting place a bright light appeared and rose straight toward the heavens, and two days passed before it finally dispersed. The prefect of Shao-chou, Wei Ch'ü, erected a memorial stone,[286] and to this day offerings have been made before it.

55. This *Platform Sutra* was compiled by the head monk Fa-hai, who on his death entrusted it to his fellow student Tao-ts'an.[287] After Tao-ts'an died it was assigned to his disciple Wu-chen.[288] Wu-chen resides at the Fa-hsing Temple at Mount Ts'ao-ch'i in Ling-nan, and as of now he is transmitting this Dharma.

56. When [in the future] this Dharma is to be handed down, it must be attained by a man of superior wisdom, one with a mind of faith in the Buddhadharma, and one who embraces the great compassion. Such a person must be qualified to possess this *Sutra,* to make it a mark of the transmission, and to see that in this day it is not cut off.[289]

---

[286] Both the *Shen-hui yü-lu* (Hu Shih, "Hsin-chiao-ting . . . ," p. 847; Suzuki text, p. 63) and the *Li-tai fa-pao chi,* T51, p. 182c, state that Wei Ch'ü erected a stele and later wrote the inscription. The latter work further states that in 719 Wei Ch'ü's inscription was effaced, and one written by Sung Ting inscribed in its place. The *Sōkei daishi betsuden,* zz2B, 19, 5, 486d, and Shen-hui (Hu Shih, "Hsin-chiao-ting . . . ," p. 847) state that the inscription was changed and a new one by Wu P'ing-i substituted. No texts of these inscriptions have been handed down.

[287] Unidentified.

[288] Unidentified. See Introduction, p. 91, n. 4.

[289] This and the following section are not included in the *Kōshōji* edition. The Tun-huang text is scarcely readable here, and the translation must remain highly tentative.

57. This priest [Fa-hai] was originally a native of Ch'ü-chiang hsien in Shao-chou. After the Tathāgata entered Nirvāṇa, the teaching of the Dharma flowed to the Eastern Land. Among all, non-abiding was transmitted; even our minds do not abide. This true Bodhisattva spoke the true doctrine and practiced [in accord with] the real parables.[290] To the one who vows to save all, practices continuously, does not retrogress in the face of disaster, perseveres under any suffering, and thus possesses the deepest of blessings and virtue, to such a man should this Dharma be handed down. If a person's talents are inadequate and his capacities do not suffice, he must seek[291] this Dharma. This *Platform Sutra* must not be haphazardly assigned to a person who betrays the precepts and has no virtue.

A pronouncement to all fellow students: strive to understand the secret meaning.

Southern School Sudden Doctrine Platform Sutra of the Supreme Mahāyāna Vehicle, one roll.

[290] Eight characters which are untranslatable follow here.
[291] The text appears to have dropped a negative here.

Glossary

An-feng 安豐
An-k'ang 安康
An Lu-shan 安祿山
An Tao-ch'eng 安道誠
Ānanda 阿難
Aśvaghoṣa 馬鳴
Basiasita 婆舍斯多
Bodhidharma 菩提達摩
Bodhidharmatrāta 菩提達摩多羅
Buddhamitra 佛陀蜜多
Buddhanandi 佛陀難提
Chang Ch'ang-chi 張昌期
Chang-chih hsien 長治縣
Chang Ching-man 張淨滿
Chang Hsing-ch'ang 張行昌
Chang Jih-yung 張日用
Chang Yüeh 張說
Ch'ang-shou 長壽
Ch'ao Chiung 晁迥
Ch'ao Tzu-chien 晁子健
Chen-kuan 貞觀
Chen-ti 眞諦
Chen-yen 眞言
Ch'en Ch'u-chang 陳楚璋
Ch'en Hui-ming 陳惠明
Ch'en Ya-hsien 陳亞仙
Cheng Ching-ch'i 程京杞
Cheng-tao ko 證道歌
Ch'eng ch'an-shih 澄禪師
Ch'eng-yüan 承遠
Chi-an hsien 吉安縣
Chi-chou 吉州
Ch'i-ch'un 蘄春
Ch'i-sung 契嵩
Ch'i-to-lo 耆多羅
Chiang-chou 江州
Chiang-chün shan 將軍山
Chiang-ling hsien 江陵縣

Chien-chung 建中
Ch'ien-yüan 乾元
Chih-ch'ang 智常
Chih-ch'e 志徹
Chih-ch'eng 志誠
Chih-chiang hsien 支江縣
Chih-chih ssu 制旨寺
Chih-chü 智炬
Chih-hai 智海
Chih-hsien 智詵
Chih-huang 智隍
Chih-kuang 智光
Chih-tao 志道
Chih-te 智德
Chih-t'ung 志通
Chih-t'ung 智通
Chih-yao 智藥
Ch'ih-ching 持經
Chin-chou 金州
Chin ho-shang 金和尚
Ch'in-hsien 沁縣
Ch'in-yang hsien 沁陽縣
Ching-chou 荊州
Ching-ch'üan ssu 淨泉寺
Ching-chüeh 淨覺
Ching-hsien 敬賢 (var. 景賢)
Ching-lung 景龍
Ching-ming ching 淨名經
Ching-nan fu 荊南府
Ching-shan 徑山
Ching-shan Fa-ch'in 徑山法欽
Ching-te 景德
Ching-te ch'uan-teng lu 景德傳燈錄
Ch'ing-yüan Hsing-ssu 清原行思
Chiu-chiang 九江
Chiu T'ang shu 舊唐書
Cho hsien 涿縣
Ch'u-chi 處寂

Ch'ü-chiang hsien 曲江縣
Ch'ü-chou 衢州
Ch'uan fa-pao chi 傳法寶紀
Ch'üan T'ang wen 全唐文
Chün-chai tu-shu chih 郡齊讀書志
Chung-nan shan 終南山
Chung-tsung 中宗
Daianji 大安寺
Daijōji 大乘寺
Dharmatrāta 達摩多羅
Dhṛtaka 提多迦
E-hu Ta-i 鵝湖大義
Eichō 永超
Enchin 圓珍
Engyō 圓行
Ennin 圓仁
Erh-ju ssu-hsing 二入四行
Fa-chen 法珍
Fa-ch'in 法欽
Fa-ch'üan ssu 法泉寺
Fa-ch'ung 法沖
Fa-hai 法海
Fa-hsing ssu 法性寺
Fa-ju 法如
Fa-jung 法融
Fa-lin 法琳
Fa-ta 法達
Fa-ts'ai 法才
Fa-wo 法我
Fa-yen 法眼
Fan-yang 范陽
Fang Kuan 房琯
Fang-pien 方辯
Fen-yin 汾陰
Feng-hsiang 鳳翔
Feng-kuo Shen-chao 奉國神照
Feng-mu shan 馮墓山 (var. 馮母；憑茂)
Fo-chung-hsing 佛種姓
Fo-hsin-tsung 佛心宗
Fu-ch'ing hsien 福清縣
Fu fa-tsang yin-yüan chuan 付法藏因緣傳

Fu-t'ang 福唐
Fu-t'ien 福田
Gayaśāta 迦耶舍
Gozan 五山
Gunabhadra 求那跋陀
Gyōhyō 行表
Haklenayaśas 鶴勒那
Han-chou 漢州
Ho-chih 郝志
Ho-lin Hsüan-su 鶴林玄素
Ho-nei 河內
Ho-tse ho-shang ch'an-yao 荷澤和上禪要
Ho-tse ssu 荷澤寺
Ho-tung 河東
Honrai muichimotsu 本來無一物
Hou Ching-chung 侯敬中
Hsi-ch'ien 希遷
Hsi-kuo Fo-tsu tai-tai hsiang-ch'eng ch'uan-fa chi 西國佛祖代代相承傳法記
Hsi-tsung 僖宗
Hsiang-hsia 向下
Hsiang-mo 降魔
Hsiang-yang 襄陽
Hsiang-ying 相應
Hsien-heng 咸亨
Hsien-t'ien 先天
Hsien-tsung chi 顯宗記
Hsien-tsung lun 顯宗論
Hsin-chin wen-chi 鐔津文集
Hsin-chou 新州
Hsin-hsing hsien 新興縣
Hsin-ti 心地
Hsin-t'ung 心通
Hsin-yang 潯陽
Hsin-yüan k'ung-chi 心源空寂
Hsing-ssu 行思
Hsing-t'ao 行韜
Hsiu-fu 修福
Hsiu-hsiu an 休休庵
Hsü kao-seng chuan 續高僧傳
Hsüan-chüeh 玄覺

Glossary

Hsüan-lang 玄朗

Hsüan-shih 宣什

Hsüan-su 玄素

Hsüan-tse 玄賾

Hsüan-tsung 玄宗

Hsüan-yüeh 玄約

Hsüeh Chien 薛蕑

Hu-lao 虎牢

Hua hsien 滑縣

Hua-kuo yüan 花果院

Hua-t'ai 滑臺

Hua-yen 華嚴

Huai-chi 懷集

Huai-jang 懷讓

Huai-ning hsien 懷寧縣

Huan-kung shan 峴公山

Huang ch'an-shih 瑝禪師

Huang-mei 黃梅

Hui-an 慧安

Hui-ch'ang 會昌

Hui-chi 惠紀

Hui-ching 慧靜

Hui-chü 慧炬

Hui-fu 惠福

Hui-hsiang 惠象

Hui-hsin 惠昕

Hui-hsün 惠順

Hui-k'o 慧可

Hui-ming 惠明

Hui-neng 惠（慧）能

Hui-shan ssu 會善寺

Hui-tsang 惠藏

Hung-cheng 宏正

Hung-chi ta-shih 弘濟大師

Hung-chou 洪州

Hung-jen 弘忍

I-ch'un hsien 宣春縣

I-fang 義方

I-feng 儀鳳

I-fu 義福

I-hsing san-mei 一行三昧

I-ta-shih yin-yüan 一大事因緣

Jayata 闍夜多

Ju-nan 汝南

Jung 融

Jung-ho hsien 榮河縣

K'ai-huang 開皇

K'ai-pao 開寶

K'ai-yüan 開元

Kānadeva 迦那提婆

Kao-tsung 高宗

Kao-yao hsien 高要縣

Kapimala 毘羅長者

Kattō shū 葛藤集

Ko-lao 猓玀

Kokubunji 國分寺

Kōshōji 興聖寺

Kuan-hsin 觀心

Kuan-hsin lun 觀心論

Kuang-hsiao ssu 光孝寺

Kuang-hsiao ssu i-fa t'a-chi 光孝寺瘞髮塔記

Kuang-sheng ssu 廣勝寺

Kuei-hsi 貴谿

Kumārata 鳩摩羅馱

Kuo-en ssu 國恩寺

Lang 郎

Lao-an 老安

Leng-chia jen-fa chih 楞伽人法志

Leng-chia shih-tzu chi 楞伽師資記

Leng-chia yao-i 楞伽要義

Li Ch'ang 李常

Li-tai fa-pao chi 歷代法寶記

Liang hsien 梁縣

Lin-chi 臨濟

Ling-nan 嶺南

Ling-t'ao 令韜

Ling-yün 靈雲

Liu-ch'en 六塵

Liu Chih-lüeh 劉志略

Liu Ch'u-chiang 劉楚江

Liu Ch'ung-ching 劉崇景

Liu K'o 劉軻

Liu-shih 六識

Liu-tse 六賊

Liu-tsu fa-pao chi hsü 六祖法寶記叙

Liu-tsu ta-shih fa-pao t'an-ching 六祖大
　　師法寶壇經略序

Liu-tsu ta-shih yüan-ch'i wai-chi 六祖
　　大師緣起外記

Liu-tsu t'an-ching 六祖壇經

Liu Tsung-yüan 柳宗元

Liu-wen 六門

Liu Yü-hsi 劉禹錫

Lo-fu 羅浮

Lu Chen 盧珍

Lu I 盧弈

Lung-hsing ssu 龍興寺

Ma-su 馬素

Ma-tsu Tao-i 馬祖道一

Madhyāntika 末田地

Mahākāśyapa 大迦葉

Manorhita 摩拏羅

Mei hsien 郿縣

Meng-shan 蒙山

Mi-to 蜜多

Miccaka 彌遮迦

Mien-chou 綿州

Mien-yang hsien 緜陽縣

Ming-hsiang 明象

Nāgārjuna 龍樹

Nan-ch'ang hsien 南昌縣

Nan-ch'üan P'u-yüan 南泉普願

Nan-t'ien-chi i-ch'eng tsung 南天竺一
　　乘宗

Nan-tsung 南宗

*Nan-tsung tun-chiao tsui-shang ta-ch'eng
　　t'an-ching* 南宗頓教最上大乘壇經

Nan-yang 南陽

*Nan-yang ho-shang tun-chiao chieh-t'o
　　ch'an-men chih-liao-hsing t'an-yü* 南
　　陽和尚頓教解脫禪門直性了壇經

Nan-yang Hui-chung 南陽慧忠

Nan-yang wen-ta tsa-cheng i 南陽問答
　　雜徵義

Nan-yüeh Huai-jang 南嶽懷讓

Niu-t'ou shan 牛頭山

Pa-hsieh 八邪

Pai-chang Huai-hai 百丈懷海

P'an-yü hsien 番禺縣

Pao-chih ho-shang 寶誌和尚

Pao-en kuang-hsiao ssu 報恩光孝寺

Pao-lin chuan 寶林傳

Pao-lin ssu 寶林寺

Pao-t'ang ssu 保唐寺

Pao-tz'u ho-shang 報慈和尚

Pao-ying 寶應

Paramārtha 眞諦

Pārśva 脇比丘

Pen-chou 本州

Pen-chüeh 本覺

Pen-lai wu-i-wu 本來無一物

Pi-an 彼岸

Pi-yen lu 碧巖錄

Pien 變

Pien-hsiang 變相

Pien-wen 變文

P'o-hsiang lun 破相論

P'o-t'ou shan 破頭山

P'o-yang 鄱陽

Prajñāmitra 般若蜜多羅

P'u-chi 普寂

P'u-t'i-ta-mo Nan-tsung ting shih-fei lun
　　菩提達摩南宗定是非論

Punyamitra 不若蜜多羅

Puṇyayaśas 富那奢

Rāhulata 羅睺羅

Ryōnen 了然

Saichō 最澄

San-chang 三障

Śaṇavāsa 舍那波斯

Śaṇavāsa 商那和修

Saṅghānandi 僧迦那提

Saṅgharakṣa 僧迦羅

Seng-ts'an 僧璨

Shan-chien ssu 山間寺

Shan-chih-shih 善知識

Shan-ku ssu 山谷寺

Shan-pei ssu 山北寺
Shang-na-ho-hsiu 商那和修
Shang-tang 上黨
Shang-yüan 上元
Shao-chou 韶州
Shao-lin ssu 少林寺
She-na-p'o-ssu 舍那婆斯
Shen-hsiu 神秀
Shen-hui 神會
Shen-hui yü-lu 神會語錄
Shen-lung 神龍
Sheng-chou chi 聖胄集
Sheng-ssu shih-ta 生死事大
Shih-chüeh 石角
shih-chüeh 始覺
Shih-chün 使君
Shih-fang 什邡
Shih-hsin 識心
Shih-lang 侍郎
shih-o 十惡
Shih-ssu k'o-sung 十四科頌
Shih-t'ou Hsi-ch'ien 石頭希遷
Shih-tzu hsieh-mo chuan 師資血脈傳
Shou-chou 壽州
Shu-chou 舒州
Shuang-feng shan 雙峯山
Shuang-feng shan Ts'ao-hou-ch'i Pao-lin chuan 雙峯山曹侯溪寶林傳
Shuo-t'ung 說通
Siṁha bhikṣu 師子比丘
Sohō 祖芳
Sōkei daishi betsuden 曹溪大師別傳
Ssu-hui 四會
Ssu-shui hsien 氾水縣
Su-tsung 肅宗
Śubhamitra 須婆蜜
Sung Chih-wen 宋之問
Sung Ching 宋璟
Sung kao-seng chuan 宋高僧傳
Sung-shan 嵩山
Sung Ting 宋鼎
Sung-yüeh 嵩岳

Sung Yün 宋雲
Ta-ch'ang ssu-ch'eng 大常寺丞
Ta-ch'eng ch'i-hsin lun 大乘起信論
Ta-ch'eng san-k'o 大乘三寠
Ta-ch'eng tsan 大乘讚
Ta-ch'eng wu fang-pien Pei-tsung 大乘五方便北宗
Ta-chi ch'an-shih 大寂禪師
Ta-chien 大鑑
Ta-chien chih-jen 大鑑至人
Ta-chih 大智
Ta-fan ssu 大梵寺
Ta-hsiao ch'an-shih 大曉禪師
Ta-jung 大榮
Ta-liang 大梁
Ta-mo ch'an-shih lun 達摩禪師論
Ta-mo lun 達摩論
Ta-mo-to-lo ch'an-ching 達摩多羅禪經
ta-shih 大師
Ta-t'ung ch'an-shih 大通禪師
Ta-yeh 大業
Ta-yü ling 大庾嶺
Ta-yün ssu 大雲寺
Tai-tsung 代宗
T'ai-ho 太和
T'ai-hu hsien 太湖縣
T'ai-tsung 太宗
T'an-ching 壇經
T'an-lin 曇林
Tang-yang hsien 當陽縣
T'ang ho-shang 唐和尙
Tao-heng 道恒
Tao-hsin 道信
Tao-hsüan 道璿
Tao-i 道一
Tao-ming 道明
Tao-ts'an 道澯
Tao-tsung 道宗
Tao-yü 道育
Te-ch'un ssu 德純寺
Te-i 德異
Ti-i-wu 第一勿

T'i 體
Tien-chung-ch'eng 殿中丞
T'ien-kung ssu 天宮寺
T'ien-pao 天寶
T'ien-p'ing 天平
T'ien-t'ai 天台
Ts'ao-ch'i 曹溪
*Ts'ao-ch'i shan ti-liu-tsu Hui-neng ta-
    shih shuo chien-hsing tun-chiao
    chih-liao cheng-fo chüeh-ting wu-i
    fa-pao-chi t'an-ching* 曹溪山第六
    祖惠能大師說見性頓教直了成
    佛決定無疑法寶記壇經
*Ts'ao-ch'i shan ti-liu-tsu Neng ta-shih t'an-
    ching* 曹溪山第六祖能大師壇經
Ts'ao-tung 曹洞
Tso-ch'an 坐禪
Tso-ch'i Hsüan-lang 左溪玄朗
Tsu-t'ang chi 祖堂集
Tsui-shang ch'eng 最上乘
Ts'un-chung 存中
Tsung-ch'ih ssu 總持寺
Tsung-hsi 宗錫
Tsung-mi 宗密
Tsung-pao 宗寶
Tsung-t'ung 宗通
Tu Fei 杜胐
Tu-ku P'ei 獨孤沛
Tuan-chou 端州
Tun-wu wu-shang pan-jo sung 頓悟無上
    般若頌
Tung-shan fa-men 東山法門
T'ung-kuang 同光
T'ung shang-jen 通上人
T'ung-ti 銅鞮
T'ung-ying 通應
Tzu-tsai 自在
Ūich'ŏn 義天
Upagupta 優波毱多
Vasubandhu 婆修盤多
Vasumitra 婆須蜜
Wang Wei 王維

Wei Chou 韋宙
Wei Ch'u-hou 韋處厚
Wei Ch'ü 韋璩
Wei Li-chien 韋利見
Wei-shih hsien 尉氏縣
Wei-yang 潙仰
Wen-hsien t'ung-k'ao 文獻通考
Wen-yüan 文元
Wu-chen 悟真
Wu-chi ta-shih 無際大師
Wu-chin-ts'ang 無盡藏
Wu-chu 無住
Wu-ch'u 無除
Wu-chung 吳中
Wu-hsiang 無相
Wu-hsin 無心
Wu-lao 武牢
Wu-men kuan 無門關
Wu-nien 無念
Wu P'ing-i 武平一
Wu-te 武德
Yang Chien 楊珹
Yang Ch'ung-ching 楊崇景
Yang K'an 楊侃
Yao-shan Wei-yen 藥山惟儼
Yin-tsung 印宗
Ying-shih 應是
Yü-ch'üan ssu 玉泉寺
Yüan ch'an-shih 遠禪師
Yüan-chia 元嘉
Yüan-chou 袁州
Yüan-chou Meng-shan Tao-ming
    ch'an-shih 袁州蒙山道明禪師
Yüan-chüeh ching ta-shu ch'ao 圓覺經
    大疏鈔
Yüan-ho Ling-chao 元和靈照
Yüan-hui 圓會
Yüan-kuei 元珪
Yün-men 雲門
Yung 用
Yung-chi hsien 永濟縣
Yung-t'ai 永泰

Bibliography

A. EDITIONS OF THE PLATFORM SUTRA

I. Tun-huang edition

Nan-tsung tun-chiao tsui-shang ta-ch'eng Mo-ho-pan-jo po-lo-mi ching: Liu-tsu Hui-neng ta-shih yü Shao-chou Ta-fan ssu shih-fa t'an ching 南宗頓教最上大乘摩訶般若波羅蜜經六祖惠能大師於韶州大梵寺施法壇經. Photographic reproduction of original manuscript in Stein Collection (S5475).

——— In *Meisha yoin* 鳴沙餘韻, comp. by Yabuki Keiki 矢吹慶輝. Tokyo, 1930. Plates 102-3. Facsimile reproduction.

——— T48 (no. 2007), pp. 337-45.

———, edited by Ui Hakuju 宇井伯壽. In *Zenshū shi kenkyū* 禪宗史研究 (Tokyo, 1941), II, 117-71.

Tonkō shutsudo Rokuso dankyō 燉煌出土六祖壇經, edited by D. T. Suzuki 鈴木大拙 and Kuda Rentarō 公田連太郎. Tokyo, 1934.

II. Kōshōji edition

Kōshōji bon Rokuso dankyō 興聖寺本六祖壇經, edited by D. T. Suzuki 鈴木大拙 and Kuda Rentarō 公田連太郎. Tokyo, 1934.

Rokuso dankyō 六祖壇經. Kyoto, 1933. Facsimile reproduction of Kōshōji edition.

III. Daijōji edition

Kaga Daijōji shozō Shōshū Sōkeizan Roku soshi dankyō 加賀大乘寺所藏韶州曹溪山六祖師壇經. In *Komazawa Daigaku Bukkyō gakkai gakuhō* 駒澤大學佛教學會學報, no. 8 (April, 1938), pp. 1-56 (text).

Shōshū Sōkeizan Roku soshi dankyō 韶州曹溪山六祖師壇經, edited by D. T. Suzuki. Tokyo, 1942.

IV. Yüan editions

Liu-tsu ta-shih fa-pao t'an-ching 六祖大師法寶壇經. T48 (no. 2008), pp. 245-65. (Tsung-pao 宗寶 edition.)

Gen En'yū Kōrai kokubon Rokuso daishi hōbō dankyō 元延祐高麗刻本六祖大師法寶壇經. In *Zengaku kenkyū*, 禪學研究 no. 23 (July, 1935), pp. 1-63. (Te-i 德異 edition.)

Hōbō dankyō kōkan 法寶壇經肯窾. Kyoto, 1697. 5 vols.

Liu-tsu t'an-ching chien-chu 六祖壇經箋註, by Ting Fu-pao 丁福保. Shanghai, 1933.

B. INSCRIPTIONS *(by author)*

Anonymous. *T'ang Chung-yüeh Sha-men Shih Fa-ju ch'an-shih hsing-chuang pei* 唐中岳
沙門釋法如禪師行狀碑. *Chin-shih hsü-pien* 金石續編, ch. 6, pp. 5b-7a.

Chang Cheng-fu 張正甫. *Heng-chou Pan-jo ssu Kuan-yin ta-shih pei-ming ping-hsü* 衡州
般若寺觀音大師碑銘并序, CTW, ch. 619 (XIII, 7935-36).

Chang Yüeh 張說. *T'ang Yü-ch'üan ssu Ta-t'ung ch'an-shih pei-ming ping-hsü* 唐玉泉寺
大通禪師碑銘并序 CTW, ch. 231 (V, 2953-54).

Ch'ing-chou 清晝. *T'ang Hu-chou Fo-ch'uan ssu ku ta-shih t'a-ming* 唐湖州佛川寺故
大師塔銘, CTW, ch. 917 (XIX, 12062-63).

Ch'üan Te-yü 權德輿. *T'ang ku Hung-chou K'ai-yüan ssu Shih-wen Tao-i ch'an-shih
t'a-ming* 唐故洪州開元寺石門道一禪師塔銘, CTW, ch. 501 (XI, 6466-67).

Fa-hai 法海. *Liu-tsu ta-shih fa-pao t'an-ching lüeh-hsü* 六祖大師法寶壇經略序, CTW,
ch. 915 (XIX, 12032-33).

Fa-ts'ai 法才. *Kuang-hsiao ssu i-fa t'a-chi* 光孝寺瘞髮塔記, CTW, ch. 912 (XIX,
11996).

Hsü Ch'ou 許籌. *Sung-yüeh Kuei ch'an-shih ying-t'ang chi* 嵩嶽珪禪師影堂記, CTW,
ch. 790 (XVII, 10435-36).

Jen-su 仁素. *Ta T'ang Sung-yüeh Hsien-chü ssu ku ta-te Kuei ch'an-shih t'a-chi* 大唐嵩
岳閑居寺故大德珪禪師塔記, CTW, ch. 914 (XIX, 12022).

Kuo Shih 郭湜. *T'ang Shao-lin ssu T'ung-kuang ch'an-shih t'a-ming* 唐少林寺同光禪
師塔銘, CTW, ch. 441 (IX, 5685-86).

Li Chi-fu 李吉甫. *Kang-chou Ching-shan ssu Ta-chüeh ch'an-shih pei-ming ping-hsü* 杭州
徑山寺大覺禪師碑銘并序, CTW, ch. 512 (XI, 6599-61).

Li Hua 李華. *Jun-chou Ho-lin ssu ku Ching-shan ta-shih pei-ming* 潤州鶴林寺故徑山
大師碑銘, CTW, ch. 320 (VII, 4106-8).

——— *Ku Tso-ch'i ta-shih pei* 故左溪大師碑, CTW, ch. 320 (VII, 4101-2).

Li Yung 李邕. *Sung-yüeh ssu pei* 嵩岳寺碑, CTW, ch. 263 (VI, 3379-81).

——— *Ta-chao ch'an-shih t'a-ming* 大照禪師塔銘, CTW, ch. 262 (VI, 3360-63).

Liu Tsung-yüan 柳宗元. *Ts'ao-ch'i ti-liu-tsu tz'u-shih Ta-chien ch'an-shih pei* 曹溪第
六祖賜諡大鑑禪師碑, CTW, ch. 587 (XII, 7535).

Liu Yü-hsi 劉禹錫. *Ts'ao-ch'i liu-tsu Ta-chien ch'an-shih ti-erh pei ping hsü* 曹溪六祖
大鑑禪師第二碑并序, CTW, ch. 610 (XIII, 7824-25).

P'ei Ts'ui 斐漼. *Shao-lin ssu pei* 少林寺碑, CTW, ch. 279 (VI, 3584-87).

Sung Chih-wen 宋之問. *Wei Lo-hsia chu-seng ch'ing fa-shih ying Hsiu ch'an-shih piao* 爲洛下諸僧請法事迎秀禪師表, CTW, ch. 240 (V, 3076).

Sung Tan 宋儋. *Sung-shan Hui-shan ssu ku ta-te Tao-an ch'an-shih pei-ming* 嵩山會善寺故大德道安禪師碑銘, CTW, ch. 396 (IX, 5104-5).

Ts'ui Ch'i 崔琪. *T'ang Shao-lin ssu Ling-yün ch'an-shih t'a-pei* 唐少林寺靈運禪師塔碑, CTW, ch. 303 (VII, 3893-94).

Tu Yü 杜昱. *Ta-chih ch'an-shih I-fu t'a-ming* 大智禪師義福塔銘, *Chin-shih hsü-pien* 金石續編, ch. 7, pp. 17b-19a.

Tu-ku Chi 獨孤及. *Shu-chou Shan-ku ssu Chüeh-chi t'a Sui ku Ching-chih ch'an-shih pei-ming* 舒州山谷寺覺寂塔隋故鏡智禪師碑銘, CTW, ch. 390 (VIII, 5021-22).

Wang Wei 王維. *Neng ch'an-shih pei* 能禪師碑, *Wang Yu-ch'eng chi chien-chu* 王右丞集箋注, pp. 446-49.

——— *Ta T'ang Ta-an-kuo ssu ku ta-te Ching-chüeh shih t'a-ming* 大唐大安國寺故大德淨覺師塔銘, CTW, ch. 327 (VII, 4193-94).

Wei Ch'u-hou 韋處厚. *Hsing-fu ssu nei tao-ch'ang kung-feng ta-te Ta-i ch'an-shih pei-ming* 興福寺内道場供奉大德大義禪師碑銘, CTW, ch. 715 (XV, 9311-13).

Yang Yü 羊愉. *Sung-shan Hui-shan-shan ssu ku Ching-hsien ta-shih shen-t'a shih-chi* 嵩山會善山寺故景賢大師身塔石記, CTW, ch. 362 (VIII, 4649-50).

Yen T'ing-chih 嚴挺之. *Ta-chih ch'an-shih pei-ming ping-hsü* 大智禪師碑銘并序. CTW, ch. 280 (VI, 3596-98).

C. WORKS IN TRIPITAKA COLLECTIONS (*by title*)

A-mi-t'o ching 阿彌陀經. (Sukhāvatīvyūha Sutra). T12 (no. 336), pp. 346-48.

Ch'an-men shih-tzu ch'eng-hsi-t'u 禪門師資承襲圖, by Tsung-mi 宗密. ZZ2, 15, 5, pp. 433b-438b.

Ch'an-yüan chu-ch'üan-chi tu-hsü 禪源諸詮集都序, by Tsung-mi 宗密. T48 (no. 2015), pp. 397-413.

Cheng-tao ko 證道歌, attributed to Hsüan-chüeh 玄覺. T48 (no. 2014), pp. 395c-96c. Also contained in *Ching-te ch'uan-teng lu* 景德傳燈錄, ch. 30, T51, pp. 460a-61b.

Ch'ih-hsiu Pai-chang ch'ing-kuei 勅修百丈清規, by Pai-chang Hui-hai 百丈懷海, rev. and enl. by Tung-yang Te-hui 東陽德輝. T48 (no. 2025), pp. 1109-60.

Chin-kang pan-jo po-lo-mi ching 金剛般若波羅蜜經 (Vajracchedikā; Diamond Sutra). T8 (no. 235), pp. 748-52.

Chin-kang san-mei ching 金剛三昧經. T9 (no. 273), pp. 365-74.

Ching-te ch'uan-teng lu 景德傳燈錄, by Tao-yüan 道原. T51 (no. 2076), pp. 196-467.

Chishō daishi shōrai mokuroku 智證大師請來目錄, by Enchin 圓珍. T55 (no. 2173), pp. 1102-8.

Ch'uan-fa cheng-tsung chi 傳法正宗記, by Ch'i-sung 契嵩. T51 (no. 2078), pp. 715-68.

Ch'uan fa-pao chi 傳法寶紀, by Tu Fei 杜朏. T85 (no. 2838), p. 1291.

Ch'uan-hsin fa-yao 傳心法要, comp. by P'ei Hsiu 斐休. T48 (no. 2012A), pp. 379-84. Full title: *Huang-po shan Tuan-chi ch'an-shih ch'uan-hsin fa-yao*. 黃檗山斷際禪師傳心法要.

Diamond Sutra, see *Chin-kang pan-jo po-lo-mi ching*.

Fan-weng ching Lu-she-na fo-shuo p'u-sa hsin-ti chieh-p'in ti-shih 梵網經盧舍那佛說菩薩心地戒品第十. T24 (no. 1484), pp. 997-1010.

Fo-tsu t'ung-chi 佛祖統紀, by Chih-p'an 志盤. T49 (no. 2035), pp. 129-475.

Fu fa-tsang yin-yüan chuan 付法藏因緣傳. T50 (no. 2058), pp. 297-322.

Fukushū Onshū Daishū gutoku kyōritsu ronshoki gesho tō mokuroku 福州溫州臺州求得經律論疏記外書等目錄, by Enchin 圓珍. T55 (no. 2170), pp. 1092-95.

Hsien-tsung chi 顯宗記, by Shen-hui 神會. Contained in *Ching-te ch'uan-teng lu*, 景德傳燈錄 ch.30, T51, pp. 458c-459b.

Hsien-tsung lun 顯宗論, by Shen-hui. Contained in *Tsung-ching lu* 宗鏡錄, ch. 99, T48, p. 949a-b.

Hsin-chin wen-chi 鐔津文集, by Ch'i-sung 契嵩, T52 (no. 2115), pp. 646-750.

Hsü ch'uan-teng lu 續傳燈錄, by Yüan-chi Chü-ting 圓極居頂. T51 (no. 2077), pp. 469-714.

Hsü kao-seng chuan 續高僧傳, by Tao-hsüan 道宣. T50 (no. 2060), pp. 425-707.

I-ch'ieh ching yin-i 一切經音義, by Hui-lin 慧琳. T54 (no. 2128), pp. 312-932.

Jikaku daishi zai-Tō sōshin roku 慈覺大師在唐送進錄, by Ennin 圓仁. T55 (no. 2166), pp. 1076-78.

Kao-seng chuan 高僧傳, by Hui-chiao 慧皎. T50 (no. 2059), pp. 322-423.

Kuan-hsin lun 觀心論, by Shen-hsiu 神秀. T85 (no. 2833), pp. 1270-73.

Kuan wu-liang-shou ching 觀無量壽經. T12 (no. 365). pp. 340-46.

Laṅkāvatāra Sutra, see *Leng-chia a-po-to-lo-pao ching*.

Leng-chia a-po-to-lo-pao ching 楞伽阿跋多羅寶經. (Laṅkāvatāra Sutra). T16 (no. 670), pp. 479-514.

Leng-chia shih-tzu chi 楞伽師資記, by Ching-chüeh 淨覺. T85 (no. 2837), pp. 1283-91.

Lin-chi lu 臨濟錄, comp. by Hui-jan 慧然. T47 (no. 1985), pp. 495-506. Full title: *Chen-chou Lin-chi Hui-chao ch'an-shih yü-lu* 鎮州臨濟慧照禪師語錄.

Li-tai fa-pao chi 歷代法寶記. T51 (no. 2075), pp. 179-96.

Lo-yang chia-lan chi 洛陽伽藍記, by Yang Hsüan-chih 楊衒之. T51 (no. 2092), pp. 999-1022

Lotus Sutra, see *Miao-fa lien-hua ching.*

Miao-fa lien-hua ching 妙法蓮華經 (Saddharmapuṇḍarīka Sutra; Lotus Sutra). T9 (no. 262), pp. 1-61.

Mo-ho chih-kuan 摩訶止觀, by Chih-i 智顗. T46 (no. 1911), pp. 1-140.

Nihon biku Enchin nittō guhō mokuroku 日本比丘圓珍入唐求法目錄, by Enchin 圓珍. T55 (no. 2172), pp. 1097-1101.

Nihon koku Shōwa gonen nittō guhō mokuroku 日本國承和五年入唐求法目錄, by Ennin 圓仁. T55 (no. 2165), pp. 1074-76.

Nirvāṇa Sutra, see *Ta-pan nieh-pʿan ching.*

Nittō shin gushōgyō mokuroku 入唐新求聖教目錄, by Ennin 圓仁. T55 (no. 2167), pp. 1078-87.

Pi-yen lu 碧巖錄, by Yüan-wu Kʿo-chʿin 圜悟克勤. T48 (no. 2003), pp. 139-225.

Pʿu-tʿi hsin-lun 菩提心論. T32 (no. 1665), pp. 572-74.

Reiganji oshō shōrai hōmon dōgu tō mokuroku 靈巖寺和尚請來法門道具等目錄, by Engyō 圓行. T55 (no. 2164), pp. 1071-74.

Saddharmapuṇḍarīka Sutra, see *Miao-fa lien-hua ching.*

Shih-ssu kʿo sung 十四科頌, by Pao-chih 寶誌. Contained in *Ching-te chʿuan-teng lu* 景德傳燈錄, ch. 29, T51, pp. 450a-51c.

Shih-men cheng-tʿung 釋門正統, by Tsung-chien 宗鑑. ZZ2B, 3, 5.

Shōbō genzō 正法眼藏, by Dōgen 道元. T82 (no. 2582), pp. 7-310.

Shōshitsu rokumon 少室六門. T48 (no. 2009), pp. 365-76.

Sōkei daishi betsuden 曹溪大師別傳. ZZ2B, 19, 5, pp. 483-88.

Ssu-shih-erh chang ching 四十二章經. T17 (no. 784), pp. 722-23.

Sung kao-seng chuan 宋高僧傳, by Tsan-ning 贊寧. T50 (no. 2061), pp. 709-900.

Ta-chʿeng chʿi-hsin lun 大乘起信論. T32 (no. 1666), pp. 575-83.

Ta-chʿeng tsan 大乘讚, by Pao-chih 寶誌. Contained in *Ching-te chʿuan-teng lu* 景德傳燈錄, ch. 29, T51, pp. 449b-50a.

Ta-mo-to-lo chʿan ching 達摩多羅禪經. T15 (no. 618), pp. 301-25.

Ta-pan nieh-pʿan ching 大般涅槃經 (Nirvāṇa Sutra). T12 (no. 374), pp. 365-606.

Tōiki dentō mokuroku 東域傳燈目錄, by Eichō 永超. T55 (no. 2183), pp. 1145-65.

Tseng-chi hsü chʿuan-teng lu 增集續傳燈錄, by Nan-shih Wen-hsiu 南石文秀. ZZ2B, 15, 4-5.

Tsu-tʿing shih-yüan 祖庭事苑, by Mu-an Shan-chʿing 睦庵善卿. ZZ2, 18, 1.

Tsung-ching lu 宗鏡錄, by Yung-ming Yen-shou 永明延壽. T48 (no. 2016), pp. 415-957.

Vajracchedikā Sutra see, *Chin-kang pan-jo po-lo-mi ching.*

Vimalakīrti Sutra, see *Wei-mo-ch'i so-shou ching.*

Wei-mo-ch'i so-shuo ching 維摩詰所說經 (Vimalakīrti Sutra). T14 (no. 475), pp. 537-57.

Wen-shu-shih-li so-shuo mo-ho pan-jo po-lo-mi ching 文殊師利所說摩訶般若波羅蜜經. T8 (no. 232), pp. 726-32.

Wu-men kuan 無門關, by Wu-men Hui-k'ai 無門慧開. T48 (no. 2005), pp. 292-99.

Yüan-chüeh ching ta-shu ch'ao 圓覺經大疏鈔, by Tsung-mi 宗密. zz1, 14, 3-5; 15, 1.

D. EARLY WORKS
(Pre-1900, including modern editions of such works; by title)

Chin-shih hsü-pien 金石續編, by Lu Yao-yü 陸耀遹. 1874 ed. 16 vols.

Ch'ü-chiang hsien chih 曲江縣志. 1875 ed. 6 vols.

Chün-chai tu-shu chih 郡齊讀書志 (Ch'ü-chou 衢州 edition), by Ch'ao Kung-wu 晁公武, ed. by Wang Hsien-ch'ien 王先謙. Peking, 1884. 20 vols.

Chün-chai tu-shu chih 郡齊讀書志 (Yüan-chou 袁州 edition), by Ch'ao Kung-wu 晁公武. SPTK ser. 3, 19. 8 vols.

Hōrin den, see *Pao-lin chuan.*

Kanchū fukyō hen 冠註輔敎編, by Ch'i-sung 契嵩. Kyoto, n.d. (Meiji reprint o. 1695 ed. ?), 5 vols.

Kattō gosen 葛藤語箋, by Dōchū 道忠. Tokyo. 1959.

Kuang-hsiao ssu chih 光孝寺志, by Ho Ts'ung 何淙. 1935 ed. 4 vols.

Kuang-tung t'ung-chih 廣東通志. 1822 ed. 334 vols.

Naishō Buppō sōjō ketsumyaku fu 內證佛法相承血脈譜, by Saichō 最澄. *Dengyō daishi zenshū* 傳敎大師全集, II (1912), pp. 313-62.

Pao-lin chuan 寶林傳. Kyoto, n.d. 3 vols. Mimeographed edition.

Sōden haiin 僧傳排韻, by Gyōjo 堯恕. 2 vols. (1912). *Dai-Nihon Bukkyō zensho* 大日本佛教全書, vols. 99-100.

Sodō shū, see *Tsu-t'ang chi.*

Sung shu 宗書, by T'o T'o 脫脫 and others. Po-na edition.

Sung-tsang i-chen 宋藏遺珍. Peking, 1935. 120 vols, in 12 cases.

Tonkō shutsudo Jinne roku 燉煌出土神會錄. 1932. Facsimile reproduction.

Tsu-t'ang chi 祖堂集. Kyoto, n.d. 5 vols. Mimeographed edition.

Tsu-t'ang chi. In *Hyosŏng Cho Myŏng-gi Paksa hwagap kinyŏn Pulgyo sahak nonch'ong* 曉城趙明基博士華甲記念佛敎史學論叢. Seoul, 1965.

Wang Yu-ch'eng chi chien-chu 王右丞集箋注, annotated by Chao Tien-ch'eng 趙殿成. Peking, 1962.

Wen-hsien t'ung-k'ao 文獻通考, by Ma Tuan-lin 馬端臨. Taipei, 1959. 8 vols.

Zenrin shōki sen 禪林象器箋, by Dōchū 道忠. Tokyo, 1909.

Zenseki shi 禪籍志, by Gitei 義諦. *Dai-Nihon Bukkyō zensho* 大日本佛教全書, 1 (1913), 272-320.

E. MODERN WORKS
(Post 1900; by author)

Abe Hajime 阿部肇. "Nanshū Zen hōkei no ichi kenkyū" 南宗禪法系の一研究, *Tōyō shigaku ronshū* 東洋史學論集, no. 4 (November, 1955), pp. 275-324.

Aizawa Ekai 相澤惠海. *Zengaku yōkan* 禪學要鑑. Tokyo, 1907.

Andō Kōsei 安藤更生. *Ganjin dai-wajō den no kenkyū* 鑒眞大和上傳之研究. Tokyo, 1960.

Chan, Wing-tsit. *The Platform Scripture.* New York, 1963.

Chang Hsiang 張相. *Shih-tz'u-ch'ü yü-tz'u hui-shih* 詩詞曲語辭滙釋. Shanghai, 1954.

Ch'en, Kenneth. "Economic Background of the Hui-ch'ang Persecution," *HJAS* XIX (1956), 67-105.

Chikusa Masaaki 竺沙雅章. "Jōkaku katchū 'Hannya haramita shingyō' ni tsuite" 淨覺夾注「般若波羅密多心經」について, *Bukkyō shigaku* 佛教史學, VII (no. 3, October, 1958), 64-67.

———— "Tonkō no sōkan seido" 敦煌の僧官制度, *Tōhō gakuhō* 東方學報, no. 31 (March, 1961), pp. 117-98.

Conze, Edward. *Buddhist Wisdom Books.* London, 1958.

Demiéville, Paul. "Deux documents de Touen-houang sur le dhyāna chinois," *Tsukamoto hakushi shōju ki'nen Bukkyō shigaku ronshū* 塚本博士頌壽記念佛教史學論集 (Kyoto, 1961), pp. 1-27.

Dumoulin, Heinrich. *A History of Zen Buddhism.* New York, 1963.

Fujita Genro 藤田玄路. *Zudokko* 塗毒皷. Kyoto, 1957. 2 vols.

Gernet, Jacques. "Biographie du Maître Chen-houei de Ho-tsö," *Journal Asiatique,* CCXLIX (1951), 29-60.

———— "Complément aux Entretiens du Maître de Dhyāna Chen-houei (668-760)," *BEFEO,* XLIV (no. 2, 1954), 453-66.

———— *Entretiens du Maître de Dhyāna Chen-houei du Ho-tsö.* Hanoi, 1949. (Publications de l'école française d'Extrême-Orient, vol. XXXI.

Giles, Herbert. *A Chinese Biographical Dictionary.* London, 1898.

Giles, Lionel. *Descriptive Catalogue of the Chinese Manuscripts from Tun-huang in the British Museum.* London, 1957.

Hiraoka Takeo 平岡武夫. *Tōdai no koyomi* 唐代の暦. Kyoto, 1954. (Tōdai kenkyū no shiori 唐代研究のしおり, vol. I.)

────── *Tōdai no sambun sakuhin* 唐代の散文作品. Kyoto, 1960. (Tōdai kenkyū no shiori 唐代研究のしおり, vol. X.)

Ho Ko-en 何格恩. "Hui-neng chuan chih-i" 慧能傳質疑, *Ling-nan hsüeh-pao* 嶺南學報, IV (no. 2, June, 1935), 41-56.

Hsiang Ta 向達. *T'ang-tai Ch'ang-an yü Hsi-yü wen-ming* 唐代長安與西域文明. Peking, 1957.

Hsieh Fu-ya 謝扶雅. "Kuang-hsiao ssu yü Liu-tsu Hui-neng" 光孝寺與六祖慧能, *Ling-nan hsüeh-pao* 嶺南學報, IV (no. 1, April, 1935), 175-201.

Hu Shih 胡適. "An Appeal for a Systematic Search in Japan for Long-hidden T'ang Dynasty Source Materials of the Early History of Zen Buddhism," *Bukkyō to bunka* 佛教と文化 (Kyoto, 1960), pp. 15-23.

────── "Ch'an-hsüeh ku-shih k'ao" 禪學古史考, *Hu Shih wen-ts'un* 胡適文存 (Taipei, 1953), III, 255-74.

────── "Ch'an (Zen) Buddhism in China, Its History and Method," *Philosophy East and West*, III (no. 1, April, 1953), 3-24.

────── "The Development of Zen Buddhism in China," *The Chinese Social and Political Science Review*, XV (no. 4, January, 1932), 475-505.

────── "Ho-tse ta-shih Shen-hui chuan" 荷澤大師神會傳, *Hu Shih wen-ts'un* 胡適文存, IV, 245-88.

────── "Hsin-chiao-ting te Tun-huang hsieh-pen Shen-hui ho-shang i-chu liang-chung" 新校定的敦煌寫本神會和尚遺著兩種, *CYLYYC*, XXIX (no. 2, February, 1958), 827-82.

────── "Leng-chia shih-tzu chi hsü" 楞伽師資記序, *Hu Shih wen-ts'un* 胡適文存, IV, 236-44.

────── "Leng-chia tsung k'ao" 楞伽宗考, *Hu Shih wen-ts'un* 胡適文存, IV, 194-235.

────── "P'u-t'i-ta-mo k'ao" 菩提達摩考, *Hu Shih wen-ts'un* 胡適文存, III, 293-304.

────── *Shen-hui ho-shang i-chi* 神會和尚遺集. Shanghai, 1930.

────── "Shen-hui ho-shang yü-lu te ti-san-ko Tun-huang hsieh-pen". . . 神會和尚語錄的第三個敦煌寫本, *CYLYYC*, extra v. IV, pt. I (September, 1960), pp. 1-31.

────── "T'an-ching k'ao chih-i" 壇經考之一, *Hu Shih wen-ts'un* 胡適文存, IV, 292-301.

────── "T'an-ching k'ao chih-erh" 壇經考之二, *Hu Shih wen-ts'un* 胡適文存, IV, 301-18.

Hurvitz, Leon. "Chih-i" *Mélanges Chinois et Bouddhiques*, XII (1962).

Itō Kokan 伊藤古鑑. "Rokuso Enō daishi no chūshin shisō" 六祖惠能大師の中心思想, *Nihon Bukkyōgaku kyōkai nempō* 日本佛教學協會年報, no. 7 (February, 1935), pp. 198-239.

Iriya Yoshitaka 入矢義高. *Kanzan* 寒山. Tokyo, 1958. (Chūgoku shijin senshū 中國詩人選集, vol. 3.)

———— "*Tonkō hembun shū*" *kōgo goi sakuin* 「敦煌變文集」口語語彙索引. Kyoto, 1961.

Jen Erh-pei 任二北. *Tun-huang ch'ü hsiao-lu* 敦煌曲校錄. Shanghai, 1955.

Jimbo Nyoten 神保如天. *Zengaku jiten* 禪學辭典. Kyoto, 1944.

Kamio Kazuharu 神尾弌春. "Kanshin ron shikō" 觀心論私考, *Shūkyō kenkyū* 宗教研究, new ser., IX (no. 5, September, 1932), 98-106.

Kanda Kiichirō 神田喜一郎. "Dembō hōki no kanchitsu ni tsuite" 傳法寶紀の完帙に就いて, *Sekisui sensei kakōju ki'nen ronsan* 積翠先生華甲壽記念論纂 (Tokyo, 1942), pp. 145-52 & plates.

Karlgren, Bernhard. *Grammata Serica Recensa*. Stockholm, 1957. (*BMFEA*, vol. XXIX.)

Kasuga Raichi 春日禮智, "Zen Tō bun Bukkyō kankei senjutsu mokuroku" 全唐文佛教關係選述目錄, *Nikka Bukkyō kenkyūkai nempō* 日華佛教研究會年報, no. 1 (1936), pp. 20-55.

Kawakami Tenzan 川上天山. "Seikago-yaku Rokuso dankyō ni tsuite" 西夏語譯六祖壇經について, *Shina Bukkyō shigaku* 支那佛教史學, II, (no. 3, September, 1938), 61-66.

Kobayashi Enshō 小林圓照. "Ichigyō zammai shikō" 一行三昧私考, *Zengaku kenkyū* 禪學研究, no. 51 (February, 1961), pp. 176-86.

———— "Zen ni okeru ichigyō zammai no igi" 禪における一行三昧の意義, *IBK*, no. 17 (January, 1961), pp. 160-61.

Kokumin bunko kankō-kai 國民文庫刊行會. *Kokuyaku daizōkyō* 國譯大藏經. Tokyo, 1927-29. 28 vols.

Komazawa Daigaku Toshokan 駒澤大學圖書館. *Shinsan Zenseki mokuroku* 新纂禪籍目錄. Tokyo, 1962.

Kuno Hōryū 久野芳隆. "Hokushū Zen" 北宗禪, *Taishō Daigaku gakuhō* 大正大學學報, no. 30-31 (March, 1940), pp. 131-76.

Kuroda Akira 黑田亮. *Chōsen kyūsho kō* 朝鮮舊書考. Tokyo, 1940.

———— "Rokuso dankyō kō hoi" 六祖壇經考補遺, *Sekisui sensei kakōju ki'nen ronsan* 積翠先生華甲壽記念論纂 (Tokyo, 1942), pp. 153-79.

Li Chia-yen 李嘉言. "Liu-tsu t'an-ching Te-i k'an-pen chih fa-hsien" 六祖壇經

德異刊本之發現, *Ch'ing-hua hsüeh-pao* 清華學報, X (no. 2, April, 1935), 483-90.

Liebenthal, Walter. *Book of Chao.* Peking, 1948.

―――― "The Sermon of Shen-hui," *Asia Major*, new ser., III (no. 2, 1952), 132-55.

Lin, Li-kuong. *L'aide memoire de la Vraie Loi.* Paris, 1949.

Lo Ch'ang-p'ei 羅常培. *T'ang Wu-tai hsi-pei fang-yin* 唐五代西北方音. Shanghai, 1933.

Lo Hsiang-lin 羅香林. *T'ang-tai Kuang-chou Kuang-hsiao ssu yü Chung-Yin chiao-t'ung chih kuan-hsi* 唐代廣州光孝寺與中印交通之關係. Hong Kong, 1960.

―――― *T'ang-tai wen-hua shih* 唐代文化史. Taipei, 1955.

Lu, K'uan-yü (Charles Luk). *Ch'an and Zen teachings.* Series. 3. London, 1962.

Luk, Charles, *see* Lu, K'uan-yü.

Masunaga Reihō 增永靈鳳. "Sanso Sōsan to sono shisō" 三祖僧璨と其の思想, *Nikka Bukkyō kenkyūkai nempō* 日華佛教研究會年報, no. 2 (1937), pp. 36-63.

―――― *Zengo shōjiten* 禪語小辭典. Tokyo, 1957.

Matsuda Fumio 松田文雄. "Jinshū den ni okeru ni san no mondai ni tsuite" 神秀傳に於ける二・三の問題について, *IBK*, no. 9 (January, 1957), pp. 212-15.

Matsumoto Bunzaburō 松本文三郎. *Bukkyō shi zakkō* 佛教史雜考. Tokyo, 1944.

―――― *Kongō kyō oyobi Rokuso dankyō no kenkyū* 金剛經及六祖壇經の研究. Kyoto, 1913.

Matsumoto Eiichi 松本榮一. *Tonkō ga no kenkyū* 燉煌畫の研究. Tokyo, 1937. 2 vols.

Mizuno Kōgen 水野弘元. "Dembōge no seiritsu ni tsuite" 傳法偈の成立について, *Shūgaku kenkyū* 宗學研究, no. 2 (January, 1960), pp. 22-41.

Mochizuki Shinkō 望月信亨. *Bukkyō dai-jiten* 佛教大辭典. Tokyo, 1955-63. 10 vols.

Nakagawa Shōsuke 中川壯助. *Zengo jii* 禪語字彙. Tokyo, 1935.

Nakagawa Taka 中川孝. "Dankyō no shisōshiteki kenkyū" 壇經の思想史的研究, *IBK*, no. 5 (September, 1954), pp. 281-84.

―――― "Daruma zenji ron (Tonkō shutsudo) kō" 達摩禪師論（敦煌出土）考, *Shūkan Tōyōgaku* 集刊東洋學, no. 2 (1959), pp. 85-96.

―――― "Rokuso dankyō no ihon ni tsuite" 六祖壇經の異本に就いて, *IBK*, no. 3 (September, 1953), pp. 155-56.

―――― "Zenshū shi kenkyū shiryō to shite no Ryōga shiji ki no naiyō" 禪宗史研究資料としての楞伽師資記の内容, *IBK*, no. 17 (January, 1961), pp. 142-43.

———— "Zenshū shi ni okeru Tōzan hōmon no igi" 禪宗史に於ける東山法門の意義, *IBK*, no. 9 (January, 1957), pp. 112-13.

Nakamura Hajime 中村元 and Kino Kazuyoshi 紀野一義. *Hannya shingyō; Kongō hannya kyō* 般若心經, 金剛般若經. Tokyo, 1960. (Iwanami bunko 岩波文庫).

Nishida Tatsuo 西田龍雄. "Seikago to Seika moji" 西夏語と西夏文字, *Chūō Ajia kodaigo bunken* 中央アジア古代語文獻 (Kyoto, 1961), pp. 391-462. (Saiiki bunka kenkyū 西域文化研究, vol. 4.)

Ōkubo Dōshū 大久保道舟. "Daijōji-bon o chūshin to seru Rokuso dankyō no kenkyū" 大乘寺本を中心とせる六祖壇經の研究, *Komazawa Daigaku Bukkyō gakkai gakuhō* 駒澤大學佛教學會學報, no. 8 (April, 1938), pp. 57-84.

Ono Gemmyō 小野玄妙. *Bussho kaisetsu daijiten* 佛書解説大辭典. Tokyo, 1931-36. 12 vols.

Osabe Kazuo 長部和雄. "Tōdai Zenshū kōsō no shisho kyōka ni tsuite" 唐代禪宗高僧の士庶教化に就いて, *Haneda hakushi shōju ki'nen Tōyōshi ronsan* 羽田博士頌壽記念東洋史論纂 (Kyoto, 1950), pp. 293-319.

Ōta Tatsuo 太田辰夫. "*Sodō shū*" *kōgo goi sakuin* 「祖堂集」口語語彙索引. Kyoto, 1962.

Ōya Tokujō 大屋德城. "Gen En'yū Kōrai kokubon Rokuso daishi hōbō dankyō ni tsuite" 元延祐高麗刻本六祖大師法寶壇經に就いて, *Zengaku kenkyū* 禪學研究, no. 23 (July, 1935), pp. 1-29.

Rouselle, Erwin. "Sutra des Sechsten Patriarchen." Chap. 1: *Sinica*, V (1930), 174-91; chap. 2: *Chinesisch-Deutscher Almanach* (1931), pp. 76-86; chap. 3: *Sinica*, VI (1931), 26-34; chaps. 4-5: *Sinica*, XI (1934), 3-4, 131-37; chap. 6: *Sinica*, XI (1936), 5-6, 202-11.

Saijō Keiko 西條惠子. *Zen Tō bun jimmei sakuin* 全唐文人名索引. Tokyo, 1962.

Sekiguchi Shindai 關口眞大. *Daruma daishi no kenkyū* 達摩大師の研究. Tokyo, 1957.

———— "Daruma to Daruma" 達摩と達磨, *IBK*, no. 23 (January, 1964), pp. 124-31.

———— "Enō no shisō ni kansuru gigi" 慧能の思想に關する疑義, *IBK*, no. 16 (March, 1960), pp. 105-9.

———— "Godaisan to Gozu Zen" 五臺山と牛頭禪, *Tōhō shūkyō* 東方宗教, no. 16 (November, 1960), pp. 21-39.

———— "Hiniku kotsuzui" 皮肉骨髓, *IBK*, no. 22 (March, 1963), pp. 14-19.

———— "Nanshū to Nanshū Zen" 南宗と南宗禪, *IBK*, no. 20 (March, 1962), pp. 70-76.

—— "Zenshū no hassei" 禪宗の發生, *Fukui sensei shōju ki'nen Tōyō shisō ronshū* 福井先生頌壽記念東洋思想論集 (Tokyo, 1960), pp. 321-38.

—— *Zenshū shisō shi* 禪宗思想史. Tokyo, 1964.

Shimada Kenji 島田虔次. "Taiyō no rekishi ni yosete" 體用の歴史に寄せて, *Tsukamoto hakushi shōju ki'nen Bukkyō shigaku ronshū* 塚本博士頌壽記念佛教史學論集 (Kyoto, 1961), pp. 416-30.

Shinohara Hisao 篠原壽雄. "Ryōga shiji ki kōchū" 楞伽師資記校注, *Uchino Tairei sensei tsuitō rombun shū* 內野臺嶺先生追悼論文集 (Tokyo, 1954), pp. 132-64.

—— "Ryōga shiji ki ni tsuite" 楞伽師資記について, *Komazawa Daigaku kenkyū kiyō* 駒澤大學研究紀要, no. 13 (March, 1955), pp. 93-106.

Shiraishi Hōru (Kogetsu) 白石芳留 (虎月). *Zoku Zenshū hennen shi* 續禪宗編年史. Yawatahama (Ehime Prefecture), 1943.

Shishiyama Kōdō 宍山孝道. "Kōrai-ban Sodō shū to Zenshū kotenseki" 高麗版祖堂集と禪宗古典籍, *Tōyō gakuen* 東洋學苑, no. 2 (April. 1933), pp. 23-50.

Suzuki Daisetsu (Teitarō) 鈴木大拙 (貞太郎). *Daruma no zempō to shisō oyobi sono ta* 達摩の禪法と思想及其他. Osaka, 1936.

—— "Jinne oshō no dango to kangaubeki Tonkō shutsudo bon ni tsukite" 神會和尙の壇語と考ふべき敦煌出土本に就きて, *Ōtani gakuhō* 大谷學報, XVI (no. 4, December, 1935), 1-30.

—— "Kaga Daijōji shozō no 'Rokuso dankyō' to 'Ichiya Hekigan' ni tsuite" 加賀大乘寺所藏の「六祖壇經」と「一夜碧巖」について, *Shina Bukkyō shigaku* 支那佛教史學, I (no. 3, October, 1937), 1-23.

—— *Kōkan Shōshitsu issho oyobi kaisetsu* 校刊少室逸書及解說. Osaka, 1936.

—— "Rokuso dankyō ni kansuru ni san no iken" 六祖壇經に關する二・三の意見, *Ōtani gakuhō* 大谷學報, XIX (no. 1, February, 1938), 1-18.

—— "Zen: A Reply to Hu Shih," *Philosophy East and West*, III (no. 1, April, 1953), 25-46.

—— *The Zen doctrine of No-mind*. London, 1958.

—— *Zen shisō shi kenkyū* 禪思想史研究 (Tokyo, 1951), vol. 2.

——, and Kuda Rentarō 公田連太郎. *Tonkō shutsudo Jinne zenji goroku kaisetsu oyobi mokuji; Tonkō shutsudo Rokuso dankyō kaisetsu oyobi mokuji; Kōshōji bon Rokuso dankyō kaisetsu oyobi mokuji* 燉煌出土神會禪師語錄解說及目次；燉煌出土六祖壇經解說及目次；興聖寺本六祖壇經解說及目次. Tokyo, 1934.

—— *Tonkō shutsudo Kataku Jinne zenji goroku* 燉煌出土荷澤神會禪師語錄. Tokyo, 1934.

Takada Gikō 高田儀光. *Zenseki mokuroku* 禪籍目錄. Tokyo, 1928.

Takao Giken 高尾義堅. "Futatabi Zen no Namboku ryōshū ni tsuite" 再び禪宗の南北兩宗に就いて, *Ryūkoku gakuhō* 龍谷學報, no. 306 (July, 1933), pp. 97-120.

Tanaka Ryōshō 田中良昭. "Dembōge ni kansuru Tonkō shinshutsu shiryō nishu to sono kankei" 傳法偈に關する敦煌新出資料二種とその關係, *Shūgaku kenkyū* 宗學研究, no. 3 (March, 1961), pp. 106-11.

――― "Fu hōzō innen den to Zen no dentō" 付法藏因緣傳と禪の傳燈, *IBK*, no. 19 (January, 1962), pp. 243-46.

――― "Tonkō shutsudo 'Soshi dengyō seiten nijūhasso Tōrai rokuso' ni tsuite" . 敦煌出土「祖師傳教西天二十八祖東來六祖」について, *IBK*, no. 21 (January, 1963), pp. 251-54.

Tokiwa Daijō 常盤大乘. *Hōrin den no kenkyū* 寶林傳の研究. Tokyo, 1934.

――― "Hōrin den no kenkyū" 寶林傳の研究, *Tōhō gakuhō, Tokyo* 東方學報, 東京, no. 4 (November, 1933), pp. 205-307.

――― *Shina Bukkyō shi no kenkyū* 支那佛教史の研究. Tokyo, 1943. 3 vols.

――― *Shina Bukkyō shiseki ki'nen shū hyōkai* 支那佛教史蹟記念集評解. Tokyo, 1931.

Tōyō bunko 東洋文庫. *Tonkō bunken kenkyū rombun mokuroku* 敦煌文獻研究論文目錄. Tokyo, 1959.

Tsukamoto Zenryū 塚本善隆. "Kinkoku dai-zōkyō no hakken to sono kankō" 金刻大藏經の發見とその刊行, *Nikka Bukkyō kenkyūkai nempō* 日華佛教研究會年報, no. 1 (1936), pp. 167-95.

――― "Nangaku Shōen den to sono Jōdo-kyō" 南嶽承遠傳とその浄土教, *Tōhō gakuhō, Kyoto* 東方學報, 京都, no. 2 (November, 1931), pp. 186-249.

――― *Tō chūki no Jōdo-kyō* 唐中期の浄土教. Kyoto, 1933. (Tōhō bunka gakuin. Kyōto kenkyūjo kenkyū hōkoku 東方文化學院京都研究所研究報告 vol. 4.)

Ui Hakuju 宇井伯壽. *Zenshū shi kenkyū* 禪宗史研究. Tokyo, 1939-43. 3 vols.

――― , tr. *Denshin hōyō* 傳心法要. Tokyo, 1936. (Iwanami bunko 岩波文庫)

――― *Zengen shosenshū tojo* 禪源諸詮集都序. Tokyo, 1939. (Iwanami bunko 岩波文庫)

Wang Chung-min 王重民. *Tun-huang pien-wen chi* 敦煌變文集. Peking, 1957. 2 vols.

Wong, Mou-lam. *The Sutra of Wei Lang (or Hui Neng)*. New ed. London, 1957.

Yabuki Keiki 矢吹慶輝. *Meisha yoin kaisetsu* 鳴沙餘韻解說. Tokyo, 1933.

Yamada Kōdō 山田孝道. *Zenshū jiten* 禪宗辭典. Tokyo, 1913.

Yamazaki Hiroshi 山崎宏. "Tō Keishū Gyokusenji Daitsū zenji Jinshū kō" 唐荊
州玉泉寺大通禪師神秀考, *Yūki kyōju shōju ki'nen Bukkyō shisō shi ronshū*
結城教授頌壽記念佛教思想史論集 (Tokyo, 1964), pp. 465-80.

Yanagida Seizan 柳田聖山. "Daijō kaikyō to shite no Rokuso dankyō" 大乘戒經
としての六祖壇經, *IBK*, no. 23 (January, 1964), pp. 65-72.

——— "Dembō hōki to sono sakusha" 傳法寶紀とその作者, *Zengaku kenkyū*
禪學研究, no. 53 (July, 1963), pp. 45-71.

——— "Gemmon 'Shōchū shū' ni tsuite" 玄門「聖冑集」について, *Bukkyō shigaku* 佛教史學, VII (no. 3, October, 1958), 44-57.

——— "Sodō shū no hombun kenkyū (1)" 「祖堂集」の本文研究 (一), *Zengaku
kenkyū* 禪學研究, no. 54 (July, 1964), pp. 11-87.

——— "Sodō shū no shiryō kachi (1)" 「祖堂集」の資料價值 (一), *Zengaku kenkyū*
禪學研究, no. 44 (October, 1953), pp. 31-80.

——— "Soshi Zen no minamoto to nagare" 祖師禪の源と流, *IBK*, no. 19 (January, 1962), pp. 82-87.

——— "Tō-matsu Godai no Kahoku chihō ni okeru Zenshū kōki no rekishiteki
shakaiteki jijō ni tsuite" 唐末五代の河北地方における禪宗興起の歷史
的社會的事情について, *Nihon Bukkyō gakkai nempō* 日本佛教學會年報,
no. 25 (March, 1960), pp. 171-86.

——— "Tōshi no keifu" 燈史の系譜, *Nihon Bukkyō gakkai nempō* 日本佛教學會年
報, no. 19 (1954), pp. 1-46.

Yokoi Seizan, *see* Yanagida Seizan

Index

THE TUN-HUANG TEXT

Note to the Text

A PHOTOGRAPHIC REPRODUCTION of the Tun-huang manuscript of the *Platform Sutra* contained in the Stein Collection (S5475) was used as the basic text.

In correcting and emending the text, the following method has been followed:

The text of the Tun-huang manuscript, as found in the original work, is given in large-size type. Square brackets are used to indicate characters I have supplied when there is a lacuna in the text; parentheses (curves) are used to indicate superfluous characters in the text.

Corrections to the text are in smaller-size type, and are placed to the right of the text itself. These corrections are enclosed in parentheses, and they have been incorporated into the translation.

When corrections have been made or supplementary material, based on a printed source, added, the source is indicated by a small letter above the addition or correction. Thus:

K = *Kōshōji* edition of the *Platform Sutra*.
KE = *Kan'ei* edition, supplementing leaf missing in *Kōshōji* edition.
S = D. T. Suzuki's edited edition of the Tun-huang text.
U = Ui Hakuju's edited edition of the Tun-huang text.

Where there is no other indication, the correction is my own.

Corresponding passages from the *Kōshōji* edition and from modern edited versions, which supplement or present interpretations at variance with the Tun-huang manuscript, have at times been added to the left of the Tun-huang text, also in smaller-size type.

In several instances the copyist of the original Tun-huang manuscript had inverted the position of two characters, and realizing his own mistake, had placed a small mark (∨) to the right of the characters to indicate the error. In such instances the characters have been placed in their correct order when copying the text. In one instance the mark (⊢) was written beside a character. This indicated a superfluous character that was to be deleted. In this instance the character is omitted from the text.

For abbreviations and variant forms of a character, the modern written form has been used.

The original manuscript contains a great number of miswritten characters. The wrong radical or phonetic is often used; characters closely resembling the correct one are frequently substituted; and homophones are used throughout.

Examples of miswritten characters and homophones

WRONG RADICAL OR PHONETIC	CHARACTERS EASILY MISTAKEN FOR EACH OTHER	HOMOPHONES
海 = 悔	令，今	衣，依，於
記 = 訖	元，天，无（無）	之，智，諸
		起，去
		名，明，迷
		亡，妄，忘，望
		門，問，聞
		五，伍，吾，悟

五五、此壇經法海上座集。上座無常、付同學道漈（漈）。道漈無常、付門人悟真。悟真在嶺南曹

溪山法興寺、見今傳受此法。

五六、如付此法、須得上恨知、心信佛法、立大悲持此經、以爲衣承、於今不絕。

五七、和尚本是韶州曲江縣（縣）人也。如來入涅槃（槃）、法教流東土、共傳無住、即我心無住。此真

菩薩、說真示（宗）、行實喻。唯教大智人、是旨衣（依）。凡度誓、修修行行、遭難不退、遇苦能忍、福

德深厚、方授此法。如根性不堪、林量不得（材）、須求此法。違立不德者（律）、不得妄付壇經。告諸同

道者、令諸蜜意（知）（密）。

南宗頓教最上大乘壇經法一卷

三十

化身報身及淨身、三身元本是一身。若向身中覓自見、即是〔成〕佛菩提因。

本從花身生淨性、淨性常在花身中。性使花身行正道、當來員滿眞無窮。

婬性本身清淨因、除婬即無淨性身。性中但自離吾欲、見性刹那即是眞。

今生若吾頓教門、悟即眼前見性尊。若欲修行云覓佛、不知何處欲求眞。

若能身中自有眞、有眞即是成佛因。自不求眞外覓佛、去覓惣是大癡人。

頓教法者是西流、求度世人須自修。今保世間學道者、不於此是大悠悠。

帛、著孝衣。即非聖法、非我弟子。如吾在日一種、一時端坐。但無動無淨、無生無滅、無去

無來、無是無非、無住〔無住〕、但然寂淨、即是大道。吾去已後、但衣法修行、共吾在日一

種。吾若在世、汝違教法、吾住無益。大師云此語已、夜至三更、奄然遷花。大師春秋七十有

大師說偈已了、遂告門人曰、汝等好住。今共汝別。吾去已後、莫作世情悲泣、而受人弔問錢

六。

五四、大師滅度諸日、寺內異香氛氳、經數日不散。山朋地動、林木變白、日月無光、風雲

失色。八月三日滅度、至十一月、迎和尚神座於曹溪山葬。在龍龕之內、白光出現、直上衝天、

二日始散。韶州刺使韋處立碑、至今供養。

二十九

大師言、今日已後迎相傳受〔遞〕〔授〕、須有依約、莫失宗旨。

五二、法海又白、大師今去、留付何法、今後代人如何見佛。六祖言、汝聽、後代迷人、但識眾生、即能見佛。若不識眾生、覓佛萬劫、不得見也。五今教汝識〔自心〕眾生見〔自心〕佛〔性〕。更留見眞佛解脫頌。迷即不見佛、悟者即見。法海願聞、代代流傳、世世不絕。六祖言、汝聽、吾汝與說〔與汝〕。後代世人、若欲覓佛、但識佛心眾生、即能識佛。〔佛心〕即緣有眾〔生〕、離眾生無佛心。

迷即佛眾生、悟即眾生佛。愚癡佛眾生、智惠眾生佛。心劍佛眾生〔險〕、平等眾生佛。一生心若劍〔險〕、佛在眾生中。一念吾若平〔悟〕、即眾生自佛。我心自有佛、自佛是眞佛。自若無佛心、向何處求佛。

五三、大師言、汝等門人好住。吾留一頌、名自性眞佛解脫頌。後代迷〔人〕〔意〕、〔聞〕門此頌意、即見自心自性眞佛。與汝此頌、吾共汝別。頌曰、

眞如淨性是眞佛、邪見三毒是眞摩〔魔〕。邪見之人摩在舍〔魔〕、正見知人佛則過〔之〕。性眾邪見三毒生〔中〕、即是摩王來住舍〔魔〕。正見忽則三毒生〔心〕〔自除〕、摩變成佛眞無假〔魔〕。

五〇、能大師言、汝等聽吾作二頌、取達摩和尚頌意。汝迷人依此頌修行、必當見性。

第一頌曰、

心地邪花放、五葉逐根隨。共造無明業、見被業風吹。

第二頌曰、

心地正花放、五葉逐恨隨、共修般若惠、當來佛菩提。

六祖說偈已了、放眾生散。門人出外思惟、即知大師不久佳世。

五一、六祖後至八月三日、食後、大師言、汝等善位座、五今共與等別。法海聞言、此頓教

法傳受、從上已來至今幾代。六祖言、初傳受七佛、釋迦牟尼佛第七、大迦葉第八、阿難第九、

末田地第十、商那和修第十一、優婆掬多第十二、提多迦第十三、佛陁難提第十四、佛陁蜜多

第十五、脇比丘第十六、富那奢第十七、馬鳴第十八、毗羅長者第十九、龍樹第二十、迦那提

婆第廿一、羅睺羅第廿二、僧迦那提第廿三、僧迦那舍第廿四、鳩摩羅馱第廿五、闍耶多第廿

六、婆修盤多第廿七、摩拏羅第廿八、鶴勒那第廿九、師子比丘第卅、舍那婆斯第卅一、優婆

堀第卅二、僧迦羅第卅三、須婆蜜多第卅四、南天竹國王了第三子菩提達摩第卅五、唐

國僧惠可第三十六、僧璨第三十七、道信第三十八、弘忍第三十九、惠能自身當今受法第十。

二七

邪法遼亂、惑我宗旨。有人出來、不惜身命、第佛教是非、竪立宗旨、卽是吾正法。衣不合轉。

汝不信、吾與誦先代五祖傳衣付法誦。若據第一祖達摩頌意、卽不合傳衣。聽五與汝頌。頌曰、

吾大來唐國、傳橃救名清。一花開五葉、結菓自然成。

第一祖達摩和尚頌曰、

第二祖惠可和尚頌曰、

本來緣有地、從地種花生。當本願無地、花從何處生。

第三祖僧璨和尚頌曰、

花種雖因地、地上種化生。花種無生性、於地亦無生。

第四祖道信和尚頌曰、

花種有生性、因地種花生。先緣不和合、一切盡無生。

第五祖弘忍和尚頌曰、

有情來下種、無情花卽生。無情又無種、心地亦無生。

第六祖惠能和尚頌曰、

心地含情種、法雨卽花生。自吾花情種、菩提菓自成。

二十六

何道。汝今悲泣、更有阿誰、憂吾不知去處。〔吾〕若不知去處、終不別汝。汝等悲泣、即不知吾〔去〕處。若知去處、即不悲泣。_{K爲憂阿誰、若憂吾不知去處、吾自知去處}性聽無生無滅、無去無來。汝等盡座、_{K坐}吾與如一偈、_{K汝}_{K法性本無生滅去來}

真假動淨偽、_{K靜}與等盡誦取、見此偈意、汝〔與〕吾同。_{K依}於此修行、不失宗旨。僧衆禮拜請大師留偈、敬心受特。_{K持}偈曰、

一切無有真、不以見於真。若見於真者、是見盡非真。_{K於}

若能自有真、離假即心真。自心不離假、無真何處真。_{K情}

有性即解動、無性即不動。若修不動行、同無情不動。_{K情}

若見真不動、動上有不動。不動是不動、無情無佛種。_{K種}

能善分別相、第一義不動。若悟作此見、則是真如用。

報諸學道者、努力須用意。莫於大乘門、却執生死智。

前頭人相應、即共論佛語。若實不相應、合掌令勸善。_{K義}_{K歡喜}

此教本無諍、無諍失道意。執迷諍法門、自性入生死。_{K諍即}_{K若言下}

四九、衆僧既聞、識大師意、更不敢諍、依法修行、一時禮拜、即之大師不永住世。上座法海向前言、大師、大師去後、衣法當付何人。大師言、法即付了、汝不須問。吾滅後二十餘年、_{K知}

二十五

對、實與虛對、嶮與平對、煩惱與菩提對、慈與空對[K(害)]、喜與嗔對、捨與慳對、進與退對[K(情)(情)]、生與

滅對、常與無常對、法身與色身對、化身與報身對、體與用對、性與相〔對〕[K]、有清無親對。

言語與法相有十二對、(內)外境有無〔情〕[K]五對、(三身有三對)[S(自性起有十九對)]、都合成三十六對法也。此

三十六對法、解用通一經、出入即離兩邊。如何自性起用。三十六對共人言語、出外於〔相〕[K]

離相、入內於空離空。著空即惟長無名[明]、著相惟〔長〕[K唯]邪見、謗法直言不用文字。既云不用文

字、人不合言語、言語即是文字。自性上說空、正語言。本性不空、迷自惑、語言除故。暗不

自暗、以名故暗。暗不自暗、以名變暗[明]。以暗現明、來去相因、三十六對亦復如是。

四七、大師言、十弟子、已後傳法、迎[遞]相教授一卷壇經、不失本宗。不稟授[受]壇經、非我宗旨。

如今得了迎[遞]代流行、得遇壇經者、如見吾親授。拾僧得教授已、寫爲壇經、迎[遞]代流行、得者必

當見性。

四八、大師先天二年八月三日滅度。七月八日喚門人告別。大師〔先〕[K]天元年於樟州國恩寺[K(新)]

造塔、至先天二年七月告別。大師言、汝眾近前[K(吾)]。五至八月欲離世間、汝等有疑早問[K(汝)]、爲汝破

疑、當令迷者盡、使與安樂[K(汝)]。吾若去後、無人教與[K(人)][K(汝)]。法海等眾僧聞已、涕淚悲泣。唯有神會、

不動亦不悲泣。六祖言、神會小僧、却得善〔不善〕[K]等、毀譽不動。除者不得[K(餘)]、數年山中更修

二十四

K（亦不代吾迷）

代得吾迷。何不自修、問吾見否。神會作禮、便爲門人、不離曹溪山中、常在左右。

四五、大師遂喚門人法海、志誠、法達、智常、志通、志徹、志道、法珍、法如、神會。大

師言、汝等拾弟子近前。汝等不同餘人、吾滅度後、汝各爲一方頭。吾教汝說法、不失本宗。

舉〔三〕科法門、動〔用〕三十六對、出沒即離兩邊。說一切法、莫離於性相。若有人問法、

出語盡雙、皆取法對。來去相因、究竟二法盡除、更無去處。三科法門者蔭界入。

界〔是〕十八界、〔入〕是十二入。何名五蔭。色蔭、受蔭、相蔭（想）、行蔭、識蔭是。何名十八

界。六塵、六門、六識。何名十二入。外六塵、中六門。何名六塵。色聲香未獨法是。何名六

門。眼耳鼻舌身意是。法性起六識、眼識耳識鼻識舌識身識意識、六門六塵。自性含萬法、名

爲含藏識、思量即轉識、生六識、出六門〔見〕六塵、是三六十八。由自性邪、起十八邪、含

自性〔正、起〕十八正。含惡用即衆生、善用即佛。用油何等。油自性〔由有〕。

四六、外境無情對有五、天與地對、日與月對、暗與明對、陰與陽對、水與火對。語（與）

言（對）法（與）相對有十二對、有爲無爲有色無色對、有相無相對、有漏無漏對、色與空對、

動與淨對、清與濁對、凡與性對、僧與俗對、老與少對、大大與少少對、長與短對、高與下對、

自性（居）起用對有十九對、邪與正對、癡與惠對、愚與智對、亂與定對、戒與非對、直與曲

經。法達一聞、言下大悟、涕淚悲泣、自言、和尚、實未僧〔曾〕轉法華、七年被法華轉、已後轉法

華、念念修行佛行。大師言、即佛行是佛。其時聽入〔人〕無不悟者。

四三、時有一僧、名智常、來曹溪山、禮拜和尚、問〔問〕四乘法義。智常聞和尚曰、佛說三乘、

又言最上乘、弟子不解、望爲敬〔教〕示。惠能大師曰、汝自身心見〔向〕、莫著外法相。元無四乘法、人

心不量四等〔自有〕、法有四乘。見聞讀誦是小乘。悟【法】解義是中乘。依法修行是大乘。萬法盡通、

萬幸〔行〕俱備、一切無離、但離法相、作無所德〔得〕、是最上乘。乘是【最上】行義、不在口諍。汝須

自修、莫問悟〔吾〕也。

四四、又有一僧、名神會、南陽人也。至曹溪山、禮拜問言、和尚座〔坐〕禪、見亦不見。大師起

（把）打神會三下、却問、神會、吾打汝、痛不痛。神會答言、亦痛亦不痛。六祖言曰、吾亦

見亦不見。神會又問、大師、何以亦見亦不見。大師言、吾亦見〔見〕、常見自過患、故云亦見。亦

不見者、不見〔下〕天地人過罪。所以亦見亦不也〔見〕。汝亦痛亦不痛如何。神會答曰、若不痛、即同無

情木石、若痛即同凡【夫】〔夫〕、即起於恨。大師言、神會、向前〔神會〕見不見是兩邊、痛【不痛】〔不痛〕是生

滅。汝自性且不見、敢來弄人。禮拜禮拜更不言〔見〕。大師言、汝心迷〔迷〕不見。問善知識覓路、以心

悟自見、依法修行。汝自名不見自心、却來問惠能見否。吾不自知〔見〕、代汝迷不得〔豈代汝迷〕、汝若自見、

二二

經上有疑、大師智惠廣大、願爲時疑。大師言、法達、法即甚達。經上無癡、〔汝心自疑〕。汝

心自耶、而求正法。吾心正定、即是持經。吾一生已來、不識文字、汝將法華經來、對吾讀一

遍、吾問即之。法達取經到、對大師讀一遍。六祖問已、即識佛意、便汝法達說法華經。六祖

言、法達、法華經無多語、七卷盡是譬喻內緣。如來廣說三乘、只爲世人根鈍、經聞公明、無

有餘乘、唯一佛乘。大師〔言〕、法達、汝聽一佛乘、莫求二佛乘、迷却汝聖。經中何處是一

佛乘、汝與說。經云、諸佛世尊唯汝一大事因緣故、出現於世。已上十六家是正法〔此〕法如何解。此法

如何修。汝聽吾說。人心不思、本源空寂、離却邪見、即一大是因緣。內外不迷、即離兩邊。

外迷看相、內迷著空。於相離相、於空離空、即是不空迷。吾此法一念心開、出現於世、心開

何物、開佛知見、佛猶如覺也。分爲四門、開覺知見、示覺知見、悟覺知見、入覺知見。〔此

名〕開示悟入。上一處入、即覺知見、見自本性、即得出世。大師言、法達、悟常願一切世人、

心地常自開佛知見、莫開衆生知見。世人心〔邪〕、愚迷造惡、自開衆生知見。世人心正、起

智惠觀照、自開佛智見。莫開衆生智見、開佛智見、即出世。大師言、法達、此是法達經一乘

法。向下分三、爲名人故。汝但於一佛乘。大師言、法達、心行轉法華、不行法華轉、心正轉

法華、心耶法華轉、開佛智見轉法華、開衆生智見被法華轉。大師言、努力依法修行、即是轉

二十一

誰疾遲。汝第一早來、勿令吾埪〔K 恠〕。志誠奉使歡喜、遂半月中間、即至曹溪山、見惠能和當〔K 尚〕、禮

拜即聽、不言來處。志城〔K 誠〕聞法、言下便悟、即契本心。起立即禮拜、自言、和尚、弟子從玉泉

寺來。秀師處不德〔K 得〕契悟、聞和尚說、便契本心。和尚慈悲、願當散示。惠能大師曰、汝從彼〔K 彼〕來、

應是細作。志誠曰、〔K 不是。〕師曰、何得不是。〔K 對曰〕、未說時即是、說乃了即是。六祖言、〔K 說了不是〕「煩

惱即是菩提」亦復如是。

四一、大師謂志誠曰、吾聞與禪師教人、唯傳戒定惠、與和尚教人〔K 汝〕戒定惠如何、當爲吾說。

志城〔K 誠〕曰、秀和尚言戒定惠、諸惡不作名爲戒、諸善奉行名爲惠、自淨其意名爲定。此即名爲戒

定惠、彼作如是說。不知和尚所見如何。惠能和尚答曰、此說不可思議、惠能所見又別。志城〔K 誠〕

問、何以別。惠能答曰、見有遲疾。志城〔K 誠〕請和尚說所見戒定惠。大師言、（如）〔K 如〕汝聽悟〔K 吾〕說、看

悟〔K 吾〕所見處。心地無疑、非〔K 非〕自姓〔K 性〕戒、心地無亂、是〔K 是〕自姓〔K 性〕定、自姓是惠〔K 是自性慧〕。能大師言、汝

戒定惠勸小根諸人、吾戒定惠勸上人。得吾自〔K 性〕、亦不立戒定惠。志城〔K 誠〕言、請大師說不立

如何。大師言、自姓〔K 性〕無非無亂無癡、念念般若觀照、當〔K 常〕離法相、有何可立。自姓〔K 性〕頓

頓修、立有漸、〔K 亦無漸次、所以不立一切法〕此契以不立。志誠禮拜、便不離曹溪山、即爲門人、不離大師左右。

四二、又有一僧、名法達、常誦法華經七年、心迷不知正法之處、〔K 來詣曹溪、禮拜問曰〕、

二十

此但是頓教、亦名為大乘。迷來經累劫、悟則剎那間。

三七、大師言、善智識、汝等盡誦取此偈、依偈修行、去惠能千里、常在能邊。此不修對面千里。各各自修、法不相持。衆人旦散、惠能歸漕溪山。衆生若有大疑、來彼山間、為汝破疑、同見佛世。合座官僚道俗禮拜和尚、無不嗟嘆、善哉大悟、昔所未聞、嶺南有福、生佛在此、誰能得智、一時盡散。

三八、大師往曹溪山、韶廣二州行化、四十餘年。若論門人、僧之與俗、三五千人、說不盡。若論宗指、傳授壇經、以此為衣約。若不得壇經、即無稟受。須知法處年月日性名、遍相付囑。無壇經稟承、非南宗定子也。未得稟承者、雖說頓教法、未知根本、修不免諍。但得法者只勸修行。諍是勝負之心、與道違背。

三九、世人盡傳南宗、能比秀、未知根本事由。且秀禪師於南荊府堂陽縣玉泉寺住時修行、惠能大師於韶州城東、三十五里曹溪山住。法即一宗、人有南北。因此便立南北。何以漸頓、法即一種、見有遲疾。見遲即漸、見疾即頓。法無漸頓、人有利鈍、故名漸頓。

四〇、神秀師常見人說惠能法疾直旨路。秀師遂喚門人僧志誠曰、汝聰明多智、汝與吾至曹溪山、到惠能所、禮拜但聽、莫言吾使汝來。所聽德意旨記取、却來與吾說。看惠能見解與吾

十九

別。頌曰、

說通及心通、如日至虛空。〔K（處）〕

惟傳頓教法、出世破邪宗。

教即無頓漸、迷悟有遲疾。

若學頓教法、愚人不可迷。〔K（悉）〕

說即須萬般、合離還歸一。〔K（雖）K（理）〕

煩惱暗宅中、常須生惠日。〔K（慧）〕

邪來因煩惱、正來煩惱除。

邪正俱不用、清淨至無餘。〔K（俱）〕

菩提本清淨、起心即是妄。〔K只此見性門〕

淨性於妄中、但正除三障。〔K（在）〕

世間若修道、一切盡不妨。

常現在己過、與道即相當。

色類自有道、離道別覓道。

覓道不見道、到頭還自懊。

若欲貪覓道、行正即是道。

自若無正心、暗行不見道。

若眞修道人、不見世間愚。〔K過〕

若見世間非、自非却是左。

他非我有罪、我非自有罪。〔K（不）〕

但自去非心、打破煩惱碎。

若欲化愚人、是須有方便。〔K（彼有）〕

勿令破彼疑、即是菩提見。

法元在世間、於世出世間。

勿離世間上、外求出世間。

邪見出世間、正見出世間。〔K（是）〕

邪正悉打却、□□□□。〔K菩提性宛然〕

那。不悟頓教大乘、念佛往生路遙、如何得達。六祖言、惠能與使君移西方剎那間、（聞）（目）目前便見、使君願見否。使君禮拜〔言〕、若此得見、何須往生、願和尚慈悲為現西方、大善。大師言、唐見西方無疑、即散。大眾愕然、莫知何是（事）。大師曰、大眾、大眾作意聽。世人自色身是城、眼耳鼻舌身即是城門、外有六門（五）、內有意門。心即是地、性即是王。性在王在、性去王無、性在身心存、性去身〔心〕壞。佛是自性作、莫向身〔外〕（直）求。自性迷佛即眾生、自性悟眾生即是佛。慈悲即是觀音、喜捨名為勢至、能淨是釋迦、平真是彌勒、人我是須彌、邪心是大海、煩惱是波浪、毒心是惡龍、塵勞是魚鱉、虛妄即是神鬼、三毒即是地獄、愚癡即是畜生、十善是天堂、我無人（無人我）、須彌自倒、除邪心、海水竭、煩惱無、波浪滅、毒害除、魚龍絕。自心地上（放）覺性如來、施大智惠光明、照曜六門、清淨照波（破）六欲諸天、下照（自性內照）三毒若除、地獄一時消滅、內外明徹、不異西方。不作此修、如何到彼。座下聞說（聞）、讚聲徹天、應是迷人人然便見（了）。使君禮拜、讚言善哉善哉、普願法界眾生、聞者一時悟解。

三六、大師言、善知識、若欲修行、在家亦得、不由在寺。在寺不修、如西方心惡之人、在家若修行、如東方人修善。但願自家修清淨、即是惡方（西）。使君問、和〔尚〕、在家如何修、願為指授。大師言、善智識（知）、惠能與道俗作無相頌。盡誦取、衣此修行（依）、常與惠能（說）一處無

十七

大師言是。弟子見說達磨大師伐梁武諦（K化）（K帝）、問達磨、朕（K已）一生未來造寺布施供養有（有）功德否。

達磨答言、並無功德。武帝惆悵、遂遣達磨出境。未審此言、請和尚說。六祖言、實無功德。

使君（朕）勿疑達磨大師言。武帝著邪道、不識正法。使君問、何以無功德。和尚言、造寺布

施供養只是修福。不可將福以爲功德、〔功德〕在法身、非在於福田。自法性有功德、〔見性是

功〕、平眞是德、〔內見〕佛性、外行恭敬。若輕一切人、吾（K吾）我不斷、即自無功德。自性虛妄、（K自性虛妄不實、）
（K平等是德）

法身無功德、念念德行、平等眞心、德即不輕、常行於敬。自修身即功、自修（身）心即德。
（即自無德）

功德自心作、福與功德別。武帝不識正理、非祖大師有過。

三五、使君禮拜又問、弟子見僧〔衆〕道俗、常念阿彌大佛（K陀）、願往生西方。請和尚說得生彼（K得）

否、望爲破疑。大師言、使君聽、惠能與說。世尊在舍衛國、說西方引化、經文分明、「去此

不遠」。只爲下根說近。說遠只緣上智。人自兩重、法無不〔同〕。名悟有殊、見有遲疾。迷人（K種）（K同）（K迷）

念佛生彼、悟者自淨其心。所以佛言「隨其心淨、則佛土淨」。使君、東方但淨心無罪、西方

心不淨有愆。迷人願生東方西者、〔悟人〕所在處並皆一種。心但無不淨、西方去此不遠。心（K方）（K悟人）

起不淨之心、念佛往生難到。除〔十〕惡即行十萬、無八邪即過八千。但行眞心、到如彈指。（K十）（K直）（K彈）

使君但行十善、何須更願往生。不斷十惡之心、何佛即來迎請。若悟無生頓法、見西方只在刹

十六

頌曰、

愚人修福不修道、謂言修福而是「道」。K（道）

布施供養福無邊、心中三業元來在。K（造）K（惡）

若將修福欲滅罪、後世得福罪無造。K（還在）

若解向心除罪緣、各自世中眞懺海。K（性）K（悔）

若悟大乘眞懺海、K（悔）除邪行正造無罪。

學道之人能自觀、即與悟人同一例。

大師令傳此頓教、願學之人同一體。

若欲當來覓本身、三毒惡緣心中洗。

努力修道莫悠悠、忽然虛度一世休。

若遇大乘頓教法、K（至）虔誠合掌志心求。

大師說法了、韋使君官寮僧衆道俗、讚言無盡、昔所未聞。

三四、使君禮拜自言、和尚說法實不思議、弟子當有少疑、K（疑）K（問）欲聞和尚。K（問）望意和尚、大慈大悲、爲弟子說。大師言、有議即聞、K（問）何須再三。使君聞、法可不（不）是西國第一祖達磨祖師宗旨。

十五

法、皆因大善知識能發起。故三世諸佛十二部經、云在人性中、本自具有、不能自姓悟（性）、須得善知識示道見性。若自悟者、不假外善知識。若取外求善知識、望得解說、無有是處。識自心內善知識、即得解〔脫〕。若自心邪迷、妄念顛倒、外善知識即有教授〔救不可得〕。汝若不得自悟、當起般若觀照、剎那間妄念俱滅。即是自眞正善知識、一悟即知佛也。自性心地以智惠觀照、內外名徹（明）、識自本心。若識本心、即是解脫。既得解脫、即是般若三昧。悟般若三昧、即是無念。何名無念。無念法者見一切法、不著一切法、遍一切處、不著一切處、常淨自性、使六賊從六門走出、於六塵中、不離不染、來去自由、即是般若三昧、自在解脫、名無念行。

K（若）莫百物不思、當令念絕、即是法傳、即名邊見。悟無念法者、萬法盡通。悟無念法者、見諸佛境界。悟無念頓法者、至佛位地。

三二、善知識、後代得悟法者、常見吾法身不離汝左右。善知識將此頓教法門、同見同行、發願受持、如是佛故、終身受持而不退者、欲入聖位。然須縛受時、從上已來、嘿然而付於法。（嘿）K（默）發大誓願、不退菩提、即須分付。若不同見解、無有志願、在在處處、勿妄宣傳、損彼前人、究竟無益。若遇人不解、謾此法門、百劫萬劫千生斷佛種性。（姓）K（姓）

三三、大師言、善知識、聽悟說無相訟、令汝名者罪滅、亦名滅罪頌。K（迷）

長。少根之人亦復如是。有般若之智〔人〕與大智之人、亦無差別、因何聞法即不悟。緣邪

見障重、煩惱根深。猶如大雲蓋覆於日、不得風吹、日無能現。般若之智、亦無大小。為一切

衆生、自有迷心、外修覓佛、來悟自性。即是小根人、聞其頓教、不信外修、但於自心、令自

本性常起正見、煩惱塵勞衆生、當時盡悟。猶如大海納於衆流、小水大水合為一體、即是見性。

內外不住、來去自由、能除執心、通達無礙。心修此行、即與般若波羅蜜〔經〕、本無差別。

〔有〕愚有智。愚為少故、智為大人、問迷人於智者、智人與愚人說法、令使愚者悟解深開。

迷人若悟心開、與大智人無別。故知不悟、即〔是〕佛是衆生。一念若悟、即衆生〔不〕是佛。

故知一切萬法、盡在自身心中。何不從於自心頓現真如本姓。菩薩戒經云、「我本願自姓清淨」。

我若無智人、一切萬法、本無不有。故知萬法本從人興、一切經書因人說有。緣在人中有

三〇、一切經書及文字、小大二乘、十二部經、皆因〔人〕置。因智惠性故、故〔然〕能建

立。

誠心見性、自成佛道、「即時豁然、還得本心」。

三一、善知識、我於忍和尚處、一聞言下大伍、頓見真如本性。是故汝教法、流行後代、今

學道者頓悟菩提、各自觀心、令自本性頓悟。若〔不〕能自悟者、須覓大善知識亦道見姓。何

名大善知〔識〕。解最上乘法直是正路、是大善知識。是大因緣、所為化道令得見佛。一切善

十三

最上第一、無住無去無來。三世諸佛從中出、將大知惠（智）到彼岸、打破五陰煩惱塵勞。最尊最上

第一、讚最上（最上）乘法修行、定成佛。無去無住無來往、是定惠等、不染一切法、三世諸

佛從中變三毒、爲戒定惠。

二七、善知識、我此法門、從八萬四千智惠。何以故。爲世有八萬四千塵勞。若無塵勞、般

若常在、不離自姓（性）。悟此法者、即是無念無億（憶）無著。莫去誑妄、即自是眞如姓（性）。用知惠觀照（智）、

於一切法、不取不捨、即見姓（性）成佛道。

二八、善知識、若欲入甚深法界、入般若三昧者、直修般若波羅蜜行。但持金剛般若波羅蜜

經一卷、即得見性入般若三昧。當知此人功德無量。經中分名讚嘆（明）（歎）、不能具說。此是最上乘法、

爲大智上根人說。少根（小）智人、若聞〔此〕法、心不生信。何以故。譬如大龍若下大雨、雨衣閻

浮提、〔城邑聚落、悉皆漂流〕、如漂草葉。若下大雨、雨放大海（於）、不增不減。若大乘者、聞說（天）

金剛經、心開悟解。故知本性自有般若之智（智）、自用知惠觀照、不假文字。譬如其雨水不從無有（於）、

元是龍王於江海中、將身引此水（小）、令一切衆生、一切草木、一切有情無情、悉皆像潤（蒙）、諸水衆

流、却入大海（小）、海納衆水、合爲一體。衆生本性、般若之智（小）、亦復如是。

二九、少根之人聞說此頓教、猶如大地草木根性自少者（小）、若被大雨一沃、悉皆自到（倒）、不能增

十二

能與說、各各聽。摩訶般若波羅蜜者、西國梵語、唐言大智惠彼岸到。此法須行、不在口〔念〕。

口念不行、如〔幻〕如化。修行者法身與佛等也。何名摩訶。摩訶者是大、心量廣大、猶如虛

空。莫定心座、即落無既空。〔虛空〕能含日月星辰、大地山何（河）、一切草木、惡人善人、惡法

善法、天堂地獄、盡在空中。世人性空、亦復如是。

二五、〔自〕性〔能〕含萬法是大。萬法盡是自姓（性）。見一切人及非人、惡知與善、惡法善法、

盡皆不捨、不可染著、由如虛空、名之為大。此是摩訶行。迷人口念、智者心〔行〕。又有名

人、空心不思、名之為大、此亦不是、心量〔廣〕大、不行是少（小）。莫口空說、不修此行、非我

弟子。

二六、何名般若。般若是智惠、一〔切〕時中、念念不愚、常行智惠、即名般若行。一念愚、

即般若絕、一念智、即般若生。（心中常愚）〔自言〕我修般若、無形相、智惠性即是。何名波

羅蜜。此是西國梵音、言彼岸到。解義離生滅、著竟生滅去。如水有波浪、即是於此岸。離境

無生滅、如水承長流。故即名到彼岸、故名波羅蜜。迷人口念、智者心行。當念時有妄、有妄

即非眞有。念念若行、是名眞有。悟此法者、悟般若法、修般若行。不修即凡、一念修行、法

身等佛。善知識、即煩惱是菩提、捉前念迷即凡、後念悟即佛。善知識、摩訶般若波羅蜜最尊

〔生〕般若、除却迷妄、即自悟佛道成。行誓願力。

二二、今既發四弘誓願訖、與善知識無相懺悔、〔滅〕[K]三世罪障。大師言、善知識、前念後

念及今念。念〔念〕不被愚癡染。從前惡行一時〔□〕。自姓若除即是懺〔悔〕[K性]。前念後念及〔今念〕[K]。念念不

被癡疾染。除却從前矯誑心。永斷名為自性懺。前念後念及〔今念〕[K]。念念不[K疽姤]

悔者知於前非惡業、恒不離心。諸佛前口說無益。我此法門中、永斷不作、名為懺悔。[K疽姤]

二三、今既懺悔已、與善知識受無相三歸依戒[K授]。大師言、善知識、歸衣覺兩足尊、歸衣正離欲[K知][K依]

〔尊〕、歸衣淨眾中尊[K覺]。從今已後、稱佛為師、更不歸衣餘邪名外道[K迷]。願自〔性〕三寶慈悲燈名[K明]。
（以自性三寶常自證明）

善知識、惠能勸（善）善知識歸衣〔自性〕三寶[K依]。佛者覺也。法者正也。僧者淨也。自心歸依

覺、邪名不生、少欲知足、離財離色、名兩足尊。自心歸正、念念無邪故、即無愛著、以無愛[K迷]

著、名離欲尊。自心歸淨、一切塵勞妄念、雖在自姓、自姓不染著、名眾中尊。凡夫〔不〕解、[K性][K性]

從日至日、受三歸衣戒。若言歸佛、佛在何處。若不見佛、即無所歸。既無所歸、言却是妄。

善知識、各自觀察、莫錯用意。經中只即言自歸依佛、不言歸他佛。自姓不歸、無所〔歸〕處。[K性]

二四、今既自歸衣三寶、惣各各至心、與善知識說摩訶般若波羅蜜法。善知識雖念不解、惠

十

善知識開眞法、吹却名妄內外名徹、於自姓中、萬法皆見、一切法自在姓[性]、名爲清淨法身[佛]。

自歸衣者除不善行、是名歸衣[依]。何名爲千百億化身佛。不思量、性即空寂、思量即是自化。思

量惡法、化爲地獄。思量善法、化爲天堂。毒害化爲畜生、慈悲化爲菩薩、智惠化爲上界、愚

癡化爲下方、自姓[性]變化甚名[多]、迷人自不知見。[念念起惡、常行惡道、廻]一念善、知惠即生。

[此名自性化身佛。何名圓滿報身]。一燈能除千年闇、一智能滅萬年愚、莫思向前、常思於後、

常後念善、名爲報身[佛]。一念惡報却千年善心、一念善報却千年惡滅。無常已來後念善、

名爲報身[佛]。從法身思量即是化身。念念善、即是報身。自悟自修、即名歸衣[依]也。皮肉是

色身、[色身]是舍宅、不在歸衣[依]也。但悟三身、即識大億[意]。

二、今既自歸依三身佛已、與善知識發四弘大願。善知識一時逐惠能道。衆生無邊誓願度、

煩惱無邊誓願斷、法門無邊誓願學、無上佛道誓願成。（三唱）善知識、衆生無邊誓願度、不是惠能

度善知識、（心中）衆生各於自身、自姓[性]自度。何名自姓[性]自度。自色身中邪見煩惱愚癡名妄、

自有本覺性、將正見度。既悟正見、般若之智除却愚癡迷妄、衆生各各自度。邪見正度、迷來

悟度、愚來智度、惡來善度、煩惱來菩提度。如是度者、是名眞度。煩惱無邊誓願斷、自心除

虛妄。法門無邊誓願學、學無上正法。無上佛道誓願成、常下心行、恭敬一切、遠離迷執覺知

九

迷人自身不動、開口即說人是非、與道違背。看心看淨、却是障道因緣。

一九、今記汝是〔性〕、〔既知〕此法門中、何名座禪〔坐〕。此法門中一切無碍、外於一切境界上念不去爲坐〔起〕、見本姓不亂爲禪〔性〕。何名爲禪定。外雜相曰禪〔離〕、內不亂曰定。外若有相〔外若著相，內心即亂，外若離相，心即不亂〕、本自淨自定。只緣境觸〔動〕、觸即亂〔離相不亂即定〕。外離相即禪、內〔源〕不亂即定〔外〕。外禪內定〔心〕、故名禪定。維摩經云、「即是谿然、還得本心」。菩薩戒云、「本須自姓清淨」〔性〕。善知識、見自姓〔性〕自淨、自修自作、自姓法身〔性〕、自行佛行、自作自成佛道。

〔內〕

二〇、善知識、惣須自體與受無相戒、一時逐惠能口道、令善知識見自三身佛。於自色身歸衣〔依〕清淨法身佛、於自色身歸衣〔依〕千百億化身佛、於自色身歸衣當來圓滿報身佛。已上三唱 色身是舍宅、不可言歸。向者三身在自〔法〕性。世人盡有、爲名不見〔迷〕、外覓三〔身〕如來、不見自色身中三性佛〔身〕。善知識聽〔汝善知識〕、令善知識衣自色身見自〔法〕性有三世佛〔性〕〔身〕。此三身佛從性上生。〔善知識、聽說，令善知識於自身中見〕

何名清淨〔法〕身佛。善知識、世人性本自淨、萬法在自姓〔性〕。思量一切〔惡〕事、即行衣惡〔於〕、思量一切善事、便修於善行〔慧〕。知如是一切法盡在自姓〔性〕、自姓常清淨〔性〕、日月常名〔明〕、只爲雲覆蓋、上名下晲〔明〕、不能了見日月西辰、忽遇惠風吹散〔慧〕、卷盡雲霧、萬像參羅〔森〕、一時皆現。世人性淨〔性〕、猶如清天、惠如日、智如月。智惠常名〔明〕、於外看敬〔著境〕、妄念浮雲蓋覆、自姓不能明〔性〕。故遇

八

〔何明爲相〕 無相〔者〕 於相而離相。 無念者於念而不念。 無住者爲人本性。 念念不住、前念

念念後念〔今〕、念念相讀〔續〕、無有斷絕。 若一念斷絕、法身即是離色身、念念時中、於一切法上無住。

一念若住、念念即住、名繫縛。 於一切法上、念念不住、即無縛也。〔是〕以無住爲本。 善知

識、外離一切相是無相。 但能離相、性體清淨是。 是以無相爲體。 於一切境上不染、名爲無念。 於

於自念上離鏡〔境〕、〔不〕不於法上念生、莫百物不思〔若〕、念盡除却。 一念斷、即〔無〕別處受生。

學道者用心、莫〔不〕息法意、自錯尚可、更勸他人。 迷不自見〔迷自迷不見〕、又謗經法。 是以立無

念爲宗。 即緣名人於鏡上有念、念上便去耶見〔起邪見〕。 一切塵勞妄念、從此而生。 然此教門立無念爲

宗。 世人離見、不起於念。 若無有念、無念亦不立。 無者無何事。 念者〔念〕何物。 無者離二

相諸塵勞。〔念者念眞如本性〕、眞如是念之體、念是眞如之用。〔自〕姓起念、雖即見聞覺之〔知〕、眞如自

不染萬鏡〔境〕、而常自在。 維摩經云、「外能善分別諸法相、內於第一義而不動」。

一八、善諸識、此法門中、座禪元不著心〔坐〕、亦不著淨、亦不言〔不〕動。 若言看心、心元是

妄、妄如幼故〔幻〕、無所看也〔著〕。 若言看淨、人姓本淨、爲妄念故、蓋覆眞如。 離妄念、本姓淨〔性〕。 不

見自姓本淨〔性〕、心起看淨、却生淨妄。 妄無處所、故知看者〔看〕却是妄也。 淨無形相、却立淨

相、言是功夫、作此見者、章自本姓〔性〕、却被淨縛。 若不動者、〔不〕見一切人過患、是性不動。

七

意、莫言先定發惠、先惠發定、定惠各別。作此見者法有二相、口說善、心不善、惠定不等。

心口俱善、內外一(衆)種、定惠即等。自悟修行、不在口諍。若諍先後、即是〔迷〕人、不

斷勝負、却生法我、不離四相。

一四、一行三昧者、於一切時中、行住座(坐)臥、常眞心是。(行直)(常行一直心是也)

淨名經云、「眞心是道場、眞心是淨土」。莫心行諂曲(曲)、口說法直。口說一行三昧、不行眞心(情)、非佛弟子。但行眞心(直)、於一切

法、無(上)有執著、名一行三昧。迷人著法相、執一行三昧、眞心(直)坐不動、除妄不起心、即

是一行三昧。若如是、此法同無情、却是障道因緣。道順(須)通流、何以却滯。(心不住法、道即通流、心若住、心住即通流住)

即彼縛。(法、名爲自縛)若坐(坐)不動是、維摩詰不合呵舍利弗宴座(坐)林中。善知識、又見有人教人座(坐)看心看淨、不

動不起。從此置(致)功。迷人不悟、便執成顚、即有數百盤(般)。如此教道者、故(固)之(知)大錯。

一五、善知識、定惠猶如何等。如燈光。有燈即有光。無燈即無光。燈是光知(之)體、光是燈之(之)

用。〔名〕即有二、體無兩般。此定惠法、亦復如是。

一六、善知識、法無頓漸、人有利鈍。明(迷)即漸勸、悟人頓修。識自本〔心〕、是見本性。悟

即元無差別、不悟即長劫輪廻。

一七、善知識、我自法門、從上已來、(頓漸)皆立無念無(爲)宗、無相無(爲)體、無住(無)爲本。

六

便傳頓法及衣、汝爲六代祖、衣將爲信、稟代代相傳、法以心傳心、當令自悟。五祖言、惠能、

自古傳法、氣如懸絲、若住此間、有人害汝、汝即須速去。

一○、能得衣法、三更發去。五祖自送能於九江驛。登時便悟。〔五〕祖處分、汝去努力、將法向南、三年勿弘、此法難去、在後弘化、善誘迷人。若得心開、汝悟無別。辭違已了、便發向南。

一一、兩月中間、至大庾嶺。不知向後有數百人來、欲擬頭惠能、奪於法、來至半路、盡惣却廻。唯有一僧、姓陳、名惠順。先是三品將軍、性行麁惡、直至嶺上、來趁犯著。惠能即還法衣、又不肯取。我故遠來求法、不要其衣。能於嶺上、便傳法惠順。惠順得聞、言下心開。能使惠順即却向北化人來。

一二、惠能來衣此地、與諸官奪道俗、亦有累劫之因。教是先性所傳、不是惠能自知。願聞先性教者、各須淨心、聞了願自餘迷、於先代悟。惠能大師喚言、善知識、菩提般若之知、世人本自有之、即緣心迷、不能自悟。須求大善知識示道見性。善知識、遇悟即成智。

一三、善知識、我此法門、以定惠爲本。第一勿迷言惠定別。定惠體一不二、即定是惠體、即惠是定用。即惠之時定在惠、即定之時惠在定。善知識、此義即是〔定〕惠等。學道之人作

八、有一童子、於碓房邊過、唱誦此偈。惠能一聞、知未見姓（性）、即識大意。能問童子、適來誦者是何言偈。童子答能曰、儞不知、大師言、生死是大（事）、欲傳於法、令門人等各作一偈、來呈看、悟大意即付衣法、稟爲六代褐（祖）。有一上座名神秀、忽於南廊下、書無相偈一首、五褐令諸門人盡誦、悟此偈者即見自姓（性）、依此修行、即得出離。惠能答曰、我此踏碓八箇餘月、未至堂前、望上人引惠能至南廊下、見此偈禮拜、亦願誦取、結來生緣、願生佛地。童子引能至南廊下。能即禮拜此偈、爲不識字、請一人讀。惠（能）問已、即識大意。惠能亦作一偈、又請得一解書人、於西間壁上提著（題）、呈自本心。不識本心、學法無益、識心見姓（性）、即吾大意。惠能偈曰、

菩提本無樹、明鏡亦無臺、佛姓（性）常青淨（清）、何處有塵埃。

又偈曰、

心是菩提樹、身爲明鏡臺、明鏡本清淨、何處染塵埃。

院內徒衆見能作此偈盡埪（恠）。惠能却入碓房。五褐（祖）忽見惠能（但即）善（知）識大意、恐衆人知、五祖乃謂衆人曰、此亦未得了。

九、五祖夜知三更（至）、喚惠能堂內、說金剛經。惠能一聞、言下便伍（悟）、其夜受法。人盡不知。

四

解深淺、我將心偈上五祖呈意、即善求法、覓祖不善、却同凡心奪其聖位。若不呈心、修不得
（K間）若不呈偈、終不得法。

法。良久思惟、甚難甚難、甚難甚難。夜至三更、不令人見、遂向南廊下中間壁上、題作呈心

偈、欲求於法。若五祖見偈、言此偈語〔…〕、我宿業障重、不合得法。聖意

難測、我心自息。秀上座、三更、於南廊下中間壁上、秉燭題作偈、人盡不和（知）。偈曰、（K喚）

身是菩提樹、心如明鏡臺。時時勤佛拭、莫使有塵埃。（K拂）

七、神秀上座題此偈畢、歸房臥、並無人見。五祖平旦遂喚盧供奉來、南廊下畫楞伽變。五（讀訖）（K留）

祖忽見此偈、請記乃謂供奉曰、弘忍與供奉錢三十千、深勞遠來、不畫變相也。金剛經云、凡

所有相、皆是虛妄、不如流此偈、令迷人誦、依此修行、不墮三惡、依法修行、人有大利益。

大師遂喚門人盡來、焚香偈前、人衆人見、皆生敬心。五祖遂喚秀上座於堂內、（方得見（入）（K祖）（K間）門是

姓）、於此修行、即不墮落。門人盡誦、皆生敬心、喚言善哉。五祖曰、汝等盡誦此偈者、（K依性）

汝作偈否。若是汝作、應得我法。秀上座言、罪過、實是神秀作、不敢求祖、願和尚慈悲、看（未）（K依）

弟子有小智惠識大意否。五祖曰、汝作此偈、見即來到。只到門前、尚未得入。凡夫於此偈修

行、即不墮落。作此見解、若覓無上菩提、即未可得。須入得門、見自本姓。汝且去、一兩日（K性）

來思惟、更作一偈來呈吾。若入得門、見自本姓、當付汝衣法。秀上座去、數日作不得。（K性）

三

三、弘忍和尚問惠能曰、汝何方人、來此山、禮拜吾、汝今向吾邊、復求何物。惠能答曰、

弟子是領南人（K嶺）、新州百姓、今故遠來、禮拜和尚、不求餘物、唯（K唯）求佛法（作）。大師遂責惠能

曰、汝是領南人（K嶺）、又是獦獠、若爲堪作佛。惠能答曰、人即有南北、佛姓（K性）即無南北。獦獠身與

和尚不同、佛姓（K性）有何差別。大師欲更共議、見左右在傍邊、大師更不言、遂發遣惠能、令隨衆

作務。時有一行者、遂差惠能於碓房、踏碓八箇餘月。

四、五祖忽於一日、喚門人盡來。門人集記（訖）。五祖曰、吾向與說（K汝）、世人生死事大、汝等門人、

終日供養、只求福田、不求出離生死苦海。汝等自姓（K性）迷門、福何可救。汝等各去（K自性若迷、福何可救、汝等各去…）。有

知惠者白取本姓（K性）般若知之（智）（K自）（K之知）、各作一偈呈吾、吾看汝偈、若吾大意者、付汝衣法、禀爲六代、火

急急。

五、門人得處分、却來各至自房、遞相謂言、我等不須呈心（K澄）用意作偈、將呈和尚。神秀上座

是教授師、秀上座得法後、自可於止（K依）、請不用作。諸人息心、盡不敢呈偈。時大師堂前有三間

房廊、於此廊下、供養欲畫楞伽變、并畫五祖大師傳授衣法、流行後代爲記、畫人盧玲（K珍）看壁了、（K及五祖血脉圖）

明日下手。

六、上座神秀思惟、諸人不呈心偈、緣我爲教授師。我若不呈心偈、五祖如何得見我心中見

二

南宗頓教最上大乘摩訶般若波羅蜜經

六祖惠能大師於韶州大梵寺施法壇經一卷

兼受無相戒、弘法弟子法海集記

一、惠能大師、於大梵寺講堂中、昇高座、說摩訶般若波羅蜜法、受（授）無相戒。其時座下僧尼道俗、一萬餘人。韶州刺史（韋璩）等據、及諸官寮（僚）三十餘人、儒士（三十）餘人、同請大師說摩訶般若波羅蜜法。刺史遂令門人僧法海集記、流行後伐（代）與學道者、承此宗旨、遞相傳授、有所於約（依）。

（以爲禀承、說此壇經）。

二、能大師言、善知識、淨（靜）心念摩訶般若波羅蜜法。大師不語、自淨心神。良久乃言、善知識淨聽。惠能慈父、本官范陽、左降遷流〔嶺〕南新州百姓。惠能幼小、父（又）小早亡、老母孤遺移來〔南〕海、艱辛貧之（乏）、於市買（賣）柴。忽有一客買柴、遂領惠能、至於官店。客將柴去、惠能得錢、却向門前。忽見一客、讀金剛經。惠能一聞、心名（明）便悟。乃問（問）客曰、從何處來、持此經典。客答曰、我於蘄州黃梅縣（縣）東馮墓山、禮拜五祖弘忍和尚、見今（今）在彼、門人有千餘衆。我於彼聽見大師勸道俗、但特（持）金剛經一卷、即得見性、直了成佛。惠能聞說、宿業有緣、便即辭親、往黃梅馮墓山、禮拜五祖弘忍和尚。

一